ON PRIVILEGE, FRAUDULENCE, AND TEACHING AS LEARNING

From one of the world's leading voices on white privilege and anti-racism work comes this collection of essays on complexities of privilege and power. Each of the four parts illustrates Peggy McIntosh's practice of combining personal and systemic understandings to focus on power in unusual ways. Part I includes McIntosh's classic and influential essays on privilege, or systems of unearned advantage that correspond to systems of oppression. Part II helps readers to understand that feelings of fraudulence may be imposed by our hierarchical cultures rather than by any actual weaknesses or personal shortcomings. Part III presents McIntosh's Interactive Phase Theory, highlighting five different world views, or attitudes about power, that affect school curriculum, cultural values, and decisions on taking action. The book concludes with powerful insights from SEED, a peer-led teacher development project that enables individuals and institutions to work collectively toward equity and social justice. This book is the culmination of forty years of McIntosh's intellectual and organizational work.

Peggy McIntosh, Ph.D. is Senior Research Scientist of the Wellesley Centers for Women at Wellesley College in Massachusetts. She has taught at the Brearley School, Harvard University, Trinity College (Washington, D.C.), the University of Denver, the University of Durham (UK), and Wellesley College. She is Founder of the National SEED Project on Inclusive Curriculum (Seeking Educational Equity and Diversity) which she co-directed with Emily Style during the Project's first twenty-five years. McIntosh is author of forty book chapters and articles, including the seminal paper "White Privilege: Unpacking the Invisible Knapsack." She consults widely in the United States and throughout the world with organizations and educators who are creating more gender-fair, multicultural, and relational workplaces and schools.

"It is rare that one gets the chance to meet or read in one's lifetime the originator of a new way of thinking or believing in the world of ideas. The legendary Peggy McIntosh is such a transformative figure. Her work is fundamental and foundational to our thinking on white privilege, and the subtle and myriad ways that race operates to the advantage of white folk while denying benefit and advantage to nonwhite people. She is also on par with the most gifted translators of complicated ideas and complex concepts we have had in a generation, and millions of people can trace their thinking about whiteness and privilege to her lucid and creative essays. Peggy McIntosh is a national treasure, and this powerhouse collection of her finest thinking and most brilliant reflections over the last few decades will solidify her sui generis stature as an American Original."
—Michael Eric Dyson, Professor of Sociology, Georgetown University

"What a gift to have this collection of Peggy McIntosh's papers! She has been a foundational leader who has already transformed our thinking and teaching, but her work will now be available to new audiences. This collection of her essays gives us her long-range view of white privilege, fraudulence, and the advancement of education through inclusion. Her work can now inspire new generations of thinkers, teachers, social justice advocates, and anyone dreaming of a more just world."
—Dr. Margaret L. Andersen, Rosenberg Professor of
Sociology Emerita, University of Delaware

"This collection serves as a reminder that systemic power and privilege are weakened when we reignite our humanity's natural curiosity, vulnerability, and longing for one another's well-being. Where whiteness pressures us to be experts produced by hierarchical systems and structures, these essays invite us to consider the world of knowledge we tap into when we remain grounded in one another's life experiences and inner knowledge. This compilation is a call to co-create a more humane and connected world."
—Debby Irving, Racial Justice Educator and Writer

"Peggy McIntosh's transformative thought is deep, engaging, and vitally important for our times."
—Hugh Vasquez, National Equity Project

"These writings reveal the heart and mind of a great student of life, a great teacher, and revolutionary social thinker. Her contribution to emerging social justice discourse is incalculable."
—Victor Lee Lewis, Radical Resilience Institute

ON PRIVILEGE, FRAUDULENCE, AND TEACHING AS LEARNING

Selected Essays 1981–2019

Peggy McIntosh

Routledge
Taylor & Francis Group

NEW YORK AND LONDON

First published 2020
by Routledge
52 Vanderbilt Avenue, New York, NY 10017

and by Routledge
2 Park Square, Milton Park, Abingdon, Oxon OX14 4RN

Routledge is an imprint of the Taylor & Francis Group, an informa business

Illustrations by Shebani Rao

Library of Congress Cataloging-in-Publication Data
A catalog record for this title has been requested

ISBN: 978-0-8153-5404-8 (hbk)
ISBN: 978-0-8153-5411-6 (pbk)
ISBN: 978-1-351-13379-1 (ebk)

Typeset in Bembo
by Taylor & Francis Books

I dedicate this book to its readers.

I give it to you in appreciation, solidarity, respect, and friendship.

CONTENTS

CONTRIBUTORS

Peggy McIntosh, Ph.D. Harvard University, was born in Brooklyn, NY and grew up in New Jersey. She attended public schools and George School in Pennsylvania before getting her B.A. at Radcliffe College. She has taught at The Brearley School, Harvard University, Trinity College (Washington, D.C.), the University of Denver, the University of Durham (UK), and Wellesley College. She is the author of forty book chapters and articles, including the classic essay *White Privilege: Unpacking the Invisible Knapsack*. McIntosh founded the National SEED Project on Inclusive Curriculum (Seeking Educational Equity and Diversity), which she co-directed with Emily Style from 1987 to 2011. She has spoken at more than 600 colleges, universities, and organizations around the world. She has four honorary degrees and the Klingenstein Award for Distinguished Educational Leadership from Columbia University.

Emily Style, B.A. Calvin College, M.A. New York University, grew up in Michigan and became a high school English teacher in New Jersey. She is author of the 1982 book *Multicultural Education and Me* and the influential 1988 essay "Curriculum as Window & Mirror." She has done adjunct teaching at colleges and consulting in schools across the United States. From 1987 to 2016, she co-directed the National SEED Project on Inclusive Curriculum (Seeking Educational Equity and Diversity). She also directed the New Jersey SEED Project from 1994 to 2002. Semi-retired, she now lives in Massachusetts where she continues to write poetry and do other kinds of thinking as well.

Hugo Mahabir, B.A. Sarah Lawrence College, M.A. University of Chicago, grew up in Trinidad and Tobago. He is head of the high school at Grace Church School (New York City).

Bob Gordon, B.A. Colby College, M.A., Ph.D. University of Colorado, is a white man who taught Spanish language, literature, and culture for twenty-three years at three liberal arts colleges and subsequently ten years at the Columbus Academy (Ohio). He is now retired and lives in Tucson, AZ.

Ruth Mendoza, M.Ed. Lesley University, grew up in Bolivia. She is a kindergarten teacher and a faculty, staff, and parent SEED co-facilitator at The Meadowbrook School of Weston (Massachusetts). She is now one of the Associate Directors of the National SEED Project based at the Wellesley Centers for Women.

ACKNOWLEDGMENTS

Dear Reader,

If you do not already know of Florence Howe, this acknowledgment can be your introduction. Florence and her husband Paul Lauter co-founded The Feminist Press in 1974. They were in residence as visiting scholars when I started to work at the Wellesley College Center for Research on Women in 1979. One day Florence was passing through my office and spotted something I had written on top of a heap of papers. She said, "This is good! You should publish." I said, "I have trouble writing." She said scornfully, "You don't have trouble writing. You just don't write! You should write to commission!" I have been doing that ever since, writing when invited. Knowing that someone wants to read your words lessens the internalized voices of "Be quiet!" and "No one is interested." I thank Florence for her uninvited, emphatic mentoring, for the Feminist Press, and for her 1974 publication of *Who's Who and Where in Women's Studies*. When it landed in my University of Denver office, its shiny red cover was the only spot of excitement for me on a desk heaped with black and white notes for meetings, classes, and academic business. That little nationwide directory felt like a salvation.

Understanding editors have played a major role in bringing forth this collection of essays. I am indebted to our enthusiastic editorial team at Routledge, Catherine Bernard, Matthew Friberg, and Rachel Dugan. I am grateful to the editors who solicited my work for *Independent School Magazine*: Blair McElroy and James Brosnan. I thank Patrick Bassett and Jonathan Cohen, who solicited the two essays co-written with Emily Style that are published here.

I owe a debt of thanks to Roberta Spivek, who had the idea of condensing my original nineteen-page paper, *White Privilege and Male Privilege* (1988), into three pages. She plucked the knapsack metaphor from the text and put it into the subtitle of the short paper. The final result was *White Privilege: Unpacking the*

Invisible Knapsack (1989), published in Peace and Freedom, the magazine of the Women's International League for Peace and Freedom. Roberta, this was a wonderful gift to the world. I thank you also for condensing Feeling Like A Fraud, Parts II and III for this collection.

Three years ago, I said to the Centers' Administrative Director, Karen Lachance, "I would like to find a research assistant who is wonderful with technology and also completely understands the work I do." Karen said dubiously, "I think you are looking for a unicorn." Four days later she called back to say, in a tone of disbelief, "I think we've found a unicorn." Rachel Nagin is indeed wonderful with technology (and gifted in teaching others about it) and deeply conversant with all the matters of head, heart, and power that this book is about. She combines intellectual strength with kindness, patience, honesty, learning, resourcefulness, and soul. Rachel, here are my devout thanks to you for shaping and shepherding my chapters. I could not have done it without you. I am grateful also that you introduced me to Shebani Rao, who did the artwork for this book. Thank you, Shebani, for your imaginative and effective illustrations.

In the early days of feminist publishing, I was inspired by many women I still feel indebted to today, many decades later: Annette Kolodny, Catharine Stimpson, Elizabeth Janeway, Adrienne Rich, Audre Lorde, Elaine Hedges, Mary Helen Washington, Tillie Olsen, Beverly Guy Sheftall, Johnella Butler, Kate Millett, Sally Gearhart, and Ruth Hubbard. In the early 1980s, one of the most important contributions to Women's Studies was being readied for publication right in the Wellesley Centers by Patricia Bell Scott, Barbara Smith, and Akasha Gloria Hull: *All the Women are White, All the Blacks are Men, But Some of Us Are Brave: Black Women's Studies*. Through it, I learned about many powerful Black authors and about the Combahee River Collective, with its brilliantly groundbreaking Statement on intersecting oppressions, written in 1977 by Demita Frazier, Barbara Smith, and Beverly Smith.

I have a great debt to women who joined the Mellon Seminars I led at the Wellesley College Center for Research on Women over seven years, 1979–1985. I was inspired especially by the thoughts and writings of Celia Alvarez, Margaret Andersen, Patricia Bell Scott, Joanne Braxton, Phyllis Cole, Anne Fausto-Sterling, Evelyn Fox Keller, Linda Gordon, Evelynn Hammonds, Sandra Harding, Mary Ann Hirsch, Akasha Gloria Hull, Saj-Nicole Joni, Jane Martin, Julie Matthaei, Sue Rosser, Patrocinio Schweickart, Eve K. Sedgwick, and Linda Gardiner, who went on to become the founding editor of the *Women's Review of Books*. This group of listeners and thinkers, together with eighty other very gifted Mellon scholars, has influenced countless academic fields in the years since we met together in monthly seminars.

I have a huge debt of gratitude to the Wellesley Centers for Women for furthering work that makes a difference to social justice and to scholarship in many fields. In the words of the previous Executive Director Susan Bailey, "A world that is good for women is good for everyone." I have been blessed by working for forty years with people at a place where you do not have to justify doing work that puts women's perspectives at the center. My perspectives have found a supportive "holding container" and growing place in this institution that I admire and love. I give special thanks to all four scholars who have held the role of Executive Director of the Centers: Carolyn Elliott, Laura Lein, Susan Bailey, and Layli Maparyan, and to Wellesley College President Barbara Newell, who bravely founded the Centers in 1974. I was fortunate to meet Jean Baker Miller during my first days at the Centers. Her influence on me has been indelible. Carol Gilligan had just left the Centers, but I am also much indebted to the paradigm-changing work she did here and subsequently. We are all indebted to the generosity of Katherine Stone Kaufmann for her continued and maternal support of those of us who work at the Centers. I give much gratitude to all the members of the core staff who support and put a shine on the Centers as a whole: Megan Cassidy, Luiza deCamargo, Anna Dore, Gretchen Eckert, Kajahl Fitzgerald, Christie Kim, Karen Lachance, Liz Meister, Jean Murphy, Janet Saad, Marnee Saltalamacchia, Sue Sours, Donna Tambascio, Kenji Thrash-Correia, Keng Wai Woo, and Hsin Hsin Yang. With Paula Johnson as Wellesley College's President and Layli Maparyan's leadership at the Centers, I have great hopes for many more decades of the Centers' work. President Johnson has worked for women strategically not only at the College, but in the medical professions for many years before she came to Wellesley. Layli's womanist work continues to expand her and the Centers' influence internationally, for the betterment of people everywhere. It is exciting to see the Centers' next phases unfolding.

When school teachers began to ask for monthly women's studies' seminars like the ones for college teachers, I found funding for the first four years of these thanks to the openness of Scott McVay of the Geraldine R. Dodge Foundation. Scott understood that the pressing problems of the whole world were intertwined. I am grateful to the dozens of K-12 teachers who joined the Dodge Seminars. One of my biggest debts of gratitude is to Emily Style, who co-led the fourth year of the Dodge Seminars and went on to co-lead the National SEED Project with me for twenty-five years, from 1987 to 2012. Emily, thank you forever for your collaborations over the years. Your intellect, knowledge, good heart, and welcoming soul have inspired hundreds of teachers to keep on keeping on, ever expanding their ability to relate to students, to themselves, to the vast resources you put at their disposal, and to the rest of the world. I am proud that together with Brenda Flyswithhawks, we built the National SEED Project into the nation's largest K-12 faculty development project covering all subject areas. Brenda, your guiding leadership, scholarship, intuition, wisdom, and generosity made the SEED Project and its workshops into a place of spiritual discovery and re-grounding for everyone who took part over the years. Brenda and Emily, I cannot imagine my personal or professional life without your sustaining friendships.

We are indebted to SEED's current and formidable Lead Team of Co-Directors: Emmy Howe, Gail Cruise-Roberson, and Jondou Chase Chen, all of them seasoned longtime SEED Seminar Leaders. This team has expanded the Project tremendously, increased the number of trained SEED Leaders, created regular

Re-SEED sessions for returnees, and appointed as Associate Directors Motoko Maegawa and Ruth Mendoza, both of whom are strong, creative and empathetic teachers. I thank this team for their impressive work and ongoing commitment to the SEED Project. I also thank Dana Rudolph for her crucial role as SEED's online content manager. I applaud all of the 2,700 leaders of SEED Seminars and the remarkable SEED staff that has shepherded them through their intensive summer New Leaders Weeks. I give particular thanks to some SEED Leaders, whom I have kept track of over the years: Rachel Allen, Cali Anicha, Chris Avery, Kathie Bach, Pat Badger, Kerwin Bell, Barbara Blackdeer MacKenzie, Kalifa Bonnivier, Bill Broderick, Keith Burns, Donald Burroughs, Rebecca Chase Chen, Michelle Cloud, Willa Cofield, Dan Cohen, Winston and Laina Cox, Alvin Crawford, Alvin Crawley, Raquel David-Ching, Diane Dana, Joan Dauphinee, Beverly Smith Davis, Richard Davis, Sandra Dickerson, Cristy and Peter Dratz, Chris Dunlap, Betty Eng, Carolina Goodman, Liz Hirsch, Havva Houshmand, Ora Jonasson, YunChi Maggie Hsu James, Seema Kapani, Linda Kaufman, Alphonse Keasley, Janice Koch, Shirley Kountze, Lori Kuwabara, Nancy Letts, Nancy Livingston, Judy Logan, Marcia Lovelace, Rachel Luce-Hitt, Nancy Marbury, Glenabah Martinez, Phyllis May-Machunda, Mary Jo Merrick-Lockett, Maryanne Michaels, Evelyn Moore, Loren Moye, Merrie Najimy, Cathy Nelson, Elaine Pace, Lily Pang, Melissa Patrick, Saburah Posner, Dena Randolph, Susan Rinker and Henry Schwartz, Peggy Rivage-Seul, Cheryl Robinson, Paula Roy, Joseph Russo, Pat Savage-Williams, Christine Saxman, Ellen D. Stern, Hazel Symonette, Adrienne Thunder, Eloise Tinley, Jan Westrick, Kim Wilson, Brian Wise, and Kari Xiong. Odie Douglas achieved the astonishing feat of having more than 100 SEED Seminar Leaders trained for his Elk Grove Unified School District in California. With colleagues Francie Teitelbaum and Kathy Orihuela, he supported and spread the SEED work far and wide. SEED is especially indebted to the wisdom of Reverend Linda Powell Pruitt, and to Sister Gervaise Valpey, an angel of SEED and of the wonderful San Domenico School. I'd also like to thank Ruth Mendoza, Bob Gordon, and Hugo Mahabir for their beautiful autobiographical contributions to this book.

I do not cry often, but in a given New SEED Leaders week in the summer, I have sometimes felt my eyes watering all day long. I am moved to see the devotion of the seasoned staff members who know what courage and character it takes for a teacher to lead a year-long seminar for their colleagues and to make it good for everyone. This is a SEED ideal.

The projects I have worked on have benefitted from very generous foundation grants and key program officers who have supported the work of curriculum change: Claire List of the Andrew W. Mellon Foundation, Alison Bernstein of the Ford Foundation, Greg and Maria of Jobin-Leeds, Rosa Smith, Shirley Mark, and Korynn Schooley of the Schott Foundation for Public Education, Richard Curcio of the Lucent Technologies Foundation, Nadia Brigham of the W.K. Kellogg Foundation, Lydia Spitzer of The Canaday Family Trust, Phoebe

Valentine of the Valentine Foundation, and Rowzat Shipchandler of the Saint Paul Foundation. I appreciate the generosity of the Rockefeller Foundation, especially Gianna Celli at the Villa Serbelloni in Bellagio. And I am grateful to our many other funders and donors over the years, including Anna Emory Hanson and Sally Wiseley as well as Elizabeth Luce Moore, Shirley Miske, and the United Board for Christian Higher Education in Asia.

Thank you Eddie Moore Jr., for your spectacular energy, influence, and good heart, and for founding the White Privilege Conference, which has drawn thousands of people into its orbit. I appreciate your indefatigable commitment to achieving so much collaboration between people of all races, across all generations and sexual orientations. I also feel special gratitude to Victor Lee Lewis, Hugh Vasquez, and the cast of *The Color of Fear*, who have so strengthened understanding of race relations in the United States. It has been one of the great honors of my life to work with you, Victor and Hugh. The films of World Trust, including *Cracking the Codes: Making Whiteness Visible*, have been instrumental to new understandings; I thank Shakti and Rick Butler for your influence on the climate of this country. I also want to thank the makers of the six-part PBS series, *Race: The Power of an Illusion*; it is another foundational documentary contribution to comprehension and analysis of race in the U.S. Jean Kilbourne's *Killing Us Softly* has done invaluable service to the analysis of gender and race in advertising as well. I appreciate all ten descendants of the DeWolf family who cooperated with Katrina Browne in making the important and candid documentary, *Traces of the Trade*, about the slave trade which is part of the family's and this nation's history.

Owing to the UN Decade for Women, UNESCO, and the East Asia Regional Council of Overseas Schools (EARCOS), I have come to count as friends and acquaintances scholars from many other nations. I thank you for your far-reaching words and works: Berit Ås of Norway, Gloria Bonder of Argentina, Chang Pilwha of South Korea, Mona Eliasson of Sweden, Betty Eng of Hong Kong, Fujieda Mioko of Japan, Chryssi Inglessi of Greece, Yenlin Ku of Taiwan, Li Xiao Zhang of China, Dorothy Smith of Canada, Dale Spender of Australia, Dagmar Schultz of Germany, Siu Mi Maria Tam of Hong Kong, and, last but not at all least, Tao Jie of China.

I have been strengthened and inspired over the last fifty years by a host of other authors, visionaries, teachers, elders, mentors, administrators, assistants, students, activists, theorists, friends, colleagues, companions, correspondents, and well-wishers. I apologize to the hundreds I have left out, but some names that come to mind in this season of my life are: Chimamanda Ngozi Adichie, Amer Ahmed, Brenda J. Allen, Joyce Allen-Beckford, Bob Amico, Margaret Andersen, Maya Angelou, Tomas Atencio and Consuelo Pacheco, Marilou Awiakta, James Baldwin, James and Cherry Banks, Mary Catherine Bateson, Tamara Beauboeuf, Jayne Blankenship, Charlotte Bunch, Kim Case, Cyrus Cassells, Mariam Chamberlain, Barbara Chase, Gail Christopher, Ta-Nehisi Coates, Carol Cohn, Johnnetta Cole, Chuck

Collins, Patricia Hill Collins, Susan Cooper, Kimberlé Crenshaw, Margaret Cruik-
shank, Karen Dace, Joy DeGruy, Makiko Deguchi, Toi Dericotte, Robin DiA-
ngelo, Emily Dickinson, W.E.B. DuBois, Randall Dunn, Michael Eric Dyson,
Cynthia Enloe, Adele Quincy Ervin, Marnie Evans, Richard Ewing, John and
Mary Felstiner, Abby Ferber, Bill and Lesleigh Forsyth, Anne Fuller, Bill Gardiner,
Valerie Graham, Diane Goodman, Joan Goldmann, Will Gravely, Ilsa Govan,
Vincent Harding, Jean Hardisty, Nancy and Roscoe Hill, Amy Hoffman (former
editor of the *Women's Review of Books*), bell hooks, Gary Howard, Debby Irving,
Charlotte Kasl, Jackson Katz, Frances Kendall, Paul Kivel, Sue Klein, Ruth Jacobs,
Stuart James, Amy Joe, Camara Jones, Judith Jordan, Carole DeBoer Langworthy,
Paul Lauter, Lilo Leeds, Justin Lincks, John Livingston, Jim Loewen, Lindy Lyman
and Charlie Potts, Frances Maher, Jean-Paul Marchand, Paul Marcus and Pat Shine,
Amy Marx, Patti Marxsen, Charles Mason, James and Judith Meredith, Phil
McGraw, Mary McKinney, Joyce Miller and Mary Norris, Elizabeth Minnich,
Toni Morrison, LeRoy Moore, Michael Malahy Morris, Amy Nadel, Pari Navabi,
Zora Neale Hurston, Peter Neumann, Donald and Bonnie Newman, Gil Noble,
Mary Oliver, Louise Pajak, Suzanne Pharr, Jodi Picoult, Charlotte Pierce-Baker,
Joseph and Elizabeth Pleck, Eleni Potaga-Stratou, john a. powell, Janis Pryor, Susan
Reverby, Rosalind Richards, Bob Richardson, David Roediger, Nicola Rolloff,
Penny Rosenwasser, Mary Rowe, Marguerite Rupp, Dena Samuels, Cynthia
Secor, Horace Seldon, Victoria Shorr, Jo and Howard Schuman, the Shelton
family, Ellen Shockro, Ajarn Sulak Sivaraksa, Tilman and Michael Smith, William
"Smitty" Smith, Richard and Lynne Spivey, Andy Stein, Shay Stewart-Bouley,
Melissa Steyn, Shannon Sullivan, Janet Surrey, Mary Kay Tetreault, Robert
Tenorio, Gwendolyn Thomas, Becky Thompson, Adrienne Thunder, J. Ann
Tickner, Martha Tolpin, Marty and Gus Trowbridge, Gwendolyn VanSant, Alice
Walker, Maureen Walker, Karen Weekes, Paula Lawrence Wehmiller, David
Wellman, Joella Werlin, Judith White, Tim Wise, and Catherine Wong. I thank
the founders of Black Lives Matter: Alicia Garza, Patrisse Cullors, and Opal
Tometi – this country owes you a continuing debt of gratitude.

I am grateful to the Quaker education that influenced the methods of
the SEED Project. After the United States dropped the atomic bombs on
Hiroshima and Nagasaki, my parents were appalled by the killing of so
many civilians. They became pacifists and members of the Society of
Friends. They sent my sister and me to a Quaker school in hopes that
Friends' values would rub off on us. It was not until decades later that I
realized my continuing debts to some of the patient, multiculturally
attuned, far-seeing Quaker teachers at George School in Pennsylvania.
Whereas I felt as a teenager that I was ahead of them, I know now that
they were way ahead of me. The values of one's religious upbringing are
often transmuted in SEED into less doctrinal and more spiritual understandings of human life. One part of Quaker teaching that has stayed with
me and been useful in all SEED work is the belief that in all people there
is spirit, soul, sacredness – "that of god in every person."

I am indebted to Winthrop and Margaret Means, my steady, interesting, supportive, talented, and ethical parents, who in their scarce free time were devoted to the natural world and caring for plants. My mother, who was forthright in many ways, once sent from suburban New Jersey a heartfelt question for my Greek professor at college. She asked what *The Iliad* had to say to a person whose required role was to do six or eight things at once. She embarrassed me. I thought her question was off the wall. My professor never answered, but she reached me. I notice that when writing about power in the curriculum and the society, I am likely to focus in part on the demanding, down to earth work of domestic care-taking of young and old people, of households, of land, and of communities.

I am indebted to my aunt and uncle, Caroline Ware and Gardiner Means, labor economists in Washington, D.C. They worked with Franklin and Eleanor Roosevelt in the 1930s and 1940s. My aunt's long interracial friendship with Pauli Murray is captured in the volume of their letters, *Pauli Murray and Caroline Ware: Forty Years in Black and White*. My aunt and uncle passed on to our family a commitment to inclusive thinking and the making of policy which does the greatest good for the greatest number.

I am in awe of my favorite (and only) sister, Helen Armstrong. Helen, your mind, heart, wit, generosity, compendious knowledge, and sacred center have steadied many people in their lives. Your quiet, ceaseless activism is inspiring. You've been a loyal support to me and to our witty, serious, professionally well-known geologist brother, Winthrop. I am grateful for my extended family, so full of people of learning, action, imagination, and goodwill: Millicent and Rustin McIntosh, Carey McIntosh and Joan Ferrante, Jim McIntosh and Elaine Gazda, Susan McIntosh Lloyd and Bob Lloyd, Dick and Marjorie K. McIntosh, Judith Hyde, Winthrop and Marilyn Means, and all of our friendly relatives in the next generation.

To my dear husband, Kenneth McIntosh, and our dear daughters, Kate Helen Carey McIntosh and Janet Susan McIntosh, I owe a special debt of gratitude for allowing me to think my thoughts without arguing with me. I know families in which a wife, mother, aunt, or grandmother has been discouraged from intellectual work by the stress of arguing with relatives. Thank you, Kate and Janet, and your families. I appreciate your rich, full, engaging lives, your partners, and your wonderful children. Ken, you are loved by everybody who knows you. You are very modest about your talents. Your kind, intelligent, patient, intuitive, and supportive nature has permeated your parenting, teaching, music, medicine, and science. You have made my life better in all ways. I thank you for our fifty-four years of marriage and your tendency to look for the greatest good for the greatest number in all things. You once told me that as an accompanist for singers, or in chamber music, you "try to put a shine on the other people." You put a shine on everyone always.

With lasting appreciation,
Peggy
January, 2019

AN OPENING LETTER

Dear Reader,

I hope that this book will be of some use to you in helping you to live your life. I am trying to write sentences that sometimes make it seem as if I am talking *with you*. I believe in my words more when I think you are there.

In these pages, you will find sets of essays on four themes I think about: privilege, fraudulence, hierarchies, and schools. The essays have in common my habit of re-seeing what I look at, doubting, revising, and supplanting what I was taught, usually by exploring questions of power. Another habit is offering pluralness in what I see and say. My method is testimonial more than analytical. I base my ideas on what I have observed.

The Privilege papers counter the myth that everybody ends up with what they wanted, worked for, earned, and deserved. Pluralness in the Privilege work has to do with seeing many different kinds of advantage and disadvantage that grant or limit people's power within our social systems.

The Fraud papers are about learning to appreciate your own complex authenticity in a world full of fakery. Pluralness in the Feeling Like A Fraud series is about countering self-doubt and the erosions of one's power by recognizing that power itself often rests on fraudulent claims.

Pluralness in the Phase Theory is about developing five different ways of making knowledge and using power in schooling. The Phase Theory may shed light on your own circumstances, and on some ways in which elders and teachers may have underestimated the magnitude of your own life experiences.

The chapters on the SEED Project describe an uplifting, collaborative project dear to my heart that I started in 1986. It supports the inner growth and adult development of teachers as well as learners of any age in any kind of school. It adds to some of the traditions of progressive education. The pedagogy of SEED is rooted in seeing plurally and in democratically hearing power in many voices.

If the processes of coming to see systems of power more clearly or pluralizing your sense of self help you as a reader, then I will feel that publishing this book has been worthwhile.

Although I am describing four thematic parts in this book, the individual articles were written one by one as they were solicited by readers from different audiences. I start each part of this book with the first paper I wrote on a given theme, as it was originally published. Over the years, the thematic ideas cross-pollinated with each other, influencing future papers. The Privilege papers, for example, would not have emerged without Phase Theory, Feeling Like a Fraud, and the SEED Project interacting with my day-to-day work at home and at the Wellesley Centers for Women.[1] The most recent Fraud paper reflects the multiplicity cherished in SEED. I keep reflecting on these themes, so all the essays in this book still feel like work in progress to me.

What do I hope for you as a reader moving, looking through these pages?

- I hope you will find useful perspectives on some of the things that bother you.
- I hope you will be strengthened in understanding ways in which history has shaped you and your world.
- I hope that my essays will give you staying power to survive bad news and terrible times.
- I hope you will respect any effort you have put into making and mending the fabrics of the world: agricultural, civic, domestic, political, religious, intellectual, emotional, artistic, educational, or philanthropic.
- I hope you will consider using some of your power to weaken unjust power systems that may have privileged you.
- I hope the book will connect you to authors, films, poets, ideas, or sources you did not know before.
- I hope the book will release you from some of the pressure to see yourself as others see you.
- I hope that your non-arguing soul is freed up to find its own power in the world.
- I hope you may find greater confidence in writing and speaking from the grounds of your own complex life.

You may have picked up this book because you heard about my work on white privilege. That theme ties together the first seven pieces in this book, and it threads into all of the essays in the volume. All of them have to do with trying to get power distributed more evenly in our society. All of them have to do with the damage to the society when power gets concentrated in the hands of few people, assumptions, ideas, and institutions.

Can this book help you to earn a living? Maybe, if it has the steadying effect that I hope for and try to encourage. I hope you will see the sources of your own balance and find even more.

If you apologize a lot, I hope that parts of this book will lessen that habit. If you feel disappointed in yourself and feel you do less with your time than you intend to, some of these essays may help you feel better. You did not create the society you have been born to. It was not engineered for your full growth and development. It is wonderful if you are able to resist some of the pressures against your wholeness – the pressures of competition, manipulation, repression, violence, and consumerism. May your resistance sustain you, foster action, and allow your wholeness to thrive.

- I hope you are interested as you witness changes in the history of ideas about power.
- I hope you will become quite sensitive to the ways power works in and around you, or what Adrienne Rich calls your "politics of location," especially by learning about women's studies and about cultures other than your own (Rich, 1984).
- I hope you will be able to speak better about efforts at diversity, inclusion, and equity, both in and outside of schools.
- I hope you will be proud of times when you acted on the values of doing "the greatest good for the greatest number."[2]
- I hope if you choose to have children, you will cherish them, be honest with them, and inspire them to be savvy, curious, and reflective people.
- I hope you will create spaces for adult development that can result in all the young people in our care feeling that they are integral to their families, to their communities, and to human life generally.

I hope you will come to share Einstein's conviction that:

Our task must be to free ourselves from the prison [of separateness] by widening our circle of compassion to embrace all living creatures and the whole of nature in its beauty ... We shall require a substantially new manner of thinking if humanity is to survive.[3]

I hope my essays make a contribution to that "substantially new manner of thinking."

Sincerely,

Peggy

January, 2019

Notes

1 Wellesley College created the Center for Research on Women (CRW) in 1974 and the Stone Center for Developmental Services and Studies (SCDSS) in 1981. From 1974 until 1995, researchers and staff referred to the CRW as "the Center" and the SCDSS as "the Stone Center." In 1995, the two centers came together to form the Wellesley Centers for Women, commonly referred to as "the Centers" or WCW.

2 This is an ideal often attributed to Jeremy Bentham, an 18th century utilitarian English philosopher. It paraphrases and combines elements from several other Enlightenment era thinkers who proposed principles of government and of morality.
3 Beginning in 1946, Einstein spoke out against atomic warfare and militarism. In his role as chair of the Emergency Committee of Atomic Scientists, he tried to rally the scientific community around supporting non-proliferation and ending the perceived need for nuclear weapons altogether. In many letters and speeches, Einstein proclaimed that "our task … [requires] a substantially new manner of thinking if humanity is to survive."

Reference

Rich, A. (1984). Notes toward a politics of location. In *Blood, bread, and poetry: Selected prose 1979–1985*. New York: W. W. Norton & Company. 210–231

PART I

The Privilege Papers

A LETTER ABOUT THE PRIVILEGE PAPERS

Dear Reader,

   After I have spoken on Privilege, the question I get from the audience most often is, "What made you see white privilege?" On the chance that you are interested, I will go ahead and answer the question here. It is not a pleasant story, but it changed my life immensely for the better. What made it unpleasant? Being destabilized; having to throw away my main assumptions about myself and other people; having to change my sense of who, what, and where I am. In the end, those changes put my life on a different and better base.

   Three years in a row (1982–1985), men and women had a kind of falling out in a seminar I was facilitating at my workplace, Wellesley College Center for Research on Women. The seminar participants were college teachers from all over New England and also New York, New Jersey, and Connecticut. We met once a month during an academic year. The men who joined these seminars were nice people and also brave, to come to a women's college to discuss our feminist topic, new scholarship on women, and how it could be brought into all of the liberal arts disciplines, including math and science.

   We started every September in great shape, with the twenty-two men and women appreciating each other and all appreciating the topic, which was end-lessly interesting. Each year, some of us teachers described the ways in which we were already bringing materials on women into our college courses. But each year, some women would bring up the question of why we couldn't put materials on women into the introductory courses.

   In those days, I took a lot of notes. One man answered the question by saying, "When you are trying to lay the foundation stones for knowledge, you can't put in soft stuff." Like all of us, he had been reading many hardback books and refereed journal articles on women's studies, but his comment showed he still felt anything on women was "soft." He was a perfectly nice man. I wrote down his comment. None of us challenged his word "soft."

In the seminar two years later, a professor said she didn't want students to have to wait for a senior year feminist seminar to read materials on women. Another very nice man explained why materials on women couldn't be brought into the courses of first-year students. He said, "In that first year, the students are trying to choose their major. That's their discipline. If you want a student to think in a disciplined way, you can't put in extras." Reader, if you were born before the 1970s, you probably will not be surprised that none of the twenty-two university faculty in the group questioned his wording. This man, like every other person in the history of the world, was born of a woman, but somehow something had been done to his mind to make him think that the one who gave him birth and life was "extra." I wondered what had been done to his mind to make our half of the world's population vanish. I just wrote down his comment because I had no words to say.

But in those days, I did think I had to decide whether these were nice men or oppressive men. I knew they were nice men, and brave, to attend this five-hour feminist seminar, spending many hours each month traveling to and from it. I *knew* they were nice, but their comments made me *feel* oppressed. It had not yet occurred to me that people could be both nice (even brave) and oppressive at the same time. I spent a couple of years confused about this, but then suddenly I remembered back to 1979 when I read the Combahee River Collective Statement from 1977. In it, brilliant black women scholars and activists wrote, "the major systems of oppression are interlocking." They had gone on to say,

> One issue that is of major concern to us and that we have begun to publicly address is racism in the white women's movement. As Black women we are made constantly and painfully aware of how little effort white women have made to understand and combat their racism, which requires among other things that they have a more than superficial comprehension of race, color, and Black history and culture.

They implied that not *some* white women, but white women *as a whole group* were oppressive to work with. I heard this sentiment echoed by black women at conferences and in the corridors of Boston area colleges. My first response, I remembered now, had been a kind of mental whine: "I don't see how they can say that about us – I think we're nice." And my second internal and unspoken response was downright racist: "I especially think we are nice if we work with *them*."

I realized then that I was expecting thanks for working with people I had been taught to look down on. Did that make me oppressive to work with? It took me about two years of dithering before I finally resigned myself to the answer. Yes, I am oppressive for black women to work with. I had hoped that I had disguised my racism by being nice – so nice. Now, I came to admit that of course my racism does show. It occurred to me the reason that black women worked with me was probably that at least I seemed to be *trying*. At University of Denver, I had taught black women's literature, but had not taught about the ways *white people's systems* created the hardships and conditions for the lives of the black characters and authors I focused on.

So in the mid-1980s, I suddenly realized this ugly parallel between the male seminar members' oppressiveness and my own racial oppressiveness. This was a pit-of-the-stomach unpleasant shock. Then the history of thinking by the men in the seminars became clearer to me. I decided they were nice men and they had simply been very good students of what they had been taught. It was a litany of assumptions they (and I) absorbed from the curriculum and the society: Men have knowledge. Men make more knowledge. Men publish and profess knowledge, as professors. Men run the best-known research universities. Men run the biggest university presses. And we have internalized the idea that men are Knowers and that Knowledge itself is male.

Up until this point, I had thought that the reason I got grants for my work on curriculum change, when my colleagues of color couldn't, was because I wrote better grant proposals than they did. Now suddenly I read it differently. I had to face my own litany of assumptions about whiteness: White people have knowledge. White people make more knowledge. White people publish and profess knowledge, as professors. White people run the best-known research universities. White people run the biggest university presses. I realized that I had internalized the idea that white people are Knowers and that Knowledge itself is white.

This was sickening. Then I came to understand what I believe to this day – niceness has nothing to do with it. I saw that the seminar itself was being funded by the Andrew W. Mellon Foundation and all the people I had dealt with at the Foundation were white. All the people I had spoken with at any foundation were white. I realized that not only did I have the whole Knowledge system on my side, I had the Grant-making system and the Money system on my side as well.

This blew away the myth of meritocracy for me. I had been brought up on the myth of meritocracy, which has two parts: First, the only unit of society is the individual. Second, whatever an individual ends up with at death must be what that individual wanted, worked for, earned, and deserved. Seeing my white privilege was wrecking my assumption that I had earned all that I had.

I did not want to face the looming questions, but I thought I had seen something very big about my life: that the Knowledge system and the Money system were working *for me*. So I asked what else I had that I hadn't earned. My conscious mind refused to answer. I asked again, urgently: "By contrast with my black colleagues at Wellesley, what do I have that I didn't earn, except the Knowledge system and the Money system working for me?" Once again, my conscious mind, the one with all the degrees and honors, wouldn't answer. I was in the habit of asking questions of my mind and having it respond. This time, it balked. My mind said, "I won't go there," or "There is no *there* there." But finally, one night as I fell asleep, feeling that I was in a spiritual crisis over this, I more or less shouted to the nameless powers-that-be, "On a day-to-day basis, by contrast with my black friends, if I have anything else I didn't earn, SHOW ME."

In the middle of that night, up swam an example. It woke me. I turned on the light and wrote it down. I was very disappointed. It seemed trivial. I think I was looking for the Next Big Thing, like the Money system or the Knowledge system. The message was this: "I can, if I wish, arrange to be in the company of people of my race most of the time." In the morning, I looked at it and still found it trivial. Now, I think it is huge. It keeps me from having to be "the lonely" or "the only." My feeling that it was trivial was a very white judgment. This statement became the first of forty-six examples that swam up over the next three months.

As I wrote in the first privilege paper that carries all of those forty-six examples, if I did not write them down immediately, they disappeared by morning. I did not want to know them. I was writing down things I did not want to recognize. It amuses me now that the examples swam up to me fully worded and grammatically correct. I am an English teacher from way back, which helps to explain that, but also shows me how close to the surface of my mind the examples were – how accessible to my subconscious. I suggest to you, dear reader, and to any student I talk with nowadays, that you ask your subconscious mind to answer your questions. I think that formal education suppresses most of what our subconscious minds have noticed. As children, we get a keen sense of unfairness, and how unfairness is obvious in lives and schools. But most schools do not teach us about racial power dynamics, nor do many parents easily discuss the terrible subject of racial power with their children, families, neighbors, local and state governments, and others in the world. I did not understand why black women found us white women oppressive until I dreamt on it after *demanding* truth. I found these wells of subconscious, suppressed information gave me dozens of grammatical, intelligible examples from my own life.

Each example was accompanied by a voice, neither male nor female, that worded the example so exactly that it did not need editing. In other words, this voice was instructing me about my experience. The voice was not inviting me to conjure up a fiction, but simply supplying words for what I already knew. The voice was answering my demand, "SHOW ME!"

After about three months, the examples stopped appearing. One night, I heard the same voice that had given me most of the examples say, "You need to write this down and publish it. It is probably the most important work you will do in your life."

I wrote down my examples and my analysis of them and sent them to some friends and colleagues in Women's Studies, Black Studies, Sociology, and Psychology in various parts of the country. They advised me to publish. But the Working Papers Committee of the Center for Research on Women, where I worked, refused to accept the paper for publication. The Committee said that it was "merely anecdotal," had no footnotes, and was not really research.

I presented it anyway as a talk at many conferences and received requests to use it in courses in many fields. I charged $0.50 per copy that people made, but I thought that the Center could make money for us all if they published it and charged $6 a copy. So the next year, I went back to the Working Papers

Committee and they turned it down again, emphasizing that our institution had a reputation *for research* to uphold and that a personal narrative could not be considered significant data. I understood their position, for I had received all of my degrees working with such academic assumptions; for example, I had carefully left the personal pronoun out of all of the papers I wrote in college and graduate school. I now believe that the omission of individual voices does immense damage to knowledge-making.

I was surprised when the same voice that gave me most of the examples woke me up about three months after the second rejection by the Working Papers Committee. The voice said, "Freud did not have footnotes!" I asked to attend another of the quarterly meetings of the committee and said that though I understood their dilemma, "Freud did not have footnotes! This is original work." They looked at each other, my colleagues with Ph.D.s in the social sciences, and then said, "Okay." As Working Paper #189,[1] it quickly became one of the Center's best-selling papers and remains at the top of the list, along with Nan Stein's important work on gender violence in schools and society. It added a necessary dimension to the all-white syllabi of feminist and male-centered courses.

Soon after the paper was published, I got a call from the *Harvard Educational Review* asking to reprint it. I said yes, on condition that the editors would solicit an article from a person of color, who does not have white privilege. They said they did not have space for another article. I offered to cut my paper in half and share the space. After a long pause, they said that the *Review* doesn't publish "short articles," so I turned down the invitation.

In 1989, Roberta Spivek, a skilled editor of *Peace and Freedom* magazine, published by the Women's International League for Peace and Freedom, asked whether she could condense the article. She reduced the list of examples from forty-six to twenty-six and brilliantly highlighted the salient points and images of my nineteen-page paper. She pulled my metaphor of the invisible knapsack out of the body of the essay and titled the three-page excerpt *White Privilege: Unpacking the Invisible Knapsack*.[2]

In the years since 1989, this work has turned out to be useful to a great many readers. I never expected it to make such an impression, especially because I felt a little bit crazy while writing from subconscious prompts. I think part of the secret of its effectiveness is that Roberta Spivek's *Knapsack* version is so brief. Many assignments in school and graduate school are of lengthy articles and books, whereas my readers can pick up the kernel of this work very quickly. In retrospect, I think most readers are drawn in by the factual quality of the individual examples of privilege that I give to describe my own life. I do not speak for other white people, but I suggest readers look at their own circumstances of advantage and disadvantage in a very detailed, detached, and down-to-earth way. Many people have told me over the years that they remember exactly where they were sitting when they first read the *Knapsack*. Some say it is the only thing they remember from a course, or a major, or all their years in college! I do think the sky high costs of college are outrageous − but I feel this little paper is worth paying tuition for. I am grateful to all the brave teachers who have ever assigned it and to all people who have ever given or recommended it to someone else. Thirty years later, my individual testimony still sparks willingness in many people to look at systemic injustice at a time when most Americans are still taught that systems of injustice do not exist here.

I have been thanked by white people and people of color for very different reasons. Frequently, white people, especially those born before the 1960s and 1970s, thank me by saying, "I never thought of any of this before." People of color thank me for a very different reason – my paper confirmed that they are not crazy; they *knew* there was something working against them that was not outright discrimination, but my paper helped to provide words and a conceptual frame that validated the truths of their experience. When I wrote my white privilege papers, I had not heard of David Wellman or his brilliant study, *Portraits of White Racism*, published in 1977. Wellman wrote the very useful explanation of white privilege as a system of advantage based on race. I think this important and analytically sharp study of the racial attitudes of five white Americans deserves a wider readership than it currently has.

The original paper of 1988 described male privilege, white privilege, and heterosexual privilege. In this way, its analysis was intersectional. In teaching about privilege, I try to create exercises that draw on these and many other kinds of privilege and disadvantage. The exercises free up audiences or classmates to stay with this many-sided complexity, which is all about power, without dropping the subject due to feelings of blame, shame, or guilt. I remind audiences that we did not invent the systems we were born into; we are taught to assimilate into them or punished for not doing so. I also say what I believe: that everybody has been born into a combination of unearned disadvantage and unearned advantage. No one is solely an oppressor, or solely an oppressed person. In *Some Notes to Facilitators of my Work on White Privilege*, [3] I suggested many additional factors beyond race that can affect one's positioning in life with regard to privilege or disadvantage.

Reading the essays on privilege that I have included in this book, you may return to moments in your childhood in which you saw some kids suffering and you had an essential empathy for them. In the big patterns of cruelty you saw, very likely the adults didn't know how to talk to you about them. It is literally too painful for words. Through work on privilege systems, you may return to that earlier, clearer moral sense and, now in retrospect, you may also come to empathize with those who didn't want to talk with you about how power works in our worlds. By courageously studying privilege, you may learn about how much power you were given by the circumstances you were born to, but also how much disempowerment was visited on you to make sure that you "knew your place."

If you are wondering why race relations are in such a bad state, the privilege analysis can help you both to understand and to act. I should begin with this recognition: just taking the privilege idea seriously for the first time can be the greatest action a person can take and it may be all that a mind can manage at first. But our minds are huge and changing them significantly will affect millions of our daily actions, interactions, and decisions. I hope you will not get paralyzed by the enormity of privilege – reflection without action – but will use what power privilege gives you to take action against some of the misuses of power that are shaping our lives and communities every day.

If you are wondering why the world is so full of injustice, the privilege analysis might make you more discouraged. It multiplies the types of injustice that you will observe. But it can clarify your own political location in the world relative to many variables and inspire you to be more conscious of how you are using your power. I hope all can see the damage done to others by the holders of privilege and also the damage to the holders themselves through dominating. The privilege work tells me that I cannot hope to stay in languid conversation about race; the hardest and most necessary work is taking action to weaken the racial and economic systems that gave me so much unearned advantage. For me, that action chiefly was co-developing the National SEED Project on Inclusive Curriculum, which I describe in the last part of this book and which has been central to the past three decades of my life.

If you are a person of color, in a sense my white privilege work will not tell you anything you don't already know. You have been oppressed all of your life by white privilege and its institutions. I hope that my essays, or those of James Baldwin, W.E.B. DuBois, the Combahee River Collective, Audre Lorde, or Ta-Nehisi Coates, will help you to name still more of what eats at you and help you to peer into the minds of those who *think* they are morally superior. I hope my essays will assure you that you are not the crazy one and that Black Lives Matter is a crucial, long overdue correction to the fact that unexamined white privilege says black lives don't matter.

If you are a white person, whiteness is your hard drive but you can devise alternative software. I hope my analysis will help you to understand that people of color, whom we have been taught to fear, dominate, and discount, are brave in expressing their anger and in demanding a more just world for all of us. I hope my analysis will help you as a white person to understand, empathize with, and respect experience that is so unlike our own.

What made me go on to write the 1998 essay *White Privilege, Color, and Crime*[4] was outrage on the part of many white people when the prominent African American athlete O.J. Simpson was acquitted of the charge that he murdered his wife. I had seen so many white people acquitted of crimes they were accused of committing, despite strong evidence of their guilt. I realized one white privilege I had was to be seen (by white people) as entitled to any legal defense I could afford. My *White Privilege, Color and Crime* essay provides thirty-seven additional examples of my privilege in the U.S. relative to the courts, the police, the security systems, and the law itself. In many ways, the Color and Crime paper is more upsetting than my first papers on privilege because of the power of the law itself to destroy people illegally and unconstitutionally. The laws get used unfairly for the protection of the property and safety of white people. For many people of color, to live in fear of the supposed protector is like being in an abusive relationship with an authority figure – one may be killed by the abuser. The Black Lives Matter movement is an example of standing up to the abuse and trying to change the power relations altogether. The movement's mantra highlights the relative disadvantage of people of color in dealing with the courts, the police, the security systems, and the law, that is, places where people of color currently "matter" as threats first, and as citizens second (if they are lucky). Organizing against police brutality needs the commitment of white people using our power to strengthen the chances for justice in all communities.

Many people ask, "So what can I do with my white privilege?" I wrote some answers to that question in the essay *White Privilege: An Account to Spend* [5] at the request of the St. Paul Foundation in Minnesota. The Foundation mounted an impressive campaign in the 1990s to counter racism in the Twin Cities. They told me that my white privilege essay made white people feel bad about themselves and gloomy about the U.S. The Foundation staff asked me if I would write something that gave more reassurance and hope. I slept on the question and was waked up next morning by a new metaphor: white privilege is like a bank account I was given at birth. I can spend it down to weaken the system that gave it to me. And because it is white privilege, it will keep refilling. So I will never go bankrupt spending down my bank account of white privilege. I gave sixteen examples of actions I have taken that reduce white privilege and distribute power more fairly. This is a good paper to give to white people who have learned about white privilege and ask, "What can I do?" It is, however, about my circumstances, not theirs, and should be read as a call to reflect on one's own circumstances and move from there.

Later, the St. Paul Foundation came back and said they wanted 40,000 people in their anti-racism workshops. They had only 4,000. Why weren't more white people signing up? I wrote *White People Facing Race: Uncovering the Myths that Keep Racism in Place.* [6] Most white people don't want to give up the myths that give white people power. Each of what I named as the five myths was based on my own experience of cultural mythologies in white America. Each of the myths props up white privilege, white dominance, or white supremacy. They protect white people's sense of virtue and normalcy. The myths run very deep in white psyches.

I am glad that I wrote the privilege papers and am glad when people decide to take part in discussions on privilege. I have seen many discussions lead to emotional, social, political, institutional, legal, and cultural change. If you use my work, I ask that you not take my examples out of context; the examples are about my personal experience, placed against the backdrop of systemic racism. Write your own lists. Try to see both individually and systemically at the same time. For white people, I advise that you try not to drift into feelings of shame, blame, or guilt. You need a certain cool-headedness to study your racial advantage, instead of being defensive about what you may feel as an attack on you by those who describe privilege. The aim of my work is to give us a better grip on how we came to be placed as we are in social and racial systems, and what any of us can do with unearned advantage to make the world more just.

I wish people clarity as we reflect on our own advantages and the power they put into our hands. I wish people courage as they act conscientiously and radically. I wish people from marginalized groups self-respect, staying power, and survival skills when dealing with so many entitled people who cannot yet understand how systems of privilege and power are at work in and around us.

Yours,

Peggy

Notes

1 This paper is included in this volume as Chapter 1.
2 This paper is included in this volume as Chapter 2.
3 This paper is included in this volume as Chapter 3.
4 This paper is included in this volume as Chapter 4.
5 This paper is included in this volume as Chapter 5.
6 This paper is included in this volume as Chapter 6.

Reference

Wellman, D. (1977). *Portraits of white racism*. Cambridge: Cambridge University Press.

1

WHITE PRIVILEGE AND MALE PRIVILEGE: A PERSONAL ACCOUNT OF COMING TO SEE CORRESPONDENCES THROUGH WORK IN WOMEN'S STUDIES (1988)[1]

Through work to bring materials and perspectives from Women's Studies into the rest of the curriculum, I have often noticed men's unwillingness to grant that they are over-privileged in the curriculum, even though they may grant that women are disadvantaged. Denials that amount to taboos surround the subject of advantages that men gain from women's disadvantages. These denials protect male privilege from being fully recognized, acknowledged, lessened, or ended.

Thinking through unacknowledged male privilege as a phenomenon with a life of its own, I realized that since hierarchies in our society are interlocking, there was most likely a phenomenon of white privilege that was similarly denied and protected, but alive and real in its effects. As a white person, I realized I had been taught about racism as something that puts others at a disadvantage, but had been taught not to see one of its corollary aspects, white privilege, which puts me at an advantage.

I think whites are carefully taught not to recognize white privilege, as males are taught not to recognize male privilege. So I have begun in an untutored way to ask what it is like to have white privilege. This paper is a partial record of my personal observations and not a scholarly analysis. It is based on my daily experiences within my particular circumstances.

I have come to see white privilege as an invisible package of unearned assets that I can count on cashing in each day, but about which I was "meant" to remain oblivious. White privilege is like an invisible weightless knapsack of special provisions, assurances, tools, maps, guides, codebooks, passports, visas, clothes, compass, emergency gear, and blank checks.

Since I have had trouble facing white privilege, and describing its results in my life, I saw parallels here with men's reluctance to acknowledge male privilege. Only rarely will a man go beyond acknowledging that women are disadvantaged to acknowledging that men have unearned advantage, or that unearned privilege has not been good for men's development as human beings, or for society's development, or that privilege systems might ever be challenged and changed.

I will review here several types or layers of denial that I see at work protecting, and preventing awareness about, entrenched male privilege. Then I will draw parallels, from my own experience, with the denials that veil the facts of white privilege. Finally, I will list forty-six ordinary and daily ways in which I experience having white privilege, by contrast with my African American colleagues in the same building. This list is not intended to be generalizable. Others can make their own lists from within their own life circumstances.

Writing this paper has been difficult, despite warm receptions for the talks on which it is based.[2] For describing white privilege makes one newly accountable. As we in Women's Studies work reveal male privilege and ask men to give up some of their power, so one who writes about having white privilege must ask, "Having described it, what will I do to lessen or end it?"

The denial of men's over-privileged state takes many forms in discussions of curriculum change work. Some claim that men must be central in the curriculum because they have done most of what is important or distinctive in life or in civilization. Some recognize sexism in the curriculum but deny that it makes male students seem unduly important in life. Others agree that certain individual thinkers are male-oriented but deny that there is any systemic tendency in disciplinary frameworks or epistemology to over-empower men as a group. Those men who do grant that male privilege takes institutionalized and embedded forms are still likely to deny that male hegemony has opened doors for them personally. Virtually all men deny that male over-reward alone can explain men's centrality in all the inner sanctums of our most powerful institutions. Moreover, those few who will acknowledge that male privilege systems have over-empowered them usually end up doubting that we could dismantle these privilege systems. They may say they will work to improve women's status, in the society or in the university, but they can't or won't support the idea of lessening men's. In curricular terms, this is the point at which they say that they regret they cannot use any of the interesting new scholarship on women because the syllabus is full. When the talk turns to giving men less cultural room, even the most thoughtful and fair-minded of the men I know will tend to reflect, or fall back on, conservative assumptions about the inevitability of present gender relations and distributions of power, calling on precedent or sociobiology and psychobiology to demonstrate that male domination is natural and follows inevitably from evolutionary pressures. Others resort to arguments from "experience" or religion or social responsibility or wishing and dreaming.

After I realized, through faculty development work in Women's Studies, the extent to which men work from a base of unacknowledged privilege, I understood that much of their oppressiveness was unconscious. Then I remembered the frequent charges from women of color that white women whom they encounter are oppressive. I began to understand why we are justly seen as oppressive, even when we don't see ourselves that way. At the very least, obliviousness of one's privileged state can make a person or group irritating to be with. I began to count the ways in which I enjoy unearned skin privilege and have been conditioned into oblivion about its existence, unable to see that it put me "ahead" in any way, or put my people ahead, over-rewarding us and yet also paradoxically damaging us, or that it could or should be changed.

My schooling gave me no training in seeing myself as an oppressor, as an unfairly advantaged person, or as a participant in a damaged culture. I was taught to see myself as an individual whose moral state depended on her individual moral will. At school, we were not taught about slavery in any depth; we were not taught to see slaveholders as damaged people. Slaves were seen as the only group at risk of being dehumanized. My schooling followed the pattern which Elizabeth Minnich has pointed out: whites are taught to think of their lives as morally neutral, normative, and average, and also ideal, so that when we work to benefit others, this is seen as work that will allow "them" to be more like "us."[3] I think many of us know how obnoxious this attitude can be in men.

After frustration with men who would not recognize male privilege, I decided to try to work on myself at least by identifying some of the daily effects of white privilege in my life. It is crude work, at this stage, but I will give here a list of special circumstances and conditions I experience that I did not earn but that I have been made to feel are mine by birth, by citizenship, and by virtue of being a conscientious law-abiding "normal" person of goodwill. I have chosen those conditions that I think in my case attach somewhat more to skin-color privilege than to class, religion, ethnic status, or geographical location, though these other privileging factors are intricately intertwined. As far as I can see, my African American co-workers, friends, and acquaintances with whom I come into daily or frequent contact in this particular time, place, and line of work cannot count on most of these conditions.

1. I can, if I wish, arrange to be in the company of people of my race most of the time.
2. I can avoid spending time with people whom I was trained to mistrust and who have learned to mistrust my kind or me.
3. If I should need to move, I can be pretty sure of renting or purchasing housing in an area which I can afford and in which I would want to live.
4. I can be reasonably sure that my neighbors in such a location will be neutral or pleasant to me.
5. I can go shopping alone most of the time, fairly well assured that I will not be followed or harassed by store detectives.
6. I can turn on the television or open to the front page of the paper and see people of my race widely and positively represented.
7. When I am told about our national heritage or about "civilization," I am shown that people of my color made it what it is.
8. I can be sure that my children will be given curricular materials that testify to the existence of their race.

9. If I want to, I can be pretty sure of finding a publisher for this piece on white privilege.

10. I can be fairly sure of having my voice heard in a group in which I am the only member of my race.

11. I can be casual about whether or not to listen to another woman's voice in a group in which she is the only member of her race.

12. I can go into a book shop and count on finding the writing of my race represented, into a supermarket and find the staple foods that fit with my cultural traditions, into a hairdresser's shop and find someone who can deal with my hair.

13. Whether I use checks, credit cards, or cash, I can count on my skin color not to work against the appearance that I am financially reliable.

14. I could arrange to protect our young children most of the time from people who might not like them.

15. I did not have to educate our children to be aware of systemic racism for their own daily physical protection.

16. I can be pretty sure that my children's teachers and employers will tolerate them if they fit school and workplace norms; my chief worries about them do not concern others' attitudes toward their race.

17. I can talk with my mouth full and not have people put this down to my color.

18. I can swear, or dress in secondhand clothes, or not answer letters, without having people attribute these choices to the bad morals, the poverty, or the illiteracy of my race.

19. I can speak in public to a powerful male group without putting my race on trial.

20. I can do well in a challenging situation without being called a credit to my race.

21. I am never asked to speak for all the people of my racial group.

22. I can remain oblivious to the language and customs of persons of color who constitute the world's majority without feeling in my culture any penalty for such oblivion.

23. I can criticize our government and talk about how much I fear its policies and behavior without being seen as a cultural outsider.

24. I can be reasonably sure that if I ask to talk to "the person in charge," I will be facing a person of my race.

25. If a traffic cop pulls me over or if the IRS audits my tax return, I can be sure I haven't been singled out because of my race.

26. I can easily buy posters, postcards, picture books, greeting cards, dolls, toys, and children's magazines featuring people of my race.

27. I can go home from most meetings of organizations I belong to feeling somewhat tied in, rather than isolated, out of place, outnumbered, unheard, held at a distance, or feared.

28. I can be pretty sure that an argument with a colleague of another race is more likely to jeopardize her chances for advancement than to jeopardize mine.

29. I can be fairly sure that if I argue for the promotion of a person of another race, or a program centering on race, this is not likely to cost me heavily within my present setting, even if my colleagues disagree with me.

30. If I declare there is a racial issue at hand, or there isn't a racial issue at hand, my race will lend me more credibility for either position than a person of color will have.

31. I can choose to ignore developments in minority writing and minority activist programs, or disparage them, or learn from them, but in any case, I can find ways to be more or less protected from negative consequences of any of these choices.

32. My culture gives me little fear about ignoring the perspectives and powers of people of other races.

33. I am not made acutely aware that my shape, bearing, or body odor will be taken as a reflection on my race.

34. I can worry about racism without being seen as self-interested or self-seeking.

35. I can take a job with an affirmative action employer without having my co-workers on the job suspect that I got it because of my race.

36. If my day, week, or year is going badly, I need not ask of each negative episode or situation whether it has racial overtones.

37. I can be pretty sure of finding people who would be willing to talk with me and advise me about my next steps, professionally.

38. I can think over many options, social, political, imaginative, or professional, without asking whether a person of my race would be accepted, or allowed to do what I want to do.

39. I can be late to a meeting without having the lateness reflect on my race.

40. I can choose public accommodation without fearing that people of my race cannot get in or will be mistreated in the places I have chosen.

41. I can be sure that if I need legal or medical help, my race will not work against me.

42. I can arrange my activities so that I will never have to experience feelings of rejection owing to my race.

43. If I have low credibility as a leader, I can be sure that my race is not the problem.

44. I can easily find academic courses and institutions that give attention only to people of my race.

45. I can expect figurative language and imagery in all of the arts to testify to experiences of my race.

46. I can choose blemish cover or bandages in "flesh" color and have them more or less match my skin.

I repeatedly forgot each of the realizations on this list until I wrote it down. For me, white privilege has turned out to be an elusive and fugitive subject. The pressure to avoid it is great, for in facing it I must give up the myth of meritocracy. If these things are true, this is not such a free country; one's life is not what one makes it; many doors open for certain people through no virtues of their own. These perceptions mean also that my moral condition is not what I had been led to believe. The appearance of being a good citizen rather than a troublemaker comes in large part from having all sorts of doors open automatically because of my color.

A further paralysis of nerve comes from literary silence protecting privilege. My clearest memories of finding such analysis are in Lillian Smith's unparalleled *Killers of the Dream* and Margaret Andersen's review of Karen and Mamie Fields' *Lemon Swamp*. Smith, for example, wrote about walking toward black children on the street and knowing they would step into the gutter (Smith, 1949); Andersen contrasted the pleasure that she, as a white child, took on summer driving trips to the south with Karen Fields' memories of driving in a closed car stocked with all necessities lest, in stopping, her black family should suffer "insult, or worse" (Andersen, 1984; Fields & Fields, 1983). Adrienne Rich also recognizes and writes about daily experiences of privilege, but in my observation, white women's writing in this area is far more often on systemic racism than on our daily lives as light-skinned women.

In unpacking this invisible knapsack of white privilege, I have listed conditions of daily experience that I once took for granted, as neutral, normal, and universally available to everybody, just as I once thought of a male-focused curriculum as the neutral or accurate account that can speak for all. Nor did I think of any of these perquisites as bad for the holder. I now think that we need a more finely differentiated taxonomy of privilege, for some of these varieties are only what one would want for everyone in a just society, and others give license to be ignorant, oblivious, arrogant, and destructive. Before proposing some more finely tuned categorization, I will make some observations about the general effects of these conditions on my life and expectations.

In this potpourri of examples, some privileges make me feel at home in the world. Others allow me to escape penalties or dangers that others suffer. Through some, I escape fear, anxiety, insult, injury, or a sense of not being welcome, not being real. Some keep me from having to hide, to be in disguise, to feel sick or crazy, to negotiate each transaction from the position of being an outsider or, within my group, a person who is suspected of having too close links with a dominant culture. Most keep me from having to be angry.

I see a pattern running through the matrix of white privilege, a pattern of assumptions that were passed on to me as a white person. There was one main piece of cultural turf; it was my own turf, and I was among those who could control the turf. I could measure up to the cultural standards and take advantage of the many options I saw around me to make what white culture would call a success of my life. *My skin color was an asset for any move I was educated to want to make.* I could think of myself as "belonging" in major ways and of making social systems work for me. I could freely disparage, fear, neglect, or be oblivious to anything outside of the dominant cultural forms. Being of the main culture, I could also criticize it fairly freely. My life was reflected back to me frequently enough so that I felt, with regard to my race, if not to my sex, like one of the real people.

Whether through the curriculum or in the newspaper, the television, the economic system, or the general look of people in the streets, I received daily signals and indications that my people counted and that others either didn't exist or must be trying, not very successfully, to be like people of my race. I was given cultural permission not to hear voices of people of other races or have a tepid cultural tolerance for hearing or acting on such voices. I was also raised not to suffer seriously from anything that darker-skinned people might say about my group, "protected," though perhaps I should more accurately say prohibited, through the habits of my economic class and social group, from living in racially mixed groups or being reflective about interactions between people of differing races.

In proportion as my racial group was being made confident, comfortable, and oblivious, other groups were likely being made unconfident, uncomfortable, and alienated. Whiteness protected me from many kinds of hostility, distress, and violence that I was being subtly trained to visit in turn upon people of color.

For this reason, the word "privilege" now seems to me misleading. Its connotations are too positive to fit the conditions and behaviors which "privilege systems" produce. We usually think of privilege as being a favored state, whether earned, or conferred by birth or luck. School graduates are reminded they are privileged and urged to use their (enviable) assets well. The word "privilege" carries the connotation of being something everyone must want. Yet some of the conditions I have described here work to systemically over-empower certain groups. Such privilege simply confers dominance, gives permission to control, because of one's race or sex. The kind of privilege that gives license to some people to be, at best, thoughtless and, at worst, murderous should not continue to be referred to as a desirable attribute. Such "privilege" may be widely desired without being in any way beneficial to the whole society.

Moreover, though "privilege" may confer power, it does not confer moral strength. Those who do not depend on conferred dominance have traits and qualities that may never develop in those who do. Just as Women's Studies courses indicate that women survive their political circumstances to lead lives that hold the human race together, so "underprivileged" people of color who are the world's majority have survived their oppression and lived survivors' lives from which the white global minority can and must learn. In some groups, those dominated have actually become strong through not having all of these unearned advantages, and this gives them a great deal to teach the others. Members of so-called privileged groups can seem foolish, ridiculous, infantile, or dangerous by contrast.

I want, then, to distinguish between earned strength and unearned power conferred systemically. Power from unearned privilege can look like strength when it is, in fact, permission to escape or to dominate. But not all of the privileges on my list are inevitably damaging. Some, like the expectation that neighbors will be decent to you, or that your race will not count against you in court, should be the norm in a just society and should be considered as the entitlement of everyone. Others, like the privilege not to listen to less powerful people, distort the humanity of the holders as well as the ignored groups. Still others, like finding one's staple foods everywhere, may be a function of being a member of a numerical majority in the population. Others have to do with not having to labor under pervasive negative stereotyping and mythology.

We might at least start by distinguishing between positive advantages that we can work to spread, to the point where they are not advantages at all but simply part of the normal civic and social fabric, and negative types of advantage that unless rejected will always reinforce our present hierarchies. For example, the positive "privilege" of belonging, the feeling that one belongs within the human circle, as some Native Americans say, fosters development and should not be seen as privilege for a few. It is, let us say, an entitlement that none of us should have to earn; ideally it is an unearned entitlement. At present, since only a few have it, it is an unearned advantage for them. The negative "privilege" that gave me cultural permission not to take darker-skinned-Others seriously can be seen as arbitrarily conferred dominance and should not be desirable for anyone. This paper results from a process of coming to see that some of the power that I originally saw as attendant on being a human being in the United States consisted in having unearned advantage and conferred dominance, as well as other kinds of special circumstance not universally taken for granted.

In writing this paper I have also realized that white identity and status (as well as class identity and status) give me considerable power to choose whether to broach this subject and its trouble. I can pretty well decide whether to disappear and avoid and not listen and escape the dislike I may engender in other people through this essay, or interrupt, answer, interpret, preach, correct, criticize, and control to some extent what goes on in reaction to it. Being white, I am given considerable power to escape many kinds of danger or penalty as well as to choose which risks I want to take.

There is an analogy here, once again, with Women's Studies. Our male colleagues do not have a great deal to lose in supporting Women's Studies, but they do not have a great deal to lose if they oppose it either. They simply have the power to decide whether to commit themselves to more equitable distributions of power. They will probably feel few penalties whatever choice they make; they do not seem, in any obvious short-term sense, the ones at risk, though they and we are all at risk because of the behaviors that have been rewarded in them.

Through Women's Studies work I have met very few men who are truly distressed about systemic, unearned male advantage and conferred dominance. And so one question for me and others like me is whether we will be like them, or whether we will get truly distressed, even outraged, about unearned race advantage and conferred dominance and if so, what we will do to lessen them. In any case, we need to do more work in identifying how they actually affect our daily lives. We need more down-to-earth writing by people about these taboo subjects. We need more understanding of the ways in which white "privilege" damages white people, for these are not the same ways in which it damages the victimized. Skewed white psyches are an inseparable part of the picture, though I do not want to confuse the kinds of damage done to the holders of special assets and to those who suffer the deficits. Many, perhaps most, of our white students in the United States think that racism doesn't affect them because they are not people of color; they do not see "whiteness" as a racial identity. Many men likewise think that Women's Studies does not bear on their own existences because they are not female; they do not see themselves as having gendered identities. Insisting on the universal "effects" of "privilege" systems, then, becomes one of our chief tasks, and being more explicit about the particular effects in particular contexts is another. Men need to join us in this work.

In addition, since race and sex are not the only advantaging systems at work, we need to similarly examine the daily experience of having age advantage, or ethnic advantage, or physical ability, or advantage related to nationality, religion, or sexual orientation. Professor Marnie Evans suggested to me that in many ways the list I made also applies directly to heterosexual privilege.[4] This is a still more taboo subject than race privilege: the daily ways in which heterosexual privilege makes some persons comfortable or powerful, providing supports, assets, approvals, and rewards to those who live or expect to live in heterosexual pairs. Unpacking that content is still more difficult, owing to the deeper embeddedness of heterosexual advantage and dominance and stricter taboos surrounding these.

But to start such an analysis I would put this observation from my own experience: The fact that I live under the same roof with a man triggers all kinds of societal assumptions about my worth, politics, life, and values and triggers a host of unearned advantages and powers. After recasting many elements from the original list I would add further observations like these:

1. My children do not have to answer questions about why I live with my partner (my husband).
2. I have no difficulty finding neighborhoods where people approve of our household.
3. Our children are given texts and classes that implicitly support our kind of family unit and do not turn them against my choice of domestic partnership.
4. I can travel alone or with my husband without expecting embarrassment or hostility in those who deal with us.
5. Most people I meet will see my marital arrangements as an asset to my life or as a favorable comment on my likability, my competence, or my mental health.
6. I can talk about the social events of a weekend without fearing most listeners' reactions.
7. I will feel welcomed and "normal" in the usual walks of public life, institutional and social.
8. In many contexts, I am seen as "all right" in daily work on women because I do not live chiefly with women.

Difficulties and dangers surrounding the task of finding parallels are many. Since racism, sexism, and heterosexism are not the same, the advantages associated with them should not be seen as the same. In addition, it is hard to isolate aspects of unearned advantage that derive chiefly from social class, economic class, race, religion, region, sex, or ethnic identity. The oppressions are both distinct and interlocking, as the Combahee River Collective statement of 1977 continues to remind us eloquently (Eisenstein, 1978).[5]

One factor seems clear about all of the interlocking oppressions. They take both active forms that we can see and embedded forms that members of the dominant group are taught not to see. In my class and place, I did not see myself as racist because I was taught to recognize racism only in individual acts of meanness by members of my group, never in invisible systems conferring racial dominance on my group from birth. Likewise, we are taught to think that sexism or heterosexism is carried on only through intentional, individual acts of discrimination, meanness, or cruelty, rather than in invisible systems conferring unsought dominance on certain groups. Disapproving of the systems won't be enough to change them. I was taught to think that racism could end if white individuals changed their attitudes; many men think sexism can be ended by individual changes in daily behavior toward women. But a man's sex provides advantage for him whether or not he approves of the way in which dominance has been conferred on his group. A "white" skin in the United States opens many doors for whites whether or not we approve of the way dominance has been conferred on us. Individual acts can palliate, but cannot end, these problems. To redesign social systems, we need first to acknowledge their colossal unseen dimensions. The silences and denials surrounding privilege are the key political tool here. They keep the thinking about equality or equity incomplete, protecting unearned advantage and conferred dominance by making these taboo subjects. Most talk by whites about equal opportunity seems to me now to be about equal opportunity to try to get into a position of dominance while denying that systems of dominance exist.

Obliviousness about white advantage, like obliviousness about male advantage, is kept strongly inculturated in the United States so as to maintain the myth of meritocracy, the myth that democratic choice is equally available to all. Keeping most people unaware that freedom of confident action is there for just a small number of people props up those in power and serves to keep power in the hands of the same groups that have most of it already. Though systemic change takes many decades, there are pressing questions for me and I imagine for some others like me if we raise our daily consciousness on the perquisites of being light-skinned. What will we do with such knowledge? As we know from watching men, it is an open question whether we will choose to use unearned advantage to weaken invisible privilege systems and whether we will use any of our arbitrarily awarded power to try to reconstruct power systems on a broader base.

Notes

1 This essay was originally published as McIntosh (1988).
2 This paper was presented at the Virginia Women's Studies Association conference in Richmond, VA in April, 1986, and the American Educational Research Association conference in Boston in October, 1986, and discussed with two groups of participants in the Dodge Seminars for Secondary School Teachers in New York and Boston in the spring of 1987.
3 From 1985 to 1990, Minnich and McIntosh spoke together at a number of colleges and universities regarding bringing people of color and women into the curriculum. It was during these consultations that Minnich would regularly point out this pattern.
4 Evans gave McIntosh this feedback after McIntosh had presented her talk on white and male privilege in 1986, before this essay was published.
5 The Combahee River Collective Statement was originally published in Eisenstein (1978) but it has appeared on its own as a Kitchen Table Women of Color Press publication as well as in "Combahee River Collective" (1979), which includes a letter from Barbara Smith verifying that the attribution to Eisenstein is accurate for first publication. See also Hull, Scott, and Smith (1982); and Smith (1983).

References

Andersen, M. (1984). Race and the social science curriculum: A teaching and learning discussion. *The Radical Teacher*, (27), 17–20.
Combahee river collective: A black feminist statement. (1979). *Off Our Backs*, 9(6), 6–8.
Eisenstein, Z. (1978). The Combahee river collective statement. *Capitalist patriarchy and the case for socialist feminism*. New York: Monthly Review Press.
Fields, M. G., & Fields, K. E. (1983). *Lemon swamp and other places: A Carolina memoir*. London: Free Press.
Frazier, D., Smith, B., & Smith, B. (1977). Combahee river collective statement. In Hull, A. G., Scott, P. B., & Smith, B. (Eds.) (1982). *All the women are white, all the blacks are men, but some of us are brave: Black women's studies*. Old Westbury, NY: The Feminist Press.
McIntosh, P. (1988). White privilege and male privilege: A personal account of coming to see correspondences through work in women's studies. *Working paper 189*. Wellesley, MA: Wellesley Center for Research on Women.
Smith, B. (Ed.) (1983). *Home girls: a black feminist anthology*. New Brunswick: Rutgers University Press.
Smith, L. (1949). *Killers of the dream*. New York: W. W. Norton.

2

WHITE PRIVILEGE: UNPACKING THE INVISIBLE KNAPSACK (1989)[1]

Through work to bring materials from Women's Studies into the rest of the curriculum, I have often noticed men's unwillingness to grant that they are over-privileged, even though they may grant that women are disadvantaged. They may say they will work to improve women's status, in the society, the university, or the curriculum, but they can't or won't support the idea of lessening men's. Denials which amount to taboos surround the subject of advantages which men gain from women's disadvantages. These denials protect male privilege from being fully acknowledged, lessened, or ended.

Thinking through unacknowledged male privilege as a phenomenon, I realized that since hierarchies in our society are interlocking, there was most likely a phenomenon of white privilege that was similarly denied and protected. As a white person, I realized I had been taught about racism as something that puts others at a disadvantage, but had been taught not to see one of its corollary aspects, white privilege, which puts me at an advantage.

I think whites are carefully taught not to recognize white privilege, as males are taught not to recognize male privilege. So I have begun in an untutored way to ask what it is like to have white privilege. I have come to see white privilege as an invisible package of unearned assets that I can count on cashing in each day, but about which I was "meant" to remain oblivious. White privilege is like an invisible weightless knapsack of special provisions, maps, passports, code-books, visas, clothes, tools, and blank checks.

Describing white privilege makes one newly accountable. As we in Women's Studies work to reveal male privilege and ask men to give up some of their power, so one who writes about white privilege must ask, "Having described it, what will I do to lessen or end it?"

After I realized the extent to which men work from a base of unacknowledged privilege, I understood that much of their oppressiveness was unconscious. Then I remembered the frequent charges from women of color that white women whom they encounter are oppressive.

I began to understand why we are justly seen as oppressive, even when we don't see ourselves that way. I began to count the ways in which I enjoy unearned skin privilege and have been conditioned into oblivion about its existence.

I was taught to see racism only in individual acts of meanness, not in invisible systems conferring dominance on my group.

My schooling gave me no training in seeing myself as an oppressor, as an unfairly advantaged person, or as a participant in a damaged culture. I was taught to see myself as an individual whose moral state depended on her individual moral will. My schooling followed the pattern my colleague Elizabeth Minnich has pointed out: whites are taught to think of their lives as morally neutral, normative, and average, and also ideal, so that when we work to benefit others, this is seen as work which will allow "them" to be more like "us."[2]

I decided to try to work on myself at least by identifying some of the daily effects of white privilege in my life. I have chosen those conditions which I think in my case attach somewhat more to skin-color privilege than to class, religion, ethnic status, or geographic location, though of course all these other factors are intricately intertwined. As far as I can see, my African American coworkers, friends, and acquaintances with whom I come into daily or frequent contact in this particular time, place, and line of work cannot count on most of these conditions.

1. I can if I wish arrange to be in the company of people of my race most of the time.
2. If I should need to move, I can be pretty sure of renting or purchasing housing in an area which I can afford and in which I would want to live.
3. I can be pretty sure that my neighbors in such a location will be neutral or pleasant to me.
4. I can go shopping alone most of the time, pretty well assured that I will not be followed or harassed.
5. I can turn on the television or open to the front page of the paper and see people of my race widely represented.
6. When I am told about our national heritage or about "civilization," I am shown that people of my color made it what it is.
7. I can be sure that my children will be given curricular materials that testify to the existence of their race.
8. If I want to, I can be pretty sure of finding a publisher for this piece on white privilege.
9. I can go into a music shop and count on finding the music of my race represented, into a supermarket and find the staple foods that fit with my cultural traditions, into a hairdresser's shop and find someone who can cut my hair.

10. Whether I use checks, credit cards or cash, I can count on my skin color not to work against the appearance of financial reliability.
11. I can arrange to protect my children most of the time from people who might not like them.
12. I can swear, or dress in secondhand clothes, or not answer letters, without having people attribute these choices to the bad morals, the poverty, or the illiteracy of my race.
13. I can speak in public to a powerful male group without putting my race on trial.
14. I can do well in a challenging situation without being called a credit to my race.
15. I am never asked to speak for all the people of my racial group.
16. I can remain oblivious of the language and customs of persons of color who constitute the world's majority without feeling in my culture any penalty for such oblivion.
17. I can criticize our government and talk about how much I fear its policies and behavior without being seen as a cultural outsider.
18. I can be pretty sure that if I ask to talk to "the person in charge," I will be facing a person of my race.
19. If a traffic cop pulls me over or if the IRS audits my tax return, I can be sure I haven't been singled out because of my race.
20. I can easily buy posters, postcards, picture books, greeting cards, dolls, toys, and children's magazines featuring people of my race.
21. I can go home from most meetings of organizations I belong to feeling somewhat tied in, rather than isolated, out-of-place, outnumbered, unheard, held at a distance, or feared.
22. I can take a job with an affirmative action employer without having co-workers on the job suspect that I got it because of race.
23. I can choose public accommodations without fearing that people of my race cannot get in or will be mistreated in the places I have chosen.
24. I can be sure that if I need legal or medical help, my race will not work against me.
25. If my day, week, or year is going badly, I need not ask of each negative episode or situation whether it has racial overtones.
26. I can choose blemish cover or bandages in "flesh" color and have them more or less match my skin.

I repeatedly forgot each of the realizations on this list until I wrote it down. For me, white privilege has turned out to be an elusive and fugitive subject. The pressure to avoid it is great, for in facing it I must give up the myth of meritocracy. If these things are true, this is not such a free country; one's life is not what one makes it; many doors open for certain people through no virtues of their own.

In unpacking this invisible knapsack of white privilege, I have listed conditions of daily experience that I once took for granted. Nor did I think of any of these perquisites as bad for the holder. I now think that we need a more finely differentiated taxonomy of privilege, for some of these varieties are only what one would want for everyone in a just society, and others give license to be ignorant, oblivious, arrogant, and destructive.

I see a pattern running through the matrix of white privilege, a pattern of assumptions that were passed on to me as a white person. There was one main piece of cultural turf; it was my own turf, and I was among those who could control the turf. *My skin color was an asset for any move I was educated to want to make.* I could think of myself as belonging in major ways and of making social systems work for me. I could freely disparage, fear, neglect, or be oblivious to anything outside of the dominant cultural forms. Being of the main culture, I could also criticize it fairly freely.

In proportion as my racial group was being made confident, comfortable, and oblivious, other groups were likely being made unconfident, uncomfortable, and alienated. Whiteness protected me from many kinds of hostility, distress and violence that I was being subtly trained to visit, in turn, upon people of color.

For this reason, the word "privilege" now seems to me misleading. We usually think of privilege as being a favored state, whether earned or conferred by birth or luck. Yet some of the conditions I have described here work systematically to over-empower certain groups. Such privilege simply *confers dominance* because of one's race or sex.

I want, then, to distinguish between earned strength and unearned power conferred systemically. Power from unearned privilege can look like strength when it is in fact permission to escape or to dominate. But not all of the privileges on my list are inevitably damaging. Some, like the expectation that neighbors will be decent to you, or that your race will not count against you in court, should be the norm in a just society. Others, like the privilege to ignore less powerful people, distort the humanity of the holders as well as the ignored groups.

We might at least start by distinguishing between positive advantages, which we can work to spread, and negative types of advantage, which unless rejected will always reinforce our present hierarchies. For example, the feeling that one belongs within the human circle, as some Native Americans say, should not be seen as privilege for a few. Ideally it is an unearned entitlement. At present, since only a few have it, it is an unearned advantage for them. This paper results from a process of coming to see that some of the power that I originally saw as attendant on being a human being in the United States consisted in unearned advantage and conferred dominance.

The question is: "Having described white privilege, what will I do to end it?"

I have met very few men who are truly distressed about systemic, unearned male advantage and conferred dominance. And so one question for me and others like me is whether we will be like them, or whether we will get truly distressed, even outraged, about unearned race advantage and conferred dominance and, if so, what will we do to lessen them. In any case, we need to do more work in identifying how they actually affect our daily lives. Many, perhaps most, of our white students in the U.S. think that racism doesn't affect them because they are not people of color; they do not see "whiteness" as a racial identity. In addition, since race and sex are not the only advantaging systems at work, we need similarly to examine the daily experience of having age advantage, or ethnic advantage, or physical ability, or advantage related to nationality, religion, or sexual orientation.

Difficulties and dangers surrounding the task of finding parallels are many. Since racism, sexism, and heterosexism are not the same, the advantages associated with them should not be seen as the same. In addition, it is hard to disentangle aspects of unearned advantage which rest more on social class, economic class, race, religion, sex, and ethnic identity than on other factors. Still, all of the oppressions are interlocking, as the Combahee River Collective Statement of 1977 continues to remind us eloquently (Eisenstein, 1978).[3]

One factor seems clear about all of the interlocking oppressions. They take both active forms, which we can see, and embedded forms, which as a member of the dominant group one is taught not to see. In my class and place, I did not see myself as a racist because I was taught to recognize racism only in individual acts of meanness by members of my group, never in invisible systems conferring unsought racial dominance on my group from birth.

Disapproving of the systems won't be enough to change them. I was taught to think that racism could end if white individuals changed their attitudes. But a "white" skin in the United States opens many doors for whites whether or not we approve of the way dominance has been conferred on us. Individual acts can palliate, but cannot end, these problems.

To redesign social systems, we need first to acknowledge their colossal unseen dimensions. The silences and denials surrounding privilege are the key political tool here. They keep the thinking about equality or equity incomplete, protecting unearned advantage and conferred dominance by making these taboo subjects. Most talk by whites about equal opportunity seems to me now to be about equal opportunity to try to get into a position of dominance while denying that systems of dominance exist.

It seems to me that obliviousness about white advantage, like obliviousness about male advantage, is kept strongly inculturated in the United States so as to maintain the myth of meritocracy, the myth that democratic choice is equally available to all. Keeping most people unaware that freedom of confident action is there for just a small number of people props up those in power and serves to keep power in the hands of the same groups that have most of it already.

Although systemic change takes many decades, there are pressing questions for me and I imagine for some others like me if we raise our daily consciousness on the perquisites of being light-skinned. What will we do with such knowledge? As we know from watching men, it is an open question whether we will choose to use unearned advantage to weaken hidden systems of advantage, and whether we will use any of our arbitrarily awarded power to try to reconstruct power systems on a broader base.

Notes

1 In 1989, McIntosh gave Roberta Spivek permission to condense "White Privilege and Male Privilege" (McIntosh, 1988) for the July/August 1989 issue of *Peace and Freedom*, the magazine of the Women's International League for Peace and Freedom.
2 From 1985 to 1990, Minnich and McIntosh spoke together at a number of colleges and universities regarding bringing people of color and women into the curriculum. It was during these consultations that Minnich would regularly point out this pattern.
3 The Combahee River Collective Statement was originally published in Eisenstein (1978) but it has appeared on its own as a Kitchen Table Women of Color Press publication as well as in "Combahee River Collective" (1979), which includes a letter from Barbara Smith verifying that the attribution to Eisenstein is accurate for first publication. See also Hull, Scott, and Smith (1982); and Smith (1983).

References

Combahee river collective: A black feminist statement. (1979). *Off Our Backs*, 9(6), 6–8.

Eisenstein, Z. (1978). The Combahee river collective statement. *Capitalist patriarchy and the case for socialist feminism*. New York: Monthly Review Press.

Frazier, D., Smith, B., & Smith, B. (1977). Combahee river collective statement. In Hull, A. G., Scott, P. B., & Smith, B. (Eds.) (1982). *All the women are white, all the blacks are men, but some of us are brave: Black women's studies*. Old Westbury, NY: The Feminist Press.

McIntosh, P. (1988). White privilege and male privilege: A personal account of coming to see correspondences through work in women's studies. *Working paper No. 189*. Wellesley, MA: Wellesley Center for Research on Women.

McIntosh, P. (1989, July/August). White privilege: Unpacking the invisible knapsack. *Peace & Freedom Magazine*, 10–12.

Smith, B. (Ed.) (1983). *Home girls: A black feminist anthology*. New Brunswick: Rutgers University Press.

3

SOME NOTES FOR FACILITATORS ON PRESENTING MY WHITE PRIVILEGE PAPERS (2004, 2018)[1]

My work is not about blame, shame, guilt, or whether one is a "nice person." It's about observing, realizing, thinking systemically and personally about circumstances beyond one's control. It is about seeing privilege, the "up-side" of oppression and discrimination. It is about unearned advantage, which can also be described as exemption from some form of discrimination.

Please do not generalize from my papers. They are about my experience, not about the experiences of all white people in all times and places and circumstances. The paragraph in each paper that precedes the list of examples says this, and often allays fears of white people that a paper on white privilege will call them racist.

Please keep "the lists" in their autobiographical contexts. It is a matter of scholarly integrity and accuracy not to claim more than I did. I compared my own circumstances with those of some of the African American women I worked with. Being clear about this will actually increase one's effectiveness as a facilitator. Say, "This is from just one white woman coming to see she's white in her time and place and workspace … She's writing about herself, not about you."

The work goes best when you draw on participants' own personal experiences, not their opinions. Opinions invite argumentation. Telling about actual experience invites listening. Opinions tend to bring on conflict whereas shared experiences tend to elicit curiosity and empathy. When participants move from experiential testimony to opinion, bring them back. Note: Usual academic habits work toward abstract argumentation and against telling about one's own experience.

When exploring privilege, it is useful to use "Serial Testimony," a disciplined mode in which each participant gets to respond in turn, uninterrupted, for, say, one minute, timed. I call this "the Autocratic Administration of Time in the Service of Democratic Distribution of Time." I think that without rigorous use of a watch or timer, Serial Testimony can be as undemocratic as any other discussion form.

Understand that every participant has an intricate "politics of location" (Rich, 1984) within the systems of social power. For example, all people in a workshop, community, or class will have constantly accumulating experiences of both advantage and disadvantage, empowerment and disempowerment, discrimination or privilege, within many different systems of power.

Recognize that all people are both located in systems and also uniquely individual.

Co-presentations and panels of people speaking about their experiences one after another can be very effective. I do not usually arrange for "dialogues," since I feel they are often a veiled form of debating and fighting, rather than listening and learning. I discourage "crosstalk" after panels unless it further clarifies what the panelists have said.

My lists of unearned privileges are not "check lists" or questionnaires. The lists are not confessional readings, either.

Please see my works on the specificity of "my sample." I compared my circumstances only with what I knew of the circumstances of my African American female colleagues in the same building and line of work. This sample is very specific with regard to race, sex, time, place, region, location, workplace, nation, vocation, and access to public transportation.

Behind and within my examples are institutions and structures that bear on my experience such as schools, textbook publishers, the police, the IRS, the media, the military, the law, medical institutions, retail businesses, and corporations.

Invite people to make their own autobiographical lists of privilege and disadvantage, for example, about their:

Economic Class
Formal Education
Region and Nation
Language
Ethnicity
Employment
Religion
Gender Identity

Sexual Orientation
Social Class
Physical Ability
Parents' Nation of Origin
Parents' Relation to Money, to Formal Education, to the Dominant Language, to the Nation.

Beware of gym-exercises which position people in only one aspect of their identities, asking them to step forward or backward from a baseline at a given prompt. Such exercises can oversimplify the identities of those who participate.

Urge participants to avoid self-righteousness and preaching to family and friends about privilege, especially if they have just discovered it themselves.

Explain the word "systemic." Help participants or students to understand (or begin to understand) what it is to see society systemically, rather than only in terms of individuals making individual choices.

Explain that most U.S. people, especially white people, have trouble seeing systemically. Explain the myth of meritocracy: that the unit of society is the individual and that whatever one ends up with must be whatever that individual wanted, worked for, earned, and deserved. This myth suppresses knowledge of systemic oppression and especially its "up-side," systemic privilege.

The work on privilege can help participants to strengthen three intellectual muscles: a) the ability to see in terms of power systems as well as in terms of individuals; b) the ability to see how systemic discrimination is matched by systemic privilege, i.e., exemption from discrimination; and c) the ability to see, and feel located in, many different kinds of privilege systems.

If you are a teacher, it is a good idea to think about your own privilege work in schools and universities as making people smarter, not necessarily better. Academic institutions do not claim that making us better is their primary goal.

Some people "get" the idea of systemic privilege and ask "But what can I do?" My answer is that you can use unearned advantage to weaken systems of unearned advantage. I suggest that white privilege is like a bank account that I did not ask for,[2] but that I can choose to spend. People with unearned privilege have far more power than we have been taught to realize under the myth of meritocracy. Those with power can brainstorm about how to use unearned assets to share power; these assets include time, money, leisure, connections, space, travel, and willingness to advocate for people without institutional power. Using these assets may connect with changes in other behaviors as well, such as paying attention, making associations, intervening, speaking up, asserting and deferring, being alert, taking initiative, doing ally work, and recognizing and acting against both the external and internalized forms of oppression and privilege.

Notes

1 This essay was originally printed in 2004 to accompany McIntosh (1988) and McIntosh (1989). This version reflects many edits and updates between 2004 and 2018.
2 See Chapter 5, *White Privilege: An Account to Spend*.

References

McIntosh, P. (1988). White privilege and male privilege: A personal account of coming to see correspondences through work in women's studies. *Working paper 189*. Wellesley, MA: Wellesley College Center for Research on Women.

McIntosh, P. (1989, July/August). White privilege: Unpacking the invisible knapsack. *Peace and Freedom*, 10–12.

Rich, A. (1984). Notes toward a politics of location. In *Blood, bread, and poetry: Selected prose 1979–1985* (pp. 210–231). New York: W. W. Norton & Company. 210–231.

4

SELECTION FROM "WHITE PRIVILEGE, COLOR AND CRIME: A PERSONAL ACCOUNT" (1998)[1]

For my first paper on white privilege in 1988, I compared my racial experiences with those of African American female colleagues who work in the same time, place, building, or line of work, doing research on and programs about women. I listed forty-six ways in which I experienced daily conditions of unearned over-advantage by contrast with these colleagues. I listed conditions that seemed to me a little more connected with race than with class, region, religion, ethnicity, or sexual orientation, though I wrote that I saw all of these factors as intricately intertwined privilege systems that bear on any one person's experience.

My method remains autobiographical here, but in the 1988 paper, I compared myself only to African American women colleagues with whom I came into daily or fairly frequent contact. For this analysis on Color and Crime, I have broadened the sample to include friends and colleagues in other racial ethnic groups. It is by contrast with these women that I tell of the racial over-advantage that makes my life markedly different from theirs in matters relating to law, crime, and the courts.

In this chapter I raise again my question of 1988: Having seen unearned power or permission to dominate, how can I use my unearned power to distribute power more fairly and to weaken systems of unearned privilege?

Here are some of the conditions on my 1988 list that relate most closely to color and crime.[2]

1. I can be sure that if I need legal or medical help my race will not work against me.
2. If my day, week, or year is going badly, I need not ask of each negative episode or situation whether it has racial overtones.
3. If a cop pulls me over, or if the IRS audits my tax returns, I can be sure I haven't been singled out because of my race.

4.   If I get angry and ask to speak to the "person in charge," I can be fairly sure I will be talking to a person of my race.
5.   I did not have to educate our children to be aware of systemic racism for their own daily physical protection.
6.   I can go shopping alone in department stores near my house without being followed or harassed by store detectives on the grounds that I may be shoplifting or soliciting.

What follows here are new points explicitly related to color and crime.

1.   We were able to teach our children that the police were their allies, and that they should dial 911 if they had an emergency.
2.   In my neighborhood, I can be sure that the police will not harass me because of the color of my skin.
3.   In my neighborhood, any police officer who might need to arrest people in my family is likely to be a person of my race.
4.   Criminality is not imputed to me as a genetic component of racial character; I am not assumed to belong to a group of people predisposed to crime.
5.   The word "criminal" in the dominant culture does not conjure up the faces of people whose skin color is like that of my father, mother, brother, sister, husband, nieces, or nephews.
6.   I have never heard or read the suggestion that all the people of my color ought to be locked up or killed. Even Islamic fundamentalists do not call for the killing of all people of my ethnicity, only certain "morally corrupt" ones.
7.   In World War II, my grandparents, despite having some German ancestry, were not locked up by the U.S. government in internment camps as Japanese people were on the suspicion or pretext that they might be traitors.
8.   Nearly all of the lawyers and judges who study, write about, argue, debate, and practice law in the U.S. are people of my race.
9.   Law breaking by the U.S. government with regard to treaties with Native people was not taught to me as a criminal aspect of my racial heritage.
10.   Deceiving indigenous people is not described as a genetic or inherited trait of white people.
11.   Refusing to honor Indian treaties today is not shown to me as law-breaking by white people.
12.   The U.S. government has never made it a crime for me to speak my native language or observe the religious ceremonies of my parents and grandparents.
13.   The prison system is thoroughly controlled by people of my race.
14.   The Constitution I am subject to was created by people of my ethnic heritage to apply to some people of my ethnic heritage and to not apply to people of other races.

15. I am assumed to be entitled to whatever legal defense I can afford, even if it allows me to be acquitted of a crime I have committed.

16. If I am suspected of being guilty but am acquitted of a crime, I will be seen by the dominant group as someone who got through the cracks rather than as a person who especially deserved not to get through the cracks.

17. Those who have been able to afford the high costs of legal training have been, for the most part, people of my race.

18. Lawyers featured as experts by the media are overwhelmingly people of my race.

19. Those who have been able to pay lawyers' fees and legal costs have for the most part been people of my race.

20. A successful tax evader in my ethnic group is usually portrayed as a cheater or even a victor, but not as an innate criminal or a representative of a whole race of people who drain society.

21. A "deadbeat dad" in my ethnic group is portrayed in the media as financially but not sexually irresponsible.

22. When I walk into the courthouses of my country, I can expect respectful treatment from the receptionists.

23. As a child, I heard jokes and sound tracks that cast people of other races as habitually dumb, coarse, sneaky, shifty, sly, malicious, or underhanded, and kept people of my race protected from such typecasting.

24. The voiceovers of criminals, shifty individuals, and villains in Disney films and in ads rarely sound like people of my racial/ethnic group.

25. If I stand in line at a bank teller's window, no one looks strangely at me, as though they have a problem with my being there.

26. If I suffer damages and decide to take a case to court, the people I see in the legal system will probably be people who were trained to trust my kind and me.

27. I can stand behind another person at an ATM machine without being feared as a potential mugger.

28. If I am laughing with friends on a street at night, it is not assumed that we are in a gang.

29. A realtor has never discriminated against me to "protect property values."

30. No one has ever suggested that I might have dealt drugs in order to afford a certain car or house.

31. The men of my race who took 400 billion dollars in the 1994 U.S. Savings and Loan (S&L) scandal are not branded as criminals or seen as enemies of the U.S. people, even though the money has never been returned.

32. When I think of prisons, I do not have to think of people of my race as disproportionately serving time in them, having longer than average sentences, and being executed in greater numbers.

33. I am allowed to believe, and encouraged to believe, that people of my race are in general law-abiding rather than law-breaking.

34. TV shows and films show people of my color as the main defenders of law and order, cleverest detectives, best lawyers and judges, and wiliest outlaws.

35. Portrayals of white males on TV as criminals and violent individuals do not incriminate me as a white person; these males, even the outlaws, are usually presented as strong men of a quintessentially American type.
36. Illegal acts by the U.S. government, in the present and in the past, around the world, are not attributed by whites to white immorality and illegality.
37. Bad race relations in the United States are not attributed by whites to our criminal behavior, despite a history of race-related breaking of laws by whites over the entire span of Anglo-European life on this continent.

The list could expand much further. The examples are hard to allow into my awareness, however, because these truths are so unpleasant to face and so disruptive of my acculturated sense of myself in moral and political worlds.

My conscious mind was schooled to believe that to some extent justice will be done through the legal system of the United States; it balks at the realization that continual unnamed injustices result from whites' projection onto our race of being on the side of law or being an admirable, individualistic challenger to the law, while people of color are subtly portrayed as beyond the ethics and rules of law and order, whether by being shiftless, exploitive, unreliable, violent, or criminal.

The bad behavior of a person of color, when it occurs or is thought to occur, is unfairly projected onto his or her entire group, whether it is the stereotype of inscrutable shiftiness attributed to Asian Americans, the gangsterism attributed to Latino men, or the inscrutability attributed to Native people. Meanwhile, people of my Anglo-European ethnicity escape mass negative projections by the media and by other white citizens. Projections onto Italians that they are connected to the Mafia, onto Jews that their main value is making money, or onto the Irish as drunken drivers do occur, and "courts of public opinion" sometimes incriminate them without evidence. But the Anglo-European character perpetually bobs up, like a Weeble doll, as the norm of uprightness that negative attributions cannot destabilize, except for very short periods, in particular instances of crimes that are seen as committed by individuals.

I am struck by the magnitude of the effects of unincriminated "whiteness." As a case in point, white-collar crime is considered to be unlike other crimes. There is a lack of public acknowledgment in the media of the damage it does to the society. Men like Michael Milken and even the Savings & Loan scandal perpetrators continue to be lionized for their ruthlessness in breaking laws.[3] The $400 billion "lost" in the S&L scandal has never been traced, but the white men who are sitting on the money are not known as white crooks if they are thought of as crooks at all. Imagine what would have happened in the United States if Black or Chicano men had made so much investors' money disappear.

The reason I see a need to do the arithmetic of unearned overadvantage as a function of unearned disadvantage is that without it I am allowed to consider myself as a person neutrally placed in relation to these matters of law. Then I do not need to bother myself about "the forces for law and order" as long as I behave myself and do not run too many red lights. But in fact, the forces for law and order, because they do not deal evenly with us, are a threat both to me and to my colleagues of color, bringing them an absence of legal protection and security and bringing trepidation, anxiety, and anger, if not outright harassment and persecution. If I am let off what they endure, then I have an unearned advantage in the form of freedom from danger, fear, and anger, and I become a target for their legitimate anger. I do not think it is good to be a target of others' legitimate anger.

Several years ago, the teenage son of a black colleague of mine was stopped by the police as he drove to his family's suburban home one night. The police made him wake up both of his parents in the middle of the night to prove that he belonged in the mostly white neighborhood, that is, that his credentials were not forged. The memory of the police hostility and the humiliation will never disappear from that family and their community; for this family, I think the town's police can never be seen as allies. But can I see them as my allies? How are they my allies if they humiliate and try to intimidate my neighbors?

I visited the police station to discuss this. The police claimed they do such things in order to protect "our" neighborhood. "Ma'am, we're only trying to protect you." But I said, "It is a protection racket." They are creating a problem of bad race relations that they then claim to protect me against. Meanwhile, white privilege might be seen to insulate my family against such treatment and the knowledge of such treatment. We do get unearned freedom from fear, anger, and preoccupation with the question of what the police might do to us. But the bad race relations are not a favor to whites. They surface in the schools and in the streets, and lower the quality of life for everyone, including whites, who become targets for anger they do not understand and are kept from understanding by the silence surrounding privilege.

I fear the police sirens when I am pulled over for speeding, but even then I can observe the processes by which police officers usually decide to let me off with just a warning. I am a late middle-aged white woman with her hair in a bun who speaks with a soft voice and lives on a familiar street in a mostly white town. I can see the officers' inclination as they talk to me and look at my license, to feel that I am not as much of a danger on the road as, say, a young black man would be. Yet I am as much a danger on the road as the next speeder.

While writing this chapter, I had a vivid experience of how white privilege works in my favor in my place of work. Campus police found computer equipment on the porch of the building at 11:00 p.m., saw computer equipment in the back seat of my nearby car, and after searching the grounds called to town police and came into the building. They thought they had interrupted a robbery. I could tell by their faces, though, that they believed me when I said that I was just working late, and that earlier that day some new computer equipment was installed, and we were told we could take away old equipment if we would pay for any repairs. I think that an African American colleague found in this apparently incriminating situation would not have been so quickly believed, and would have had much more reason to be scared in the situation, if she had dared to work in this building so late at all.

In the nine years since I published the original white privilege paper, I have done more than ninety co-presentations with persons of color on the subject of privilege systems. Many co-presenters have said that within the last few days preceding our co-presentation, their financial credentials had been doubted or in stores they had been asked for more kinds of personal identification than had others. It does not matter that they might be full professors or own their own businesses; they get incriminated through whites' racial and ethnic projections onto them of financial unreliability and habitual dishonesty. I escape these projections. I can thus live naively, out of touch with life in the United States, unthinking on the question of how I reside in that society and how it resides in me.

Some well-meaning white readers of my analyses have felt that they will now just divest themselves of unearned advantage. It is not that simple. Doors will continue to open for us whether or not we want this to happen. I have, however, identified at least ten ways in which I can, in my own circumstances, use power to share power and use unearned privilege to weaken systems of unearned privilege. There are ways to collaborate, work as allies, and create change within institutions, policies, and individuals.

My own forms of activism have especially involved: choosing to work with women and men of color and trying to diversify all-white groups if I work with them; organizing for integration of my neighborhood; challenging and changing curricula, scholarship, and teaching methods to create more critical and more inclusive knowledge and education; co-presenting on white-skin privilege with persons of color to share podium time and honoraria; asking the local supermarket buyers why they will stock specialty Chinese but not specialty African American foods; writing to Hallmark and Crayola's executives about both racism and sexism in their product lines; trying to listen and then respond as an ally to participants of color in mostly white organizations; doing homework on, taking seriously, and disseminating words and works by those who do not a have white privilege; getting and using money to spread understanding of privilege systems (and denial of them) through school-based faculty development seminars, consultancies, talks, articles, letters, and conversation, including family conversation; understanding how much I have to learn from people I was taught to overlook, fear, or avoid – learning some of what they have to teach and being awed and grateful for that, and putting my life on a more inclusive and generous base, aware that white privilege both helps and hinders this effort.

There are some people of color who misread the original paper and feel it shows that white people know all about our racial status and behavior as whites. These readers think that I was saying things that all white people know. On the contrary, I was carefully taught in hundreds of ways not to know, not to see, what I wrote in that paper. I was taught that I didn't have a race. The word "race" referred to other people. I was just "normal." And I was taught to see racism only in individual acts of meanness, not in invisible systems conferring dominance on my group. People who benefit most, in the short term, from privilege systems are kept most blinded to them, for they interfere with the myth that democracy has been achieved and is working well.

I think that white people are socialized, conditioned, and educated to not know about white-skin privilege, even more thoroughly than males are raised to be oblivious to male privilege. To use a parallel and telling example with fewer political and social ramifications: most right-handed people cannot tell you about right-handed privilege. They were not taught to be aware of it. Left-handed people have a lot to say on the subject of being left-handed, which often comes as a surprise to the dominant group.

The white readers who have found my analysis most unsurprising are in general those who, through interracial relationships, cross-cultural adoptions, and other "border crossings" are positioned so as to have double or triple perspectives, seeing on both sides of lines of privilege. White women who become keenly aware of male privilege may get to parallel insights on race privilege if they are able to decenter themselves, as we have asked men to do. But in doing so, white women forego the moral high ground that many of us found so empowering in being the people with justice on our side. It can feel sickening to be decentered when you have just felt centered at least gender-wise for the first time ever.

I originally found that going into this subject deeply shook up my sense of being a moral and a nice person. It complicates the whole matter of moral worth. But it has nothing to do with niceness. It has to do with being oppressive through privilege and oblivious to one's oppressiveness, again through privilege. One white privilege is not to know about white privilege. This has nothing to do with whether one is nice. It is about the sense of entitlement with which people of my color took permission, or what we read as permission, from God, or nature, to fill the turf, the time, the payrolls, and the centers of recognized authority, including the courts of law. And then not to know that this is our racial history.

I believe that when this happens, the centers of recognized authority within the psyche also take on a cast of white dominance, and replicate the larger society in the inner self. And then the forces of law and order, or of brave domination, in the psyche can feel they are holding at bay the forces of law-lessness and all the projections that they have acquired. To me, it feels as if forces in my personality that are privileged in the wider society for whites become forces in a multiple, interior self that have license to govern, imprison, or ride roughshod over the rest of my personality and perceptions. Then what I call *interior colonization* occurs. The self gets taken over by just a segment of itself, and the rest gets identified with the Other, imprisoned, or silenced, while the authorities can deny that any repression is occurring.

Through my work on these problems, I have found it is hard to keep alert to myself as white. It requires diligent reflection on the relation between what I send out to the world in my projections and what I receive. I find that the ancient Greek idea of seeing as a two-part process is useful, though we learned about it in school in order to learn that it was inaccurate. Yes, I do seem to send out "eyebeams" that pick up some things and not others, so that what I send out bears on what I get back. My racial and other social understandings go forth and pick up what they have the capacity to see. Keeping alert to the racial origins of my eyebeams is appropriate but taxing. I was not taught to see myself as white, let alone to see my seeing as influenced by whiteness. And I was taught to see myself as on the side of the law and of fairness. It seems now that my Anglo-European eyebeams saw lawfulness where people of my color were in control and the scene was quiet.

This work on seeing privilege is epistemologically dizzying as well as emotionally hard. It is hard to learn you are being decentered when you were not aware of being central to begin with. I think that for heterosexual white males it has been especially hard, like a one-two-three punch, first having "maleness" problematized and then "whiteness" and then "straightness." I think that many people who are trying to be reflective are feeling a kind of epistemological nausea from being whirled around so suddenly, as it seems to them. And I myself find that a retreat from the subject of being consciously white is tempting. I see it as curling up and falling asleep, and sleep has its place. But nightmares will come. And I would rather be awake, and not a sleepwalker. I now feel that being a white sleepwalker through the world of white control perpetuates a zombielike incapacitation of the heart and mind.

It is only a hypothesis, but I would guess that white oblivion about, and inculturated denial of, privilege acts as a psychological prison system that costs white people heavily in terms of preventing human development. Walking obliviously through our own racial experience may perpetuate the imprisonment of the heart and intelligence in a false law-and-order of tyrannizing denial about who, what, and where we are. So the societal systems of color and crime may reside also in the psyches of white people, where an equivalent of bad race relations or white supremacy damages the civic health and balance of the soul.

Notes

1 This essay originally appeared as McIntosh (1998).
2 The numbers listed here are reflective of the edits made for this version. They differ from the numbers listed in the original.
3 References to Milken and the S&L scandal were included in the original essay in 1998, twenty-one years before this publication. It is worthwhile to note that Milken went to prison for ten years for securities fraud, among other charges. Since then, he has invested heavily in cancer research. As a result, Forbes Fortune Magazine declared Milken to be "The Man who Changed Medicine" (Daniels, 2004). Milken also maintains his status as one of the richest men in the world. Going to prison for illegal trading and tax evasion has not diminished his long-term reputation. The S&L scandal is just one of a series of major financial scandals that occurred before and after the original publication of this essay. The perpetrators of these crimes, or their identity

groups, have not been demonized in society much beyond the political moment of the scandal, partly because of the various privileges they have.

References

Daniels, C. (2004, November 29). The man who changed medicine. *Fortune Magazine.*

McIntosh, P. (1988). White privilege and male privilege: A personal account of coming to see correspondences through work in women's studies. *Working paper 189.* Wellesley, MA: Wellesley College Center for Research on Women.

McIntosh, P. (1998). White privilege, color and crime: A personal account. In Mann, C. R., & Zatz, M. (Eds.), *Images of color, images of crime* (pp. 207–216). Los Angeles: Roxbury Publishing Company.

5

SELECTION FROM "WHITE PRIVILEGE: AN ACCOUNT TO SPEND" (2009)[1]

When The Saint Paul Foundation founded the community initiative called *Facing Race*, it asked brave questions: Is it possible to improve the racial climate of a region? If so, is it possible for the change to stick? They found that teaching about privilege of any kind can be stressful, scary, disorienting, and unpleasant for any group that learns it is privileged.

They asked whether I could do anything about the guilt of white people on learning about white privilege. I decided therefore to write more about the advantages for me as white person and a person who has class privilege and it led me to a new class-based metaphor of a bank account.

White Ignorance of Systems

The phrase "white privilege" triggers anger in many people. For example, many working-class white people who have worked very hard all their lives feel frustrated to be told that they have any unearned advantages. White people who have struggled to stay afloat have trouble imagining that they have any "privilege" in relation to others. If white people have privilege, why do they have so little to show for it?

To get the answer, you need to be able to think systemically about how power works in the United States to produce different types of privilege and discrimination. A white person may not speak English well, or may not have enough money, or may face discrimination as a recent immigrant. The stresses from not having English-speaking privilege, class privilege, or U.S. privilege may make a white person feel that he or she has no privilege at all. Everything about life is hard. *Yet it is harder still for those who do not have white privilege.*

Often, to the police, to merchants, and to bankers, a disadvantaged working-class person is ranked lower than one who fits the middle-class norm. At the same time, those white working-class people who do "get ahead," against the odds, often believe their own hard work alone got them where they are. The American dream — that people individually achieve upward mobility through hard work — appears to be a valid dream for them, and they imagine it to be working for everybody else, too. They are taught not to notice anything except their individual efforts. Yet their race influenced which jobs, neighborhoods, schools, and public services they could access. Unless they can see systemically, they will not understand this.

People benefiting from a privilege system are taught not to see it, for the myth of meritocracy denies that power systems exist. Everybody succeeds on his or her own merits. According to this myth, if people do not suc-ceed, it is because they are not worthy; they aren't smart or don't work hard enough. The myth of meritocracy says that if people work hard, they get ahead.

I was taught in both subtle and overt ways that white people had earned and deserved all of our successes. I was taught to assume that we white people were "the best and the brightest" compared with people of color. I unconsciously believed that white people were superior, and that our being in charge of the society was a normal and natural sign of our superiority.

I thought it was normal for the police to be nice to us, because we were good people; it was normal to read about white people in the schoolbooks because we had created "civilization"; it made sense that we got good jobs because we were hard workers; we got rich because we saved our money. Since I believed that all people succeeded on their merits, I didn't see the invisible mechanisms of group privilege that pushed us as white people ahead. The power we held seemed perfectly appropriate and just.

This feeling of being correctly placed above others kept me and other white people of my class from seeing the ways in which everyone is born into an unfair system. It prevented me from noticing how those with the most power got to define, reward, and control "success." It kept me from seeing that whe-ther I "succeeded" had less to do with how hard I worked, or how good a person I was, than with the systemic class and race privilege that I was born with. Through this privilege I was given the benefit of the doubt and didn't have to prove that I deserved to be accepted.

I was fifty years old when I noticed I had white privilege. A slow learner you may say, but a very good student of what I had been taught, which is that pri-vilege systems did not exist. After becoming aware of privilege, the question came up, "What am I going to do with all this unearned advantage that I have?" Though I raised the question in my original papers on privilege, I am here answering it at greater length since the Saint Paul Foundation has requested that I help white people handle the guilt that many of them feel on learning that they have privilege.

I will not set aside the image of white privilege as an invisible knapsack filled with assets that I can count on cashing in each day. But I am setting beside it a second way of thinking about white privilege. It is like a bank account I did not ask for but that I may choose to spend down. One of the ways that I may choose to spend it down is to weaken the systems of unearned advantage that gave it to me. But because it is white privilege it will keep refilling through no effort of my own, so I will never go bankrupt spending down my bank account of white privilege.

Spending the Bank Account

So how do I spend down my bank account of white privilege? I organize projects, invest time and money, read, write letters and emails, intervene, spread the word, campaign, work with others against injustice, and try to influence policy. It is a mixture of raising my own awareness and trying to change the social fabric as well. For example, my work has involved:

1. Coming to see and weaken some of the habits of whiteness and white control that I was raised to take for granted in me and other white people.
2. Visiting the police in my town to protest their harassment of African Americans and immigrants.
3. Organizing for racial integration of my neighborhood.
4. Trying to diversify mostly white groups I work with.
5. Hiring and supporting people of color.
6. Co-presenting on white skin privilege with persons of color (Indigenous, Latina/o, Asian American, and African American) to share publicity, podium time, and speaking fees
7. Pressuring supermarkets to stock the foods of ethnic groups they would like to exclude from their customer base.
8. Starting conversations, including some family and public conversations, about privilege and racism.
9. Listening and then responding as an ally to participants of color in mostly white organizations rather than letting their comments hang unacknowledged in silence.
10. Doing homework on, then promoting and disseminating, the words and works of those who do not have white privilege.
11. Understanding how much I have to learn from people I was taught to overlook, fear, or avoid for reasons of race, class, religion, nationality, or sexual orientation.
12. Making presentations and organizing programs in which I am aware and honest about how much I have learned from people of color.
13. Belonging to a group of white anti-racists who meet regularly.
14. Intervening in and even ending conversations that put down vulnerable groups.
15. Choosing to live on less money so our family can give more money toward social justice or individuals in need.
16. Being more willing to use the terms "white superiority" and "white supremacy" in discussing the assumptions and outcomes of white privilege.

As in my original paper on white privilege, this list of examples is auto-biographical and relates to my own circumstances. Such a list would look different for each person who made one, depending on his or her circumstances and sphere of influence. In general, those who are privileged have more power than they use for social change; almost none realize how much power privilege gives us to act.[2]

Why Spend Down the Bank Account?

What are the payoffs for white people if we use our unearned advantage to weaken systems of unearned advantage? It feels good to stop being resented or even hated. Many of us who have racial or class power do not realize that we are so mistrusted by people who have less money or status. This mistrust may never go away even if we raise our awareness and commitment to social justice. This is understandable. We must not expect to be thanked or trusted even if we know we are working on ourselves and for others as well. It is not up to those with less power to make us feel good again.

But the payoffs are huge. To me it feels like recouping losses. One thing my privilege had cost me was the opportunity to engage in real conversations with people I was taught to look down on. They could sense I was unconsciously patronizing or scared. Working against racism and white privilege brought me a purpose in life beyond feathering my own nest or working chiefly for the happiness of my own family, friends, and students. I began to develop a stronger character and personality when I started to have working relationships with people beyond the social and racial groups I was allowed to associate with as a child. These new and authentic relationships gave me for the very first time a sense of community. Until then, the word "community" had been empty and without meaning for me as a white person who was raised in mostly white towns of single-family homes. Working for social change took me deeper into awareness of my own socialization and also made me more extroverted, even visionary, in my hopes and dreams, which were no longer so individualistic. I began to participate in making strategies to change whole institutions.

I now spend my energy on projects I could not have dreamed of when I was young. When my projects are going well, it is like finally living in a better world – a world that has reduced suffering. Using privilege on projects for social change allows me to work toward the world in which I want to live.

My life has improved so much that sometimes I wonder what kept me from seeing the big picture of privilege earlier in my life. I am indebted to activists of the 1960s, 1970s, and 1980s who woke up to systems they had not been taught about in the 1950s, and tried to shape a freer, more humane, less racist, world. Many are people of color. In the words of Victor Lewis, "People of color pay the tuition for whites to learn about racism."[3]

Once I discovered privilege, my biggest source of resistance to spending down the bank account, was fear – my fear that if I tried to use unearned power to share power for a new social ideal, I would lose status, money, respect, purpose, life plans, family, friends, pleasure, institutional support, and my existing sense of identity. I know most white people today are already feeling insecure with regard to social class, income, time, opportunity, safety, and their capacity to do what they want. Many people feel, "I'm already stretched and hurting. I can't be sure of my future. Why should I go beyond taking care of myself and my own?"

If you are feeling this way, take courage. My experience has been that even very ordinary, everyday sharing of racial and other kinds of power can have a tremendous emotional and social payoff. It can make the world seem less insecure, and more meaningful. It can create a sense of community – the knowledge that we are in this life together. Lessening white privilege feels to me like repairing lost connections. Most of the disconnections in U.S. culture and in our institutions occur along lines of power. None of us is simply part of one identity group. We all have souls and identities, and at the same time we were born with social locations and group identities that shape us and easily keep us separated from other people, especially within institutions. But we were also born into relation with others. I find that working against racism mends the social fabric, heals the soul, and reduces fear. It makes things better for everybody.

Discussions of race and privilege can help form an invaluable ability to recognize systems of power, both around us and within us. This knowledge can empower us all to know better where we came from, who and where we are, and what we can do. In the SEED Project, when we combine self-reflection with group process, we create a mysterious and powerful way for people to go much further than before in their own understanding. Speaking candidly with others about our experiences within power systems is an innovative and promising way for a group of people to get more insight into how to help everyone survive and thrive. Some think that at this time in our history a person is dangerously un-American to conceptualize race and power systemically, but I feel that in doing so one becomes a better-informed, wiser, and more humane citizen of the community, the nation, and the world.

Notes

1 This essay originally appeared as McIntosh (2009).
2 My most significant work in "spending down the bank account" has been founding and working for three decades with Emily Style and the staff of the National SEED Project on Inclusive Curriculum, in order to make school curricula, teaching methods, and climates more gender-fair, multicultural, and inclusive of all students no matter what their backgrounds are.
3 Unpublished personal communication to the author over the course of their friendship.

Reference

McIntosh, P. (2009). *White privilege: An account to spend.* St. Paul, MN: Saint Paul Foundation.

6

WHITE PEOPLE FACING RACE: UNCOVERING THE MYTHS THAT KEEP RACISM IN PLACE (2009)[1]

"A hard or scary thing about talking about racism is ..." As Victor Lee Lewis, Hugh Vasquez, and I start our sessions on race in places across the United States, we ask everyone in the participant group to pair up with another person to do this exercise that Victor Lewis devised. We ask each person to finish this oral prompt as many times as possible in one minute. Each person speaks uninterrupted. **"A hard or scary thing about talking about racism is ..."**

This is a remarkable way of getting fear and resistance into the open, as people speak only for themselves, but also feel relief in the kinship with others who have similar fears. Here are some of the responses we have heard from white participants:

- You don't want to be called a racist.
- I am afraid I may be blamed.
- I may be ashamed.
- I may make a fool of myself.
- My racism may show.
- I may shut down.
- I may get hopeless.
- Someone will get angry at me.
- I could hurt someone.
- I may find out I have a lot to learn about myself.
- I may have to say I'm part of the problem.

In these responses from white people, I hear two fears – that of saying a "wrong" or hurtful thing, and that of losing self-esteem. I've concluded that these responses are rooted in our desire to feel good about ourselves and preserve our images of ourselves and our relationships in the world. We seem to know there is something to be feared, that may get us into trouble with others if we open the lid and speak about racism in the United States.

Resistance, Privilege, and Governing Myths

The desire to keep our image of ourselves "clean" is part of white privilege. Those of us who are white people in the United States feel entitled to feel good about ourselves because we have been shielded from the negative aspects of white history. We have received assurances that we are normal, admirable, and deserving, and that we have better values and behavior than people of color here and around the world. These teachings most often come to us subliminally from our families, educational systems, and the media. We resist looking at racism because we fear damage to our perception of ourselves as "good people" in the "greatest country" in the world.

I think it is natural that anyone would resist anything that might cloud their image of their goodness. But I suggest we ask ourselves why that image hasn't already been clouded. How have whites kept such a strong sense of pride and deservedness? The answer, I think, is that white people are raised on five strong cultural myths: **meritocracy, manifest destiny, white racelessness, monoculture,** and **white moral and managerial superiority.** These lay the foundation for our feeling good about ourselves as white people, and they work in us to override and discredit counter-evidence. They also deter us from entering into serious discussions of racism on a systemic as well as individual level. One of the central elements of white privilege is not having to take the subject of racism seriously.

The **myth of meritocracy** is the myth that the individual is the only unit of society, and that whatever a person ends up with must be what he or she individually wanted, worked for, earned, and deserved. This myth rests on the assumption that what people experience – how they see, feel, think, and behave, and what they are capable of accomplishing – are not influenced by any social system or circumstance. The myth of meritocracy acknowledges no systems of oppression or privilege that, for various people and in various situations, could make life arbitrarily more – or less – difficult.

The **myth of manifest destiny** includes the idea that white people were intended by God to take the lands of indigenous people in order to possess the whole of what is now the continental United States. Under this myth, whites do not have to allow into our moral or ethical awareness the fact that we live on land taken from those who were here before us, and whose cultures and physical existences white people attempted to destroy. Believing explicitly or implicitly that God intended white people to "settle" North America has excused many white people from seeing white settlement as a matter of racial violence in which they decimated others' settlements and lives.

The **myth of white racelessness** is the notion that white people do not have race or racial experience. In this view, we are just "normal." Others have race, which we are led to believe makes problems for them, or us. We who are "normal" are racially unmarked, and we set the standard for what it is to be human. The participation of white people in systems of dominance or oppression is not seen as part of our racial history.

The **myth of monoculture** is that there is one American culture and that we all experience it more or less the same way. Anyone who is having trouble with American culture is not seeing accurately or behaving appropriately. The myth of monoculture imposes an assumption and a requirement on people of color. It requires them to learn to see and feel and behave like white people ("normal" people) – that is, to assimilate into white culture – and it assumes that they have nothing to lose by forsaking their cultures of origin, and a great deal to gain from fitting into the one "normal" culture. Under the myth of monoculture, *E pluribus unum* (Out of many, one) is understood as an ideal, but its converse, *Intra unum plures* (Within one, many), is neither respected nor acknowledged.

When white people receive these key beliefs and assumptions from our families, the educational systems, and the media, we absorb the idea that white people are superior to others. This is not said in so many words. Instead, we learn to assume that it is natural for us to be in charge of the world and its affairs, and the idea that only a very unusual person of color, unlike others of his or her kind, can be trusted with power such as ours gets instilled in the subconscious minds of whites. This is the **myth of white moral and managerial superiority**.

It is important to recognize how strong a part this cluster of myths plays in creating the psychological underpinnings for whites' refusal to face racism. The myths have been taught to white people in the United States, usually at a subconscious level, for centuries. Each of these five myths rests in part on white privilege and creates resistance in the hearts and minds of white people to facing race. Elements of the myths can be heard in the most common statements of resistance to discussing race or even raising the subject:

- Why can't we just get along? There aren't any racial problems if people don't create them.
- We're all the same.
- I'm not prejudiced.
- I don't see color. I just see people.
- Why make waves?
- Don't make people angry.
- Look on the bright side.
- Studying race is divisive, even racist.
- We all have problems. People with character overcome them. Opportunity is there for everyone.
- Some people just don't know how to fit in.
- If they're going to live here, they ought to speak English. They are lucky to even be here.
- They are just ungrateful.
- They spoil this community – this country.

To face race is to be willing to critically examine the five myths underlying these statements. White people's resistance is natural. Raised in an environment that accepts these five myths as truth, why would those of us who are white not resist upsetting our egos, our perceptions of our family and ancestors, and our ideas about this nation? Will a new awareness of our racial history and of the present improve our lives? I feel strongly that the answer is yes. But raising our awareness is not easy because the process works against so much of what we have been led to believe by education, by the media, and by the focus on individualism in U.S. culture.

Overcoming Resistance

Those who want to do their homework on race relations must give up the sunny view of monoculture, that we are all in the same system and experiencing it the same way. They must learn to pluralize their minds. They must give up the myth of meritocracy and the assumption that whites should be in charge. The more-accurate frameworks allow one to perceive and recognize the diseases of racism and other societal ills even if one is not suffering as an obvious victim (Loewen, 1996; Zinn, 1980). Developing more-accurate frameworks in the minds of students or citizens requires developing six skills that are seldom taught in American schools:

- the ability to see that we are arbitrarily placed in the world at birth
- the ability to see how the circumstances of our birth give us starting orientations within many kinds of social, linguistic, cultural, and political hierarchies
- the ability to see how our locations in those systems influence our experiences and our understanding of ourselves and the world
- the ability to recognize that preexisting systemic hierarchies have created injustice, which all of us experience to a degree
- the ability to recognize that these hierarchies of power have also created unearned advantage or privilege, which all of us have experienced to a degree
- the ability to see we can work within and despite these hierarchies, in order to limit harm and increase the common good.

In the monocultural, single-system world I was living in before I learned to see other systems, I was looking fine. But in the multicultural world that I actually live in, the truth of my history is that I am a member of both oppressive and oppressed groups. To acknowledge the oppressive part of my ancestral history is to reposition myself in the social and political world more as part of the problem than as part of the solution. I was fearful of this repositioning; I feared loss of centrality, certainty, self-esteem, confidence, entitlement, power, self-satisfaction, self- respect, pride, the sense of superiority, the sense of protection, the sense of competence, and the familiar landscape of my psyche. Like most white people, I resisted looking at race.

What can help overcome that resistance? The best way I know is to set up processes of group interaction that value and honor the stories of each person in the group. We are all arbitrarily placed in systems, but we all have our individual essences, which I feel are our sacred centers. When white people tell deep, honest stories of knowing both oppression and privilege, and when these stories are believed, my experience is that white people can open themselves to facing race, without blame, shame, or guilt. They can exchange their resistance for a profound new understanding that sustains rather than destroying the psyche and the social fabric.

At our workshops on race, after the first prompt by Victor Lee Lewis has allowed people to acknowledge what is hard and scary in talking about race, we ask the pairs of participants to take a minute each to respond to the second of his prompts: "A good and useful thing about talking about racism is ..." When we repeat this prompt once again at the close of the session, we hear responses like these from white people:

- It is such a relief to get it out in the open.
- I've never just sat and listened to people of color talking about their lives before.
- I had no idea our lives were so different – and we work in the same building.
- I learned I was dreaming that we are "all living in the same world."
- I was sure I could be heard here.
- I know I am not being blamed here.
- Talking about race showed me to myself in a hard but good new way.
- I think I will be a better person now.
- Learning about privilege is changing everything for me.
- I can learn how to work against racism in myself and others.
- I have longed for interracial community; now I think there is hope for it.
- I am getting over my fear of people of color.
- I know I am white and this has untied so many knots for me.
- I never realized I had personal power to weaken the system of white privilege.

These responses reflect my own experience. Being known and heard while telling one's experience, and listening to the experiences of others, can be transformational. It lessens resistance to facing the injustices that distort all of us and produce social myths. It lessens fear and increases compassion and empathy. It helps white people see more clearly who we are and where we came from. It helps us to understand that though our learning of what we were taught has damaged and disempowered us, we have agency, too.

Support for overcoming my own resistance to facing race came from some of the most compelling authors I have read: Frantz Fanon, Paulo Freire, Lillian Smith,

Virginia Woolf, Demita Frazier, Beverly Smith, Barbara Smith, Will Gravely, Tillie Olsen, Akasha Gloria Hull, Sylvia Ashton-Warner, Audre Lorde, Alice Walker, Howard Zinn, and James Loewen. It also came from work with my colleagues Victor Lewis and Hugh Vasquez of the film the *Color of Fear*, all of the people in the film *Mirrors of Privilege*, scholars in women's studies and ethnic studies around the world, and colleagues in the National SEED Project, especially Brenda Flyswithhawks, Odie Douglas, Willa Cofield, Nancy Livingston, Eloise Tinley, Hugo Mahabir, Glenabah Martinez, Loren Moye, Jondou Chase Chen, Gail Cruise-Roberson, Motoko Mae-gawa, Ruth Mendoza, and Emily Style. These companions have confirmed in me the sense that we are not alone and that we are all hurt by the systems we are in.

Facing race, I have learned, opens new doors to possibility and connection. My life has been transformed by walking through those doors. A glimpse of the potential for a better life can help to overcome whites' resistance to facing race.

Note

1 This essay originally was published as McIntosh (2009).

References

Ashton-Warner, S. (1963). *Teacher*. New York: Simon and Schuster.

Butler, S. (Producer, Director). (2006). *Mirrors of privilege: Making whiteness visible*. [Video/DVD] World Trust Films.

Fanon, F. (1967). *Black skin, white masks*. New York: Grove Press.

Fanon, F. (1968). *The wretched of the earth*. New York: Grove Press.

Freire, P. (1970). *Pedagogy of the oppressed*. New York: Herder and Herder.

Frazier, D., Smith, B., & Smith, B. (1977). Combahee river collective statement. In Hull, A. G., Scott, P. B., & Smith, B. (Eds.) (1982). *All the women are white, all the blacks are men, but some of us are brave: Black women's studies*. Old Westbury, NY: The Feminist Press.

Gravely, W. (2019). *They stole him out of jail: Willie Earle, South Carolinas last lynching victim*. Columbia, SC: The University of South Carolina Press.

Lee, M. W. and Stir-Fry Productions (Producer, Director). (1997). *The color of fear*. [Video/DVD] Oakland, CA: Stir Fry Seminars and Consulting.

Loewen, J. W. (1996). *Lies my teacher told me: Everything your American history textbook got wrong* (1st Touchstone ed.). New York: Simon & Schuster.

Lorde, A. (1983). *Zami: A new spelling of my name*. Trumansburg, N.Y: Crossing Press.

Lorde, A. (1984). *Sister outsider: Essays and speeches*. Trumansburg, NY: Crossing Press

McIntosh, P. (2009). *White people facing race: Uncovering the myths that keep racism in place*. St. Paul, MN: Saint Paul Foundation.

Olsen, T. (1978). *Silences*. New York: Delacorte Press/Seymour Lawrence.

Smith, L. (1949). *Killers of the dream*. New York: W. W. Norton.

Walker, A. (1983). *In search of our mothers' gardens: Womanist prose* (1st ed.). San Diego: Harcourt Brace Jovanovich.

Woolf, V. (1928). *Orlando: A biography*. New York: C. Gaige.

Woolf, V. (1929). *A room of one's own*. New York: Harcourt, Brace and Company.

Zinn, H. (1980). *A people's history of the United States* (1st Harper colophon ed.). New York: Harper & Row.

PART II
The Fraudulence Papers

A LETTER ABOUT THE FRAUDULENCE PAPERS

Dear Reader,

In these essays on feeling like a fraud, I hope you will take some comfort from my claim that the chances are you are actually not a fraud. You may have been made to feel inadequate, defeated, unsure, unseen, and unwelcome in many of your institutional and personal circumstances. I feel for you if you have had a large amount of self-doubt. But I feel that often the standards by which you are made to feel bad are fraudulent standards and were created to uplift and inflate those who already have some power. Our society is filled with fakery. We are subtly bribed or coerced into going along with systems and judgments under which only a few can feel really good about ourselves.

If you are easily intimidated and quick to apologize when the world is going badly for you, you may be comforted by this series of Fraud papers. They say that you are probably no more fraudulent than the next person, but that vertical social institutions have been set up to persuade you to sit down, be quiet, lie low, and fit in, and then (as the promise goes) you will feel you belong. But the feelings of fraudulence are so strong that they may continue to tell you that others are the "real thing" while you are a "nothing." The Author, the Star, the Pundit, the Pro, the Bestseller, and the Hero — these are the "real people." Please forget it; they may well be even more insecure than you or me. As I see it, your self-doubt may be a blessing - you have divined that your soul is complicated and reflects plural creation and you are not one thing. You have many voices, ideas, and loves.

If you are up against a self-image that keeps mirroring inadequacy to you, the Fraud papers will tell you it's okay. It's just that you are a good student of the feeling of fraudulence that powerful structures tried to give you, and that you internalized. If you hold onto that debilitating lesson, you will keep apologizing and feeling bad. I hope these papers are like mental antibiotics, restoring some of your equilibrium and energy and freeing you up to doubt any oppressively fraudulent ideals that may have infected you.

Many people feel fraudulent at the idea of speaking in public. So I want to pass on to you some words which my mother-in-law, Millicent McIntosh,[1] gave to me when I told her I was nervous about giving a talk. She said, "If you focus on what you want the people in the back row to take away, you will lose your stage fright." For me this comment was extraordinarily useful; it relocated me from the introverted question of "How am I doing?" into the extroverted, relational question, "What do I want to convey?" Her words reminded me that I am not alone in this event. The other people there are equally real. I should relate to them. My aim should be to make the talk worth their time, and worth carrying away to other places. The people farthest from you are the ones, she suggested, that you must talk to; raise your voice so you can be heard in the back row. Perhaps she also intuited that some of those in the back row may not be so keen on being there in the first place. Her twenty-two words of advice got me over my fear of public speaking, though it did not allay my justified ambivalence about the worth of my words.

For me the Moebius strip from the German mathematician August Moebius perfectly conveyed the paradox that feeling like a fraud is deplorable and, at the same time, applaudable. This metaphor accurately describes the ambivalence in my mixed feelings about "excellence" as it is usually defined. The two-ness of the Moebius strip allowed me to explore fraudulence authentically in my papers.

The first Feeling Like A Fraud talk for the Stone Center for Developmental Services and Studies[2] at Wellesley was a success, but when I was invited to do a second one four years later, I simply could not outline the talk. I tried unsuccessfully for weeks and I had piles of notes. I discovered that for me the outline itself is a fraud. My genre is the list. So in that talk, I conducted a "house tour" of different rooms in my house and explained how I think differently about fraudulence in each of them. Switching from an outline to a list of domestic spaces freed me up to write authentically and enjoy the talk, which was about identifying elements of my "home-self" that spot fraudulence in some of the public roles I am asked to play.

The third Fraud talk came out of a wish to face my own feelings of fraudulence when coming into conflict. The fourth Fraud talk traced ambivalences and complexities that are deep and meaningful and that, I believe, constitute a plural psyche in any of us.

In the academic world, I often get thanks for the first Fraud paper from people who are struggling to write a Ph.D. dissertation and are bogged down in writing a literature review. The internet has made this process easier, but even so it can be grueling to try to trace where ideas came from and how they spread. Readers have thanked me for the second paper for its combination of domestic and professional assets in the "home-self." The third paper appeals to those who have been ashamed of hating conflict. The fourth paper is somewhat untested. I presented it as a keynote address for the American Psychological Association and the Texas Psychological Association, in a Luncheon Seminar series at the Wellesley Centers for Women in 2017, and in several talks at other colleges. But will it be useful? I hope that the idea that the psyche is plural will resonate with your experience or at least be worth thinking about with some sectors of your complex mind.

Earnestly yours,
Peggy

Notes

1 Millicent McIntosh was the head of the Brearley School in New York from 1930 to 1947 and President of Barnard College from 1948 until her retirement in 1964.
2 Wellesley College founded the Center for Research on Women (CRW) in 1974 and the Stone Center for Developmental Services and Studies (SCDSS) in 1981. From 1974 until 1995, researchers and staff referred to the CRW as "the Center" and the SCDSS as "the Stone Center." In 1995, the two centers came together to form the Wellesley Centers for Women, commonly referred to as "the Centers" or WCW.

7

FEELING LIKE A FRAUD, PART I (1985)[1]

Not so long ago in Wisconsin at the Wingspread Center I attended a conference on women's leadership in higher education. Seventeen women in a row spoke from the floor during a plenary session and all seventeen started their remarks with some kind of apology or disclaimer. The self-deprecating comments ranged from "I just wanted to say ..." to "I have just one point to make ..." to "I never thought about this before, but ..." to "I really don't know what I'm talking about, but here goes!"

Ironically enough, all of us had been funded to attend the conference because we supposedly knew something about Women's Leadership. Yet we seemed to share a feeling of illegitimacy when speaking in front of women like ourselves. The apologies started me on a new train of thought which led to this talk on "Feeling Like a Fraud."

I find that this title triggers a flash of recognition in both male and female friends and colleagues. For many, it calls up a familiar feeling – the feeling that in taking part in public life one has pulled the wool over others' eyes; that one is in the wrong place, and about to be found out; that there has been a colossal mistake in the selection and accreditation process which the rest of the world is about to discover. One dreams recurrently, as I do, that one has been exposed as "not belonging," or as having "gotten in" under false pretenses. In my case, someone from Harvard University calls to say they have found out I never took the Ph.D. qualifying exam in German. Or one feels like a play actor, a hypocrite, a stager of charades, or like sixteen personalities without a common center. One feels illegitimate in doing something, or appearing as something; one feels apologetic, undeserving, anxious, tenuous, out-of-place, misread, phony, uncomfortable, incompetent, dishonest, guilty. Many women and men I know seem to share these feelings. But some research and much observation suggest they are especially severe in women, both in chronic life-long forms and in acute forms in particular situations.

I think we need to take a double look at the phenomenon of feeling like a fraud. I will discuss it here from two apparently opposed points of view. I suggest both that we mustn't let the world make us feel like frauds, and that we must keep alive in ourselves that sense of fraudulence which sometimes overtakes us in public places. I suggest that on the one hand feeling like a fraud indicates that we have, deplorably, internalized value systems that said most people were incompetent and illegitimate in the spheres of power and public life and authority. But then on the other hand, I suggest that when we apologize in public, we are at some level making a deeply wise refusal to carry on the pretense of deserving and feeling good about roles in conventional and oppressive hierarchies. I think that most feelings of personal fraudulence need to be analyzed politically and deplored, especially feelings of fraudulence in "lower caste" people. But on the other hand, I also think that feeling like a fraud is conducive to social and political change, and that some forms of it should be applauded and developed in us, so that we become better at spotting fraudulence in, and trying to alter, the forms of our culture.

You may be wondering which of these sides I will come out on. I am coming out on both sides. My talk is like a Moebius strip. On one side it says, "We must not let them make us feel like frauds." And on the other side it says, "Let us continue to spot fraudulence in the public roles we are asked to play." And when I twist over this strip which has two "opposing" sides and join it together again as a circle, I have the Moebius strip phenomenon. You run your finger along the surface. Without changing sides, you cover all surfaces of the twisted circle of tape. In the end your finger comes back to the very spot it began without having changed sides. I feel that the two kinds of argument I am making here are similarly, so to speak, both "on the same side."

Let me give some more specific examples of the feelings of fraudulence which I am talking about. In students it often takes these forms. "The Admissions Committee made a mistake. I don't belong here." Or "I got an A on this paper. So he didn't find me out." Or "I got a B on this paper. So he found me out." Or "I got a C on this paper. He really found me out." All three reactions to the grade are variants on the same feeling that one was an imposter to begin with as author of the paper. Or in reaction to the comment "You made your points beautifully in this paper," the student may think, "It can't be true. I can't even remember what I said." Or a student who works on a committee may be praised by the Dean for her organizational skill, and think guiltily of the mess on the desk which the Dean hasn't seen. Analogously, a person feeling like a fraud when told that someone likes her will feel, "Then, he must be a jerk." Or, if told she is beautiful, will think only of her faults. Likewise, a graduate student, told that she has written "the definitive work" and will very likely have a brilliant defense, is likely to think that it is all a colossal mistake, and that she couldn't "defend" a guppy. When a letter of recommendation states: "Ms. X is one of the brightest students I have taught in the last fifteen years," Ms. X is likely to think, "What a pushover! But, how long can I keep fooling her?"

When a commencement speaker says, "Medicine will be better off with people like you entering the field," the graduates are likely to think, "These speakers are all hypocrites." If an executive says, "She has set her goals high and has met them in a truly professional way," the employee may feel, "This is no picture of me. I just hold the office together. I just talk to people, for goodness sake." The book reviewer may say, "This book is a path-breaking study," while the faculty member feels, "No, I just cobbled my term papers together into a book of essays because I want to get tenure." Within life in general, one may feel like a fraud speaking in meetings, calling in to a talk show, writing to the newspaper, being praised, telling people what one thinks, claiming to know anything, being called an expert, taking a strong point of view, putting one's head up in any public place, having opinions, and, most terrifying of all, having one's opinions taken seriously.

I have begun to touch on the tip of the iceberg for a few rather privileged people in rather academic and elite situations. There are myriad other examples from spheres of experience which are more widely shared in terms of class and race and culture. But I notice as I think through feelings of fraudulence that they seem to me not to occur in some areas of life. I pat our cat and the cat purrs. I don't feel like a fraud. It's not the same as getting an A on a paper. When I bring home chocolate chip mint ice cream, the kids' appreciation doesn't throw me into a panic about who I am. I think that being praised for a good spaghetti sauce or for finding a bargain is not so unnerving as being praised for giving a speech.

I do not think that it is simply the public nature of certain activities which makes us feel fraudulent. Kiyo Morimoto of the Bureau of Study Council at Harvard/Radcliffe has said that a majority of the incoming freshmen feel that they were admitted to the college by mistake. Feeling fraudulent can infect lives even within not-very-public situations.

I have come to think of it this way. The more hierarchical the activity or institution, and the higher up we go in it, the greater our feelings of fraudulence are likely to be. People feel fraudulent especially when ascending in hierarchies in which by societal definition they do not belong at the top of the pyramid. I call hierarchies pyramidal because most resemble mountains, with far less room at the top than on the bottom. On the top there is less territory but more power, more money, more press, more praise, and more prizes. On the bottom is far more territory and more people, but less of the powers and privileges. Women and lower caste or minority men are especially few in the tops of the hierarchies of money, decision making, opinion making, and public authority, in the worlds of praise and press and prizes, the worlds of the so-called geniuses, leaders, media giants, "forces" in the culture. Women are not considered, for example, to be actors in real history, but only in women's history. Our perspectives are not featured in mainstream psychology, but only in "Psychology of Women" courses. We are featured not on the front page, but in the Living section of the newspapers. And so on and so forth through the curricular and noncurricular matrix (or should I say patrix?) of our lives. And so when we rise up in hierarchical worlds, while socialized to feel that we shouldn't be there, it is not surprising if we appear to ourselves to be fraudulent. "If this is 'one of the best colleges in the country,' then I don't belong here." "He thinks I am wonderful? Then he must be a loser." "She said I argued brilliantly? Then I fooled her." I think most people who feel like frauds have internalized systems of seeing which say most people are not valid and don't belong in the worlds of worth, distinctiveness, excellence, authority, creativity, opinion, or forceful expressiveness, positive or negative.

In recent discussions, people have used terms such as the "imposter syndrome" in "high-achieving" women. They talk about some of the problems I have been discussing, and especially about executive or highly placed women's feelings of tenuousness and illegitimacy in their careers. Very often such discussions turn to parental attitudes, particularly parental attitudes toward girl children, and some say that when parents supported nontraditional career aspirations in girls, this correlated with fewer feelings of being an imposter.

I like the phrase "imposter syndrome" (Clance and Imes, 1978). This is very useful. I also admire the work of Irene Stiver (1982) on this subject. But I think that it does not make sense to start with a unit like the nuclear family to try to account for the imposter syndrome. The unit to study, though it is much harder to study than the individual family with its individual actors, should be the whole society. Most people receive messages from every side, throughout the culture, that they are not legitimate in places of authority, not legitimate wearing the white coat, not legitimate behind the podium with the presidential seal, not legitimate as a female or minority male within frameworks of the boardroom, the corporate executive office, the banking industry, the Defense Department, or in the worlds of making and shaping technology, opinion, and policy. Adults' failures of nerve may relate, of course, to specific attitudes in specific parents. While our own parents may have failed to encourage, for example, nontraditional career aspirations in women, the society as a whole reinforced in a thousand ways its failure to encourage anyone to challenge the hierarchical winners-and-losers arrangements of the whole culture.

We have some remedies for the feeling of personal fraudulence. Particularly in the United States and over the last two decades, we have been introduced to courses on assertiveness training and confidence building, and, for some of us, courses in public speaking, or workshops on how to survive interviews. We have won greater chances at athletics, and now more women than before are developing an ability to compete in athletic situations with confidence and self-respect and enjoyment. These correctives help some women and men to feel that they are not frauds, and that they are, on the contrary, competent, whole, entitled, and legitimate, both as private persons and as public speakers and actors.

In addition, exposure to mentors and to role models apparently helps to create a feeling of competence and of being sponsored and encouraged in high places by those who "ought to know" our worth. I have benefitted very much from some of the correctives mentioned above, and especially from two courses in public speaking given by the wonderful Merelyn Reeve [Jacobs] of Dartmouth

College who told us, "Say what you want your audience to know. They have come all this distance to hear you, and you owe it to them to get to the point."[2] Such advice helped her listeners to cut down on the apologies. But such remedies do not go beyond the first way of seeing feelings of fraudulence. They help only to correct the problem as I have outlined it so far, that we feel like frauds because we were socialized to think we do not belong high in hierarchies, and that most feelings of fraudulence come when one is rising in – or appearing to rise in – hierarchical territory, by taking the pulpit, or taking the podium, or taking the front of the class, or taking a position in the news – taking positions which the world associates with people of merit and importance. The higher we go in those hierarchical structures, the more likely we are to feel, hollowly and in our inner selves, that we do not belong and the more we are likely to ask, "What am I doing here?" Assertiveness training can help us to look around and check out the people around us, and then say, "I am here because I have as much right to this podium as anyone else, as much competence in this presidency as anyone else I see around me." This translates into "I may be a fraud, but I am no more fraudulent than the next person."

Now suddenly, the plot thickens. Is the next person fraudulent? This question leads to my second perspective on feeling like a fraud. Here we move into territory where assertiveness training and speech workshops may be of no help. The next person behind that podium is, yes, very likely to be playing a role which entails fraudulence, pretense, imposter behavior. And it has less to do with that individual than with the roles which develop out of the public requirements at the tops of hierarchies as now constructed.

I now shift from the Moebius strip message "We must not let them make us feel like frauds" to the other Moebius strip message which is contiguous yet apparently opposite: "Let us continue to spot fraudulence in the public roles we are made to play in the hierarchies of power." And here I want to tell a story about a woman colleague in a large United States research university who dared, figuratively speaking, to move in public from one side of the strip to the other. Her university was holding a faculty-wide debate on whether affirmative action guidelines for hiring should also be followed for decisions about tenure and promotion. The heated meeting on this important subject included all of the undergraduate and graduate school faculties. I was not there, but I heard that, one after another, white male faculty members stood up to say they had their doubts; when it came to promotion and tenuring, the university had to be on guard against mediocrity, and not let down its high standards, and that when it came to giving people a lifetime vote of confidence, one couldn't just take "any old person" and give that vote of confidence – one must make a financial investment in excellence. The woman psychologist to whom I am grateful stood up and said,

> I am hearing a lot of talk about excellence. But then I look around me and I see a lot of mediocre men. For me the real test of affirmative action will

be whether or not I can stand up here in twenty years and see equal numbers of mediocre women and mediocre men.

She called the men on their claim to excellence, on their equation of power
with merit.

This relates to my second perspective on feeling like a fraud. We feel fraudulent, I think, partly because we know that usually those who happen to get
the high titles and the acclaim and the imagery going with them are not "the
best and the brightest," and we don't want to pretend to be so either. When we
entertain nagging thoughts about whether we belong or deserve to be at the
podium, or in the boardroom, or tenured, or giving an interview to a newspaper, or earning a good salary for what we like to do, we may be deeply wise
in feeling anxious and illegitimate and fraudulent in these circumstances. Those
men who feel the same way in such settings may be deeply wise as well, for the
public forms and institutions tend to demand that one appear to be an authority
figure, an expert, and "the best." The forms require that one appear to be a
person who sets goals and knows how to meet them, a "leader" who is superior
in certain qualities over those who are "followers." The public forms and institutions insisting on these images do require fraudulent behavior of us, and they
will turn us into frauds if we accept the roles as written. The roles are dishonest
and people who are still in touch with their humanity and with their frailty will
properly feel fraudulent in them. What the public roles entail and promote are
usually not those qualities we have really specialized in ourselves. What the systems reward in us rarely corresponds to what we are really good at, and most
humane in being.

This point brings me back to the conference of women who appeared to
disown their own ideas when they took the floor. When seventeen women in a
row apologize, then perhaps we should listen to what they are saying, particularly when the seventeen apologists are known as "leaders" but are not acting
like them. We need to listen to what they tell us about the way they want to
lead. My first response was to think that these apologetic women were testimony to women's incompetence. And that is the world's judgment on them.
But an alternative way of listening to them, on the assumption that women are
competent, brings out a message their behavior delivers, which is not that they
can't stand behind the podium, but that they can't stand the podium. And in
their apologies these women were, let us say, trying to change the forms of
public speaking to make them less fraudulent, less ridiculous, and less filled with
pretense. Conventions of public speaking entail many uses of rhetoric; the rules
of effective rhetoric require that one speaker persuade a group of followers.
What if a person at a conference simply wants to put new ideas on the table?
She may begin by saying, "You may not agree with this, but ..." In this
apparent apology, she is creating an opening which is nonrhetorical, and her
words accomplish several important ends. "You may not agree with this, but
..." This opening not only acknowledges the presence of the Other; it also

postulates the engagement of the Other in what is going on (as they say in literature, it postulates reader response). It also acknowledges the validity of the Other's ideas. "You may not agree with this, but ..." creates a tentative tone, a conversational matrix, a sense of give and take. As I see it, this opening acknowledges and strengthens the social fabric before it can be torn by rhetoric. It says, "I am not taking the floor from you. I recognize you are there. I am trying to make this more like a conversation than like a speech." The woman who says, "I have just one point to make ..." is saying also "I don't want to interrupt the flow," or perhaps "I am not saying this in opposition to what has already been said ..." Research has indicated that girls in playgrounds often break up a game rather than having it disintegrate into conflicts over rules. The woman speaker who says, "I really don't know what I'm saying, but here goes!" inspires neither confidence nor respect in the boardrooms of corporate America, but she is not pretending, and perhaps we need more of her in the boardrooms. At any rate, I find I want to make the case for some of the apologies I heard as refusals to pretend, refusals to be a fraud, refusals to carry through with the rhetorical conventions of public speaking, or writing, or performance in which one must pretend to be a strong man overcoming others, or a woman strongly identified with white males' functions and rules for power and success.

I wish to return now to undergraduate students' feelings of fraudulence, of feeling guilty and out of place. "The Admissions Committee made a mistake. I don't belong here." If one insists on defining certain colleges as "the best," any intelligent woman will feel that no one has done the tests to know whether either the college or she can be called "the best." It's a valid doubt. When she gets an A on a term paper, beyond the idea that "this means he didn't find me out" is this idea: An A is a grade absolutely better than B. Even when used together (in A-/B+), there is a slash between to show they are not the same grade. But is the student with the A absolutely better than the others who took that exam and who scored lower? A woman down the hall may have studied all month, never having had a course in this subject before, and have gotten a B. Another may never have really understood what was going on, but her questions really showed others what the course was about. Let's say she got a C. Our "A student" may not have done any work until the last two days, and then crammed all night. That puts her up, away from the others, on a pedestal. Does she belong there? A woman may say to herself, "He thinks I am beautiful. But I hate that Beauty Queen stuff; I won't get trapped by it." Or, "They call me an expert. That's because they don't know any better. They probably don't know who the experts are on this subject. I certainly don't." Or, "They call me a pathbreaker. But I don't think of myself as breaking paths. I think and write." It seems to me that the absoluteness of hierarchical rankings and ratings and of the existing metaphors of originality or strength contain many elements of fraudulence. For women, especially, this absoluteness, and those metaphors of pathbreaking and being expert don't correspond to our complex sense of the web of circumstances in which we are born, circumstances in which our lives do not have trajectories and goals, but are, rather, threads in the fabric of circumstance, only partly of our own social and emotional weaving.

We resist, in other words, the building of pedestals, and the awarding of titles which we feel are not quite appropriate and which separate us from others like ourselves and which imply that we are self-sufficient or independent loners. And this resistance is healthy for us and others. Or, rather, it can be seen both as good and bad for us, but as good for the whole society.

A colleague told me that she attended a conference in which, in the relaxed aftermath, students began to ask the visiting professors, all of whom were women, how they came to their public lives and their academic fields. One woman, in examining her past, put her distinguished present down mostly to the circumstance that she had been rich. Another, examining her past, put her distinguished present down mostly to the circumstance that she had been poor. And a third put her success down to the fact that she entered the library and the books that interested her more or less fell on her head. None of the women acknowledged her own competence or excellence or enjoyment of her field. None said, "I liked the field; I read the books; I understood them; I got my papers in on time; I became competent; I saw new possibilities; I add to the world; people appreciate my work and I do, too." These women were perhaps then, let's say, deplorably modest, rejecting credit for themselves. But on the other hand, I would say they were applaudably honest. From one point of view, they were all feeling rather like frauds as "success stories," or "notable women," so they put their lives down to circumstances. On the other hand, they were feeling a fraudulence attaching, as I think, to the myths of self-realization which go this way:

> I came up from nothing, rags to riches, from pink booties to briefcase on Wall Street. I did it all myself. I knew what I wanted and I was self-reliant. You can be, too, if you set your sights high and don't let anything interfere; you can do anything you want.

Now, it seems only honest to acknowledge that that is a myth. When women refuse to take sole credit for their midlife status and insist on mentioning circumstances of birth and color and wealth and regional and ethnic setting and rejecting the pretenses of the pedestal and the podium, they are doing something that the whole society needs. We need it, in other words, in our highest policy-makers, this sense of how circumstances of birth and status and social network more than individual selves bear on life outcomes. False pictures imply that the individual is the unit of actualization in this culture, and that self-actualization is the main business of all competent people. But most of human life is bound up in collective and social and private experience which is not linear and not filled with clear upward trajectories and not identified with the aspirations of white, upwardly mobile men. Most of human sensibility is not covered by what authoritative experts tell us because their frameworks for thought are often wrong, and are in fact, fraudulent when they claim to cover all of us.

What, then, should we teach students about feeling like a fraud? First, that it is a feeling taught to us. Second, that this teaching is no accident. Third, that it is not good for us to feel like frauds insofar as that feeling perpetuates hierarchies. And fourth, that in another sense, it is good for us to feel like frauds insofar as that feeling may help us to undermine hierarchies. I advocate in this a double vision, as I do in virtually all other kinds of work with students and in the society at large. We need a double vision both of what the dominant culture stands for, and of what we lower caste people who are undervalued can develop in the way of a critique of the dominant culture. Within the dominant culture, people who can't deliver the goods from behind the podium will look incompetent. Therefore, we need to get over the socialized feeling of being a fraud and stand behind that podium and deliver the goods. This is learning the present ways of power. But, alternatively, it is constructive for the whole society if we question why there must be a podium, and ask whether the town meeting or the Quaker meeting or the March on Washington weren't perhaps better experiments in public speaking. Only when we examine the difference between the conversation and the speech can we suggest that world leaders try conversation.

Let me turn now to the linguistic aspect of feelings about fraudulence in writing. When one writes a paper on virtually any subject, one is likely to begin with a complex of myriad ideas that constitute what William James called, in the mind of a baby, "a buzzing, blooming confusion" (James, 1890, p. 488). But one must choose among these ideas in order to put a paper together, because the rules for the sentence and the paragraph are very arbitrary. The rules insist on beginnings, middles, and ends. Within the sentence, conventions of grammar dictate that the subject act on the object through the verb. Moreover, traditional conventions of expository writing insist on something still more autocratic, that one make a case which is cohesive and clear, an argument which has no holes in it, a position from which one can take on all comers and defend one's self. This assumption about what writing is, the making of a case against the fancied attacker, permeates our teaching of writing from the expository courses through the graduate student's defense of the thesis, which is a kind of king-on-the-mountain in which you take on all attackers of your small piece of territory. It's silly, isn't it, that the paper must make a "watertight," "unimpeachable" argument, must make "points," and be like the world of boxing or dueling, holding off imagined attackers. The rules surrounding formal writing leave sensitive people with a feeling that the finished paper makes a statement which is fraudulent. Those who want to use language for other purposes are uneasy with the praise which comes with using language for making arguments. A student who says "I am such a fraud; I can't write this paper" will tend toward self-censorship or silence, and she needs help against those feelings. A student who says that one is, after all, a fraud in writing this kind of paper is in better shape. She knows life doesn't come in sentences; life doesn't come in paragraphs. And although institutions are encouraging her to use the expository essay as a kind of combination attack and defense mechanism, she wants to find alternative uses of language. I think we need to help students to have both states of mind. First, we need to help them get past the feeling that they are more fraudulent than anyone else, and help them get past the feeling that everyone else in the class is really writing a first-rate argument, whereas they are blocked individually. Second, we need to help them to project some of their feeling of fraudulence onto societal forms. They should be encouraged to see that the public forms of our lives are a construct for organizing us, and that they particularly serve to keep the present economic, political, racial, and sexual hierarchies in place. Students as actors can gradually change those forms as they use them and become successful in them. So the student may wisely repudiate that pinnacle-shaped A on the terms in which it was offered to her, as praise, for example, for "winning" argumentation. She may keep her own rich sense of connection which the subject nevertheless gave her before she wrote the "winning" paper on it, and which may enrich her life as she tries to write new scripts for her own public performance.

Likewise, students can be helped to get high grades or prizes for successful debating, learning to make a point against all comers. We need also to teach them to see fraudulence inherent in the conventions of debate, in that you become a polished expert in making the case for the side you have been assigned, rather than making a case for what you may perceive as the truth. Students need to be helped to see there is a reason why they can accept "You are good to talk to" more easily than "This is the best paper I have had in fifteen years." The letter and the conversation as forms have less of fraud in them; they don't force us into authoritativeness and gross simplification.

My husband, on hearing me work through these ideas, said, "You're saying that those who don't think they are fraudulent are the real frauds." Yes. We have been socialized to feel like frauds but have developed some strengths in the midst of that fact, and because of that fact. Those who were socialized to feel absolutely entitled have made a habit of fraudulent behavior in proportion as they have internalized the view of themselves as the best and the brightest. So our task is complex. When a student says, "I get so nervous talking in class," I think we need first to point out that she/he was set up to get nervous. Hierarchies are disempowering, and nearly all people are socialized so that they will feel like failures in public and need help to feel confident. At the same time, students are right deeply to mistrust what anyone says authoritatively, including themselves. We need that tentativeness in high places. We need it in the Pentagon, in the White House, and in makers of public policy. We need that conversation, that ability to listen, to have a nonrhetorical, a relational self.

I hope we can move students from "My voice should not be heard at all" to "I don't like the official tone I am forced to take in those situations; it misrepresents me" through "What other voice can I find to convey not an autonomous, self-confident me (which doesn't exist), but the self-in-relation, not coercive, and not deceptive, but social?" If we give students a double vision of social reality, I think they can learn both the language of power, which we use standing at the podium and delivering those straight sentences, and the language of social change, which suggests alternate visions of how to use power.

Women and others who have been disempowered are not all able to bring our truths to light yet. Many such people tend to apologize. But in doing so we are creating a voice which, though sounding tentative, has the seeds for the future in it. When we say, "You may not agree with this, but ..." we are creating an atmosphere of detente, peace, negotiation-making tentativeness, rather than using the podium for the violent act of bringing everyone over to our side. Perhaps, then, we women should be seen as canary birds attesting to carbon monoxide in the atmosphere. When seventeen women in a row apologize, there may be something wrong with the air in the nonapologetic world. The fraudulent-feeling people in the culture are perhaps our best canary birds. When they begin to keel over, we know we are really in trouble – that the air around them does not have enough life-sustaining oxygen. Those situations in which they sense the toxicity in the air most clearly are those situations connected with grades, titles, promotions, public accreditation, and public pronouncements, in the hierarchies which have the clearest absolute ranking systems, with a clear demarcation between winners and losers.

So, "which of these things do you want?" says the mind seeking only one vision. As I have said, I want two things at once: to mitigate apology which reinforces hierarchy, and to intensify revisionary tentative behavior, so that we see and criticize fraudulent forms and customs in the expert, the leader, the "self-made" man, the "self-reliant" person, the self-righteous American certain that God is on our side, and that He intends us to be a winner. We need more training in seeing the public presences of winners and authority figures as personae, fraudulent actors in high places, and in bringing the material of the private consciousness into public life, as feminists are already trying to do on so many fronts.

My theory of two ways of seeing fraudulence should be put here against my theory of the psyche and of the society in general. I see both our individual psyches and the whole society as having the shape of a broken pyramid, with a kind of geological fault running more or less horizontally through the center and dividing the top part from the lower part. The public and competitive functions of our psyches are contained in the top part of the pyramid, and the most ordinary, lateral, everyday business of simply getting along "without accomplishing anything" is, in my view, at the base of the psyche, and of civilization, and of the pyramid which I am drawing here.

All institutions and psyches have both public, competitive functions and, underlying these and making them possible, a substructure of the ordinary work of upkeep, maintenance, and making and mending of the social fabric. At the tops of the pyramids are concentrated money, power, and decision-making functions, and in the very much wider base are the more ordinary functions which have either no visibility at all in most of what we read and do and think and are told, or very little visibility, and have seldom been named and identified.

The grain in the public part of the psyche and in the public part of our institutions is vertical and contains many ladders to promotion, "success," praise, and prizes. The hidden prescription under these competitive functions of personality and society is that you win lest you lose, because those alternatives are seen to be the only alternatives: Either you are on your way up, or you're on your way down, falling toward the bottom. One wouldn't want to be on the bottom, so it is assumed one will be striving toward what the world calls the top – that is, toward "accomplishment," "achievement," "success," defined as leading to individual power. In the lateral functions of the psyche and of the society occur the experiences of washing the dishes and patting the cat, and having talks with one's friends, and earning enough money to put the bread on the table, and getting the bread on the table, and washing the dishes, and loving those who cannot help us "get anywhere." These are the functions of answering the phone, of driving home at night, of being a person intimately involved with others for the sake of the involvement. They are not what the world would call the functions of achievement or success. They have instead to do with survival. The hidden prescription in this basis of our institutions and our psyches is that one works for the decent survival of all because therein lies one's own best chance for survival. This is not an altruistic prescription; you don't simply work for others, but you live with others because that is one of the impulses and conditions we were born to. One finds one's development through the development of others. One develops, as the researchers here have defined it, a self-in-relation (Miller, 1984; Surrey, 1984).

Now, unfortunately, the functions represented by the top parts of my broken pyramids have been projected onto white males born to circumstances of cultural power, and the functions of the psyche and the institutions which I place at the base of the pyramids have been projected onto women and lower caste males. Much research is now showing, of course, that women aren't so happy with that assignment – that projection onto us – of all of the lateral functions of survival, nor men with the projection onto them of the world of winning versus losing – a world which has only two alternatives: yes/no; right/wrong; top/bottom; win/lose; self/other; success/failure.

By now it is clear to you that the first type of feeling like a fraud occurs chiefly in these top-level public functions of self and society. If one has internalized the view that only the win/lose value system and version of reality are real, women at the podium (or lower caste men) will feel fraudulent, since by definition they are losers trying to act like winners in occupying the podium. If, however, we have educated our students and ourselves to a double vision, to both the public functions of psyche and society and the hidden, lateral functions of psyche and society, the survival functions, then we can see feeling like a fraud as something else again. In its second aspect, the feeling of fraudulence is the critique of the vertical from these lateral parts of the personality, objecting both that the vertical behavior is partial and misrepresents us and that the lateral realities which are the ground of our humanity are not honored in the culture's value system or its most conventional praise.

My view of curriculum change superimposed on this diagram goes this way. In Phase I you study womanless History. In Phase II, women in History, but only as exceptions, and still on History's terms. In Phase III, women are seen as a problem, anomaly, or absence in History, as a problem for historians and also for the society, as victims, the oppressed, the losers, or the incompetent. Then one moves further to that main work of women which has been assigned to us – finding one's self through the development of others, and then one is doing Phase IV: Women As History, redefining history so as to make us central. In Phase V we will have History Redefined and Reconstructed to Include Us All. Now once one has come to see the traditional lives of women as just as real as and more plentiful than what history has documented, why then everything shifts. The feeling of fraudulence at that point is seen to arise out of the sense that all people are interconnected, and that in no absolute way is one student different from the one down the hall who studied for weeks, or the roommate who never really understood the course. Each of us has done something that cannot be absolutely ranked. When we resist that ranking system that awarded us the A, because of our consciousness of the lateral functions of life and personality, then we are resisting fraudulence in a way that may become useful to the whole society.

Now what do I mean by that? According to my dream of the next hundred years, we can, if we live that long, bring into public life with us our sense of the now-named and reconstituted survival functions, and we can call into question and change the behavior of those who see the world only in terms of winners and losers. And, of course, we need this work on a global scale to keep from blowing ourselves up. We can see already that so much of public performance is based on rules of acting and image-building, and we can spot the inaccuracy of the hierarchies in that they are not the meritocracies they claim to be. We know that our consciousness coming out of the survival aspects of personality can help us encourage the whole society not to pretend to be what it isn't. The pluralistic version of reality that comes out of seeing women as history – and that means all women, not just a few white women — also conduces to a kind of foreign policy which says that the Russians and we and the Chinese are equally valid people. The seventeen apologies come from this deeper level, and if we will listen to them and learn from them, they will bring revisionary strength to the whole culture. The apologies suggest that most leaders are poseurs, and that the "top" is not the top. I think Alice in Wonderland was right when she said to the Court, "You are nothing but a pack of cards!" Wise people go behind the screen and perceive the Wizard of Oz as a little old bald man with a wrinkled face behind the screen. Until we see the authoritative forms as forms, we will continue to deny those parts of ourselves that have no words, that don't come in paragraphs and chapters and footnotes; we will be forced to deny the wool-gatherer, the conversationalists, the imaginer, the lover of women and lower caste men, the one who likes people and joins with them without necessarily "achieving" anything. The world of neighborhoods and of human communities is the world of survival. If the public world becomes more honest, it may help us invent a form of podium behind which honest people don't have to apologize for their connectedness to others.

I wish to end with the apology, which is not only an apology, which might have introduced my talk. I appreciate the invitation to speak in this colloquium series. I am not an expert in women's development. I am only an observer, but you thought I might be a resource for the series. In the same way, in your Stone Center work you invite us all, and not just the experts, in on a process. You show us not a finished theory, but a process of reaching a theory, a process of reseeing women and renaming some of our apparent weaknesses as potential or actual strengths. Your work in reconstruing and reconstructing enabled me to do some work, personal as well as public, which goes into my observations tonight. Your work, I think, can help us convert "feeling like a fraud" into resisting fraudulence and pressures toward fraudulence which originate outside of us in absolute, hierarchical systems and in definitions of our strengths as weaknesses. To this audience I want to say that I do see myself as an amateur observer, very limited, merely human, narrowly circumstanced and therefore half blind in observing all of what I have described. But also I would like to ask whether it wouldn't have been good for us all if every expert lecturer, every general, and every leader had demonstrated an ability to appreciate the process of living more than the products of success and victory. Wouldn't it have made quite a difference to ourselves and to human life in our time?

Notes

1 This chapter was previously published as McIntosh (1985).
2 Between 1980 and 1981, Professor Jacobs held two workshops at the Wellesley Center for Research on Women. It was during one of these workshops that Professor Jacobs said this to participants.

References

Clance, P. R., & Imes, S. A. (1978). The imposter phenomenon in high achieving women: Dynamics and therapeutic intervention. *Psychotherapy: Theory, research & practice*, 15(3), 241–247.

James, W. (1890). *The principles of psychology*. New York: Henry Holt and Company.

McIntosh, P. (1985) Feeling like a fraud. *Work in progress No. 18*. Wellesley, MA: Stone Center Working Paper Series.

Miller, J. B. (1984). The development of women's sense of self. *Work in progress, No. 12*. Wellesley, MA: Stone Center Working Paper Series.

Stiver, I. (1982). Work inhibitions in women. *Work in progress No. 3*. Wellesley, MA: Stone Center Working Papers Series.

Surrey, J. (1984). The "self-in-relation": A theory of women's development. *Work in progress No. 13*. Wellesley, MA: Stone Center Working Papers series.

8

SELECTION FROM "FEELING LIKE A FRAUD, PART II" (1989)[1]

I first gave a talk on this subject in April, 1984, as part of an earlier series. I proposed a dual view of feelings of fraudulence, using a Moebius strip as metaphor. This strip, when twisted once and fastened at the ends, becomes a loop on which two apparently opposed statements turn out to be, so to speak, "on the same side." I suggested both that "We must not let them make us feel like frauds," and that "We should continue to spot fraudulence in the public roles we are asked to play." I applauded the part of the self which hesitates to claim isolating titles and rewards, and said that there are pretenses in official language and behavior which may imply that we are more than we feel we really are in terms of merit and singularity, and less than we feel we are as human beings embedded in matrices of circumstances and relationships.

I think that many of our feelings of fraudulence come from deep and wise sources. The trick is to trust the very feelings of discomfort that are giving us the most trouble, and try to follow them where they may lead. Some baseline sense of *authenticity* in us must be responsible for our registering a lack of fit between our own sense of ourselves and what is said about or around us.

This talk builds on the previous discussion. But this time I am shifting the emphasis from what's wrong with "them" to what's right with "us." I want to focus not on the pretenses of "official" worlds which may make us feel like impostors but on some authentic elements of life which seem to me fundamental and central grounds of our being.

Because of my excitement in making this shift from the subject of fraudulence to the subject of authenticity, I had been eagerly looking forward to this talk for months. I wrote page after page of new ideas. But I couldn't organize the pages. The day of the lecture approached and still I couldn't outline the talk. And so, naturally, I began feeling like ...

As I have said, the trick in this matter of fraudulence is to try to hold onto the very feelings that are giving you the most trouble, and trust them to lead you to some new ground, some new way of seeing or being. Given months' accumulation of animated notes, why could I not outline the talk? It dawned on me, then, that the outline itself makes me feel fraudulent. I realized that for me the outline is, and always has been, a fraudulent form. My genre, I realized, is the *list*.

What makes the outline give me such discomfort, the list such relief? On a list, everything matters; you need not rank, subordinate, and exclude. One cannot be generous in an outline. One must decide that which things matter a lot and which less, by degrees. The outline forces what are for me unacceptable simplifications.

The list allows me to keep everything, to expand, to add at any time. There is no pretense that everything in a list has been sorted out. The outline pretends to have a place for everything. It implies that what's left out didn't fit, and that what got in all fits together.

I knew that I wanted to talk about encounters with feelings of fraudulence and attempts to track and act on feelings of authenticity. I also knew that no single idea seemed to be more important than the others, and that starting with any one of them as *the* most important distorted my sense of the whole matter.

At that perception, the topic turned metaphorically from an argument into a house tour of places in my home where I go when I am thinking about feeling like a fraud. I will show you some of the rooms; we can start or finish anywhere. Within the house metaphor, I do not feel like a fraud. The only danger is that I will talk too much on this tour, since now I feel at home.

Though we could start the tour anywhere, I will first take you to the shelves where I have accumulated some key readings since my last talk. But to tell the truth, papers and books lie in heaps everywhere around the house. One thinks with the help of others in all rooms of life. But here are some key readings which have fetched up on the shelves of one particular room. Blythe Clinchy and Claire Zimmerman (1985), in "Growing Up Intellectually: Issues for College Women," described "connected" and "separated" knowing, and drew on Peter Elbow's (1973) contrast between playing "the doubting game" and "the believing game," as described in Elbow's book, *Writing Without Teachers*. This paper has been important to me in identifying a learning mode I find non-fraudulent. Further work is in Belenky, Clinchy, Goldberg, and Tarule (1986), *Women's Ways of Knowing*. Next comes Jane Martin's (1985) book, *Reclaiming a Conversation: The Ideal of the Educated Woman*, and several of her articles advocating that we educate for the three C's: care, concern, and connection (Martin, 1986). Here is Alfie Kohn's (1986) book, *No Contest: The Case Against Competition*, which I consider to be, along with Mark Gerzon's (1982) *A Choice of Heroes*, among the most important books by men on the damage done when socialization forces men into postures of dominance. Here is P. R. Clance's (1985) book, *The Impostor Syndrome*, which focuses, like her earlier work with Imes (1982), on the pathology of feelings of fraudulence. Next comes Carol

Cohn's (1987) paper, "Sex and Death in the World of Defense Intellectuals," and the paper by Carol Gilligan and Jane Attanucci (1988) called "Two Moral Orientations: Gender Differences and Similarities." Here is a paper on "double helix management style" by Helen Regan (1987) of Connecticut College, Jean Baker Miller's (1987) preface to the second edition of *Toward a New Psychology of Women*, and a *New York Times* article on the "impostor syndrome" in winners of Nobel and Pulitzer prizes (Berger, 1987). Then comes an article in the American Psychological Association *Monitor* on the "impostor syndrome" in therapists (DeAngelis, 1987).

I was particularly delighted with this last article. It reported on a study of sixty-two doctoral-level therapists who responded to a questionnaire about whether they ever felt like impostors in their roles as therapists. In this study, 79% of the therapists reported that they felt like impostors "occasionally," and the remainder reported that they felt like impostors "frequently" (DeAngelis, 1987, p. 15). The author implied that therapists' impostor feelings are problematical, but I think that feelings of fraudulence within our present systems can be very wise, instructive and constructive, and we need these feelings especially in "experts."

I want to take you now to the living room, where we play a lot of music, and there are a lot of instruments, records and tapes. I'm going to put on a tape of the 1984 "Feeling Like a Fraud" talk and play fragments which anticipated my present emphasis on that *authenticity* in us which evaluation systems may miss. Fast forward …

I listed some ways in which one may feel fraudulent: "One feels illegitimate in doing something, or appearing as something; one feels apologetic, undeserving, anxious, tenuous, out-of-place, misread, phony, uncomfortable, incompetent, dishonest, guilty."

I described people repudiating praise which makes them feel misread and uncomfortable. I also noted that, in my experience, feelings of fraudulence are not so common in domestic or everyday life.

I noted that feelings of fraudulence may be felt when people who were socialized to think they do not belong high in hierarchies rise up into public view in any way, but I also noted a related feeling of not trusting hierarchical reward systems to read us rightly. Thinking of ourselves not as solo pioneers, but as threads in a complex web of circumstance and interaction, some of us may be reluctant to accept special praise and the "loner" status it falsely implies.

I said that I hoped we could move students and ourselves from feeling "My voice should not be heard at all" to "I don't like the official tone I am forced to take in these situations; it misrepresents me" through "What *other* voice can I find to convey not an autonomous self-confident me (which doesn't exist), but the self-in-relation, not coercive and not deceptive, but social?" In answer, I suggested the voice of conversation, which as a form has little of fraud in it; it demands neither solo authoritativeness nor the soloist's accountability. I said that some of women's apparent apologies may be anti-rhetorical strategies for avoiding dominance, and for staying connected to listeners through a tone of conversation and dialogue.

I described an either/or, win/lose pyramidal structure of psyche and society which rests on a wide, lateral base of collaborative potential. The vertical part of our psyches and our institutions pushes us to ascend toward power and individual visibility, while the more hidden lateral functions of society and self tell us to keep working for the decent survival of all. I suggested that feelings of fraudulence may amount to a critique by wise, well-grounded, laterally oriented parts of the psyche of the too-strong emphasis on, and reward for, the vertical in present-day U.S. psyches and society.

This is why it is quite possible to feel both that we are not good enough to be taken seriously, and that there is something wrong about the systems which have excluded us from serious consideration. I know that the part of me that is at home sitting here in a dimly lit living room musing about this paradox without any single-minded focus is not the part which gets public kudos. And I am thinking of an alumna of a New England school who didn't attend her fiftieth reunion because she felt that according to the Alumnae Notes version of things, she would be seen as having done nothing of importance with her life. Yet she knew that that perception of her life was deeply wrong. She was up against a version of reality which says that those who chiefly make families and communities and private worlds are not really in the picture. For many of us, the filter systems within which we are screened, rewarded, or praised may have missed out from the very beginning on what we consider "the most genuine ground of [our] being" (Tillich, 1951). In these cases, I think we need to insist on its genuineness and its centrality to our work in the world.

As I feel this shift from an analysis of "what's wrong with them and their fraudulent forms" to "what feels important to me," I feel the positive emotion of what in faculty development groups I call the shift from Phase III study of excluded people's *issues* to Phase IV study of "ordinary" people's *experience*, seen on their own terms.[2] One shifts from anger at low status and victimization to the conviction that we are all valid, and that we in non-dominant groups may have a lot to teach, if only we can take our home-selves seriously enough to word, to name, what we observe and feel about our lives. I think that what I call the *home-self* here may correspond to my sense of baseline authenticity.

Anyone's particular search is specific in many ways, so mine may speak best to white, Anglo-American women of middle age who have economic security and who share some of my academic and personal circumstances. We need testimony and research on many diverse people's experiences of feeling like a fraud, but since I am talking here about tracking a sense of authenticity, I must, in this case, stay very close to home.

Now I want to take you to the study upstairs, and pull out some old photo albums which will show me in positions of feeling like a fraud. Here's a commencement photo from June, 1967. I am in a voluminous crimson gown signifying a Ph.D. from Harvard, and also serving as a spectacular maternity dress, for I am eight months pregnant. As Harvard's President, that pinnacle-sitter among pinnacle-sitters, has awarded our degrees, he has said, "I welcome you into the company of educated men." As women getting Ph.D.s, a great many of us have been suddenly defined right out of the picture. Here's another photo of six short, smiling fresh-faced white women at a Phi Beta Kappa initiation ten years earlier. The dean doing the honors has said kindly to all of us at once, "You don't look like Phi Beta Kappas," defining us right out of the identity we have just earned. We are politely speechless, and perhaps a little flattered, pleased not to look like a Bluestocking woman.[3] But we sorely needed then as now, for our mental health, Gloria Steinem's exemplary behavior in rejecting pictures of her which, in the guise of compliments, leave her out. She knows how to haul others' definitions of her right back to where she herself is. Told by a reporter, "You do not look 40," she said, "This is what 40 looks like" (Dullea, 1984).

Here is a photo, going back another four years, of my first college roommate. It is November, 1952, and our Greek professor has asked us to come to his office. It seems that my roommate and I have been making the same mistakes on our Greek exercises, which are otherwise very good. Yes, we do the daily homework exercises together. The aim is to learn Greek, no? No – our professor, renowned scholar of epics, explains that we must be judged alone. We can be rewarded only for solo feats on what he calls "the battlefield of learning." We feel like criminals. We work separately, and each gets C+ for the course. The reward system does not acknowledge *as* learning the kind of learning that works for us and that we did well.

Here is a plaque on the wall and a commencement photo from the seventies at the University of Denver. The plaque includes my name and reads, "Outstanding Academic Advisor." But six faculty members had done intensive advising together. We were not competing, and we consulted students as well as each other on how to do this intricate relational work. The presentation of an award created four winners and two losers, and created a mesa above two low hills where we had tried together to create a plateau. The reward system and its attendant naming system seemed to me to harm the basic nature of the work and the group effort.

The sense of fraudulence in these cases came from having my actual ways of being ignored, and a condition created in which I felt as if I must disown part of my identity. Leaving it *out*, I could paradoxically feel like one of the *in*-group. But my sense of *authenticity* had consisted in my good feelings at having a rather unorthodox, complex identity; being female, reflective, somewhat solipsistic and also effective in public or institutionally accredited ways; working with friends; collaborating in learning and in advising; and being tied in and supported. The prize-and-grade-givers at every turn were giving the prizes for versions of "excellence" alien to me, even when this entailed defining away what was standing right in front of them.

The next photo is from a private New England girls' school in June, 1982. I am sitting on the platform feeling like a fraud because my publications have been given the most prominent place in the introduction of me as commencement speaker. Conversation with other people is at the center of my work. I feel like a fraud, sitting there and hearing chiefly about the publications which set me at a distance from this audience of parents and students, rather than about the conversations which tie me in. I especially want to say this to the sixty seniors sitting there in the sun in their white dresses. They hate writing, don't they? Most of the research indicates so; the rhetorical style of expository writing they have been drilled in has worked against their trusting themselves as writers, and underrated many of the kinds of thinking they do more easily.

So I go up to the podium with a stricken feeling of a great chasm to cross. To try to tell the seniors of my respect for their experience, I say something heartfelt. I say, "We need you, *just as you are*, in the White House." The seniors look at me in disbelief, as do their fathers, who hold corporate America together. Just then, three U.S. Army helicopters, flying in close formation, swoop low over the commencement ceremony and hover in place, drowning us all out. So while they churn overhead, I'll tell you why most publication makes me feel like a fraud.

First, as you know, I trust lists, not outlines. Second, I like conversations, in time and space, in situations and with bodies. Publication locks words into place and launches them into the void. Since the author can neither imagine nor adjust to various readers' needs and reactions during the act of reading, the author must accept isolation, and must risk being *misunderstood*. For those of us who fear being misunderstood, and who like to keep the social fabric as whole as possible through conversation, presenting ourselves in black print on white pages can be daunting.

And then there is the matter of footnotes. Footnotes are a courtesy to the reader, says my colleague Elizabeth Minnich. Footnotes are for information, says Jean Baker Miller's editor. These are valid observations. But since conventions of academic footnoting have always intimidated me, I now look to see whether there is an element of fraud in them. The writer of footnotes purports to be adding a clear piece to an accumulating body of knowledge in a conscious, systematic way. But where an idea came from is often unclear, especially in the interdependent worlds of feminist thought in which I now spend so much time. Footnoting is frequently used, I think, to perpetuate the illusion that knowledge-making is systematic and rational, sequential and cumulative. At least this is true in most of the formal study I have experienced.

Now those U.S. Army helicopters have headed back to their base, and I resume telling the seniors in their white dresses that I trust them in their authentic seventeen-year-old selves. But they are young, and perhaps feel too vulnerable to believe in their own authenticity; they may have to settle, for now, for being trapped in and subtly undermined by single-minded views of what excellence is.

For those of us who are not so trapped in others' definitions, it is possible to consult our authentic, dissenting selves to arrive at some *alternative* ways of doing things. The trick here is to ask the authentic dissenting self, "What would make you feel better?" I will give you some examples, and for this we should move into a bedroom, for it is in the early morning hours and in bed that I get my best alternative ideas on how to act.

I was about to visit Pasadena Polytechnic High School in California. Having never spoken to California teachers before, I wondered what I could tell them, but felt a problem in the idea of "telling" them anything. So I decided to put the discussion period first. At the school, I listened for an hour to what faculty had to say about the topic at hand (women in the curriculum), and then identified seventeen subthemes. While we took a coffee break, I constructed the talk from those themes. The talk synthesized a conversational event. I felt wonderful about it.

Once, on being asked to give a keynote address at a conference on Women and Education, I said that I was tired of the pinnacle system of having a keynote speaker. Couldn't we have a kind of conversational plateau on which two or more people talked to each other in public? As a result, Ted Sizer, a longtime headmaster at Phillips Andover Academy, and I, who met for the first time the night before, held a public conversation for an hour and a half, sitting in two armchairs on a stage before an audience of educators at the Bryn Mawr School in Maryland. We talked back and forth. It was risky to participate in this simultaneously private-and-public exchange, but it made good on the *usually* fraudulent claim that we in education have dialogues with each other.

The elements of authenticity which I enjoyed in these two situations came from having more than one voice heard, from sharing responsibility and from creating an atmosphere for exchange rather than an argument. These were work-in-progress sessions.

In connection with the American Bicentennial, when asked to give a talk at the University of Denver on "Rugged Individualism," I was filled with ambivalence about the topic. On the one hand, we may need qualities of rugged individualism to resist much of what we are told and taught, and to tap into our authenticity. On the other hand, the idea of rugged individualism has rested on a myth, a *macho* illusion, even an infantile delusion in the United States, that the self is the main unit of society, and that selves do not have strong past and present connections. I felt fraudulent, not being able to come to a clear sense of one important "main" opinion or argument. So I devised a pluralistic form of lecture, in which the medium could be the message. I arranged twenty chairs in a semi-circle and labeled each with a different facet of myself. I gave the talk jumping from chair to chair and giving a wide variety of perspectives on the subject, e.g., as from "Granddaughter of Presbyterian Grandmother" and "Mother of Two Young Girls" and "Reader of *Field and Stream* in the Dentist's office." At the center of the horseshoe was an armchair labeled, "Central Self." The students asked afterward, "What is the central self?" I said I didn't know; I simply assumed that there must be one, to act as a kind of moderator, though not necessarily as the central authority. It keeps the personality from flying apart from centrifugal force. It moderates between various voices in the self, which are also the voices of others inhabiting the imagination. The central self does not, however, come up with "the answer," dominating or overriding some voices. All stay there, in plural variety, corresponding to what goes on in my head.

Jamaica Kincaid wrote about the many voices in her head on the subject of how to be a girl, in a tiny piece, in a genre all its own, which is found at the start of her book, *At the Bottom of the River* (Kincaid, 1984). As soon as I read her piece called "Girl," I went upstairs, got into bed, and wrote my own version of it, echoing the voices in my head from my childhood about how to be a girl. This piece of writing seemed so authentic that I decided it could provide a good opening exercise for SEED faculty development seminars. A traditional format ("My name is, I teach at and I am here because ...") separated people, because of accents, differences in perceived status and because of the semi-official accounts some people gave of themselves. Within a few minutes of beginning such introductions, a few in the room were usually feeling like frauds, whereas when I asked everybody to write a piece paralleling Jamaica Kincaid's "Girl," and used those as our sole introduction to one another, we heard the voices of our experiences *as girls and boys* coming through. This way of beginning has transformed each seminar series. It also makes me part of the group. We are all in it together, in a lateral relation, each the authority on her own experience, which none of the rest of us can know better than she.

Now I want to take you to my desk in the living room where much correspondence from my colleagues in curriculum change has piled up. A colleague at University of Michigan writes about how a group of instructors replaced a fraudulence-inducing assignment with a better one. The first assignment had been a complete failure. After the students had had several weeks of instruction in Art History, the instructors in this course provided this assignment: Go to the Museum of Classical Art in Ann Arbor, choose a Roman sculpture, and write an analytical essay on it. The papers were wooden, stilted, poorly organized, boring, and filled with the language of art criticism badly used or misused.

The faculty cancelled the assignment altogether and redesigned it. The second assignment went this way: Go to the Museum of Classical Art, choose a work of Roman art, make a copy of it in any medium you choose, and then write an essay on your experience of copying it. These papers asked students to be *authorities on their own experience*. Whereas the first papers had been written under the shadow of students' knowledge that all of the teaching assistants were getting Ph.D.s in Art History, the second put the students and the instructors in a more lateral relationship to the works of art. Students stopped asking the usual question, "What do you want?" and did not need to wonder, "How can I appear to know what I'm talking about when I really don't?" The papers were interesting, vivid, unusual, clearly organized narratives about what it was like for a student to have a particular learning experience. In terms of Belenky et al.'s (1986) description of the modes of "procedural knowing," the students had been allowed to move from "separated" to "connected" knowing.

The next piece of correspondence comes from teachers on both coasts of the country. At schools in California and Maryland, American History teachers tried to compensate for the fact that the texts that they were using omitted women's history altogether. One experiment was a valiant attempt at a corrective which did not work. The teachers invited the students to create a supplement to the American History text, focusing on the lives of women. The students said they could not do it. How were they to know about women's lives if the many editors of their thick textbook didn't? And in any case, how could they possibly imitate textbook style, which sounds as if nobody in particular wrote the book? The students were very uncomfortable with this assignment, partly, I would say, because it put them in a position of claiming more authority than they felt.

A history teacher in a similar effort at a girls' school asked each student to imagine that she was a female person in the Massachusetts Bay Colony in 1638. She said,

> Here is a ten-page questionnaire I would like you to fill out to tell about your life. We don't know a great deal about women and girls in your situation. Here are twenty American history books from which you can pick up a little information and insight on women and girls. Do consult these books; don't just make up everything. But once you've schooled yourself a little, using these as a resource, make some educated guesses and invent your personality and your life.

The students loved this assignment, whether or not they were known as "good" students. One said, as she handed in her paper, "I don't care what I get on this; it's the best thing I ever did in school." Some students said that for the very first time, they had "found a real person in history." Many got a sense of identity from the project, which they cannot get from routine assignments merely asking for their reasoned *opinions*. The only doubt they had about the assignment was that it made them *make up* so much of what they said. This raised the question, "What do you think historians do?" And that question had the effect of making them see themselves as *historians*, not readers of others' history, but into *makers* of the stories which "History" is.

In another school, an English teacher grew exasperated at giving eighth grade students repeated assignments in writing about short stories' plots, characters, settings, and themes. She felt the whole course was pointless. She transformed the course into one which turned the students into writers. Every assignment for a thirteen-week period was the same: for Monday and Wednesday the students read two short stories, and for Friday they wrote a fraction of a story themselves. She asked that whatever they wrote be in some way triggered in their imaginations by what they had read. This assignment had a transforming effect; students became for the first time *interested in the craft of writing*. Tillie Olsen, Shakespeare, and Hemingway became related to the students in that all were writers.

I think the authenticity of these assignments for students came into being when teachers at least temporarily put aside the mantle of authority and let students become the authorities on their own experience and on their own sources of creativity. It is very important to this discussion that in all of these cases the teachers reported feeling *comfortable* with the revised assignments as well as impressed with the work they inspired. The teachers felt well grounded, as they do not in the familiar situation of scrambling to "stay on top of the material."

Finally, here is a love letter from a past student, forwarded by a colleague in American Studies at the University of Denver. We faculty members from that program get such letters still, years after a profound experiment in curricular revision. Four of us who were teaching American Studies realized that we were teaching courses on "American Culture" in such a way that all ancestors of people like ourselves were left out. We decided to end the omission of people like ourselves by teaching our American culture courses twice through. First we ran through the presidents and the most famous writers of a given twenty-year period, all of whom were white and male, and generally from the eastern United States. Then we went back and asked the students to help fill in whatever had been left out in the first part of the course. Students spent the rest of the semester doing their own research on many aspects of life: dolls, tools, recipes, church services, bridges, butter churns, prayers, songs, punishment, diseases, or quilting.

In the final exam in such courses, we asked students to compare the *version* of American culture conveyed by the first few weeks with the *versions* in the latter part of the course. The letter on my desk is from one of the many students who have written thanking us for this teaching; we gave him the ability to see what he was learning as versions, rather than as truths. We helped him to see systemically (i.e., to see social *systems* at work) and to take an interest in the *politics of ways of seeing*. In learning all this, our students felt authentic, for they were able to find themselves in a way that they had never experienced in college before.

The same was, of course, true for us as teachers. For us, the authenticity came in putting ourselves – the unseen Others – into the curriculum. Most teachers in most places are passing on versions which exclude themselves – as teachers – and exclude students' experiences, reinforcing systems of power that do not serve most of us well. As the mail on this desk accumulates, I read of the changes taking place as consciousness of this problem grows.

After all this wordiness, I want to take you over into a room in this house which I love because it is so completely nonverbal: a quirky old greenhouse. I open the door and smell! It's the smell of earth and of growing things. Here, it is all growth and development. These plants don't feel they're on trial. Here they are "all bodies in the body of the world."[4] The greenhouse helps to explain to me what I so dislike about grading in education. My aim as caretaker here is not to put plants in competition with each other. Quite the reverse; in gardening, to help each plant fulfill the potential which its seed contained, you *reduce* competition. This is what I try to do in education.

Now I must confess to you about another room in the house. If you are a reader of Charlotte Brontë or Sandra Gilbert and Susan Gubar, or if you love Lily Tomlin and Jane Wagner, you will not be surprised to hear that there is a Madwoman in the Attic (Brontë, 1847; Gilbert & Gubar, 1979; Tomlin, 1985–1989; Wagner, 1986). You go up there and her room is absolutely draped with Moebius strips. She scrawls on them, in red ink, and covers the walls with angry graffiti. She is alternately *off the wall* with anger at those who have made *her* feel like a fraud, and *off the floor* with a visionary sense of her own elemental connection to the universe. You can never anticipate her mood. She harangues me if I give her any attention and harangues me if I don't. The other day she looked at me and said, "You need me. I'll be here for you." Now, I spend a lot of time taking care of her, and when I do it is very hard on my family. And here she is, telling me I need her. Thanks a lot.

Today she threw down a poem which I will read to you. She has written:

> The prize fish flops, and dies.
> I pass through the nets.
> I escape the hooks.
> I am the growing medium – water.
> The prize roses wilt and die,
> Brushed free of soil.
> I am the growing medium – earth.
> The princess swoons over the perfect
> three-star omelette.
> I am the steady stove.
> The jet assumes its power. –
> It levers against me – the air,
> The necessary body for its rise and its
> Descent.
> Water, Earth, Fire, Air,
> I am the growing medium, the
> genuine element.
> Trust me.

I want to go back to the shelves now and pick up one of the articles there. It is a paper that suggests that unless we study what we *haven't* noticed, we will never understand what we think we have noticed. According to the Gilligan and Attanucci (1988) paper, human moral development was seen by earlier researchers as simply a neutral and universal kind of development in which approximately two-thirds of the (male) sample were seen to mature fairly well and one-third seemed to be anomalous, immature. When, through research on women, Gilligan identified the "ethic of care," the previous model of "moral development" began to look like a specific model for development of what she called an "ethic of justice" (Gilligan, 1982). Until the voices of women had truly been listened to and the previously unlooked-for "ethic of care" identified, the ethic of care was not in the spectrum of moral concern; therefore men who did not fit the first norm of an ethic of justice could not be placed at all.

Most of the research on this subject of feeling like a fraud, or impostor, has been done on college students or on white, middle-class, employed American women in early middle age. I suggest that until we study the sense of fraudulence or authenticity in other people more fully, and in many cultures, we will not understand it in any of us.

Though I cannot generalize from my own explorations, I will summarize. My feelings of authenticity came with feeling physically female and being in situations of connection, uncertainty, conversation, solitude, informality, sociability, collaboration, domesticity, repetitive life, spontaneity, expressiveness, and what the world calls madness. I have often felt authentic when doing what Jean Baker Miller calls "finding one's development through the development of others,"[5] or when entertaining many contradictions and differing people, emotions and ideas.

For most men I know, feelings of fraudulence may well be triggered by the very qualities of life which seem authentic to me. At the same time, some employed white women I know say they feel somewhat fraudulent even in the home sphere, today, when confronted with superwoman images. Some people seem never to feel like frauds at all. Factors of age and class, race and region, as well as personal circumstance play into all of this. Our diverse senses of authenticity should be mined further.

For me, the shift from rhetorical argument to house tour was the breakthrough allowing me to go from feelings of fraudulence caused by separation from myself to an authentic sense of self-in-domestic-connection. The shift from that abstract Moebius strip to an imagined house allowed me to feel more comfortable, being simultaneously *at home* and *with you in public*, bringing the public life to the home ground and home-work to the world.

Going public with our sense of, or search for, authenticity seems to me an important step for people who do not thrive in the public worlds of confrontation and challenge. Once I felt only silence and misery on the subject of fraudulent feelings, and then entered what Belenky et al. (1986) call a position of "received knowing," agreeing in this case to the commonly held opinion that women simply lacked confidence. Then followed an important switch to a kind of street-wise, angry, "subjective knowing," which may remind you of the Madwoman: "There's a lot of goddamn phonies out there."

Academic training encourages me to value the abstract, "separated-knowing" analysis of the Moebius strip talk more than these homelier vignettes. But the gardening self, the half-awake person in bed, the woman who broods over old photos, and the Madwoman make essential and original observations. Connecting with these *many* parts of the self is a way of doing what Belenky et al. (1986) refer to as "constructed knowing," choosing one's versions from a wide variety of understandings, sources, voices, and guesses.

I don't think that we will be able to do what I call the *meta-doubting*, the necessary *meta-criticism* of the main invisible structures of psyche and society, until we try to get in touch with our personal senses of authenticity and talk about how things really are for us on a daily basis.

Many individuals daily bring what I have been describing as the home or friendship sense into their routine lives and into institutional worlds. A larger task is to create whole value systems, policies, and institutions which place at the center this concern for growth, development, and survival without violence and with dignity for all. Listening to voices of personal authenticity, however tentative they are, may help us to develop theories of human nature and systems which fit experiences and serve basic human needs better than most present theories and systems do. The mostly submerged baseline sense of authenticity in those who unaccountably feel like frauds may help to reveal the places in which present theory or policy do not fit with what people are, or want, or do most constructively.

Notes

1   This chapter was previously published as McIntosh (1989).
2   See Chapter 12, *Interactive Phases of Curricular Re-Vision: A Feminist Perspective*.
3   A Bluestocking person was an educated person of the 18th century who belonged to the Blue Stockings Society, but by the 19th century, the term had come to refer to educated women who were negatively stereotyped as frumpy and dirty.
4   LeRoy Moore, professor of Religion, first coined and used this phrase of self description at a faculty party at the University of Denver, "I am a body in the body of the world."
5   Jean Baker Miller used this phrase in unpublished personal communication with the author beginning in 1979.

References

Belenky, M., Clinchy, B., Goldberger, N., & Tarule, J. (1986). *Women's ways of knowing: The development of self, voice, and mind.* New York: Basic Books.

Berger, J. (1987). Prize winners find glory bittersweet. *The New York Times*, April 18, 21–22.

Brontë, C. (1847). *Jane Eyre.* In Dunn, R. (Ed.) (1971). Norton Critical Edition. New York: Norton.

Clance, P.R., & Imes, S.A. (1982). The impostor syndrome in high-achieving women. *Psychotherapy: Theory, Research, Practice*, 15, 241–247.

Clance, P.R. (1985). *The impostor phenomenon: Overcoming the fear that haunts your success.* Atlanta: Peachtree Publishers.

Clinchy, B., & Zimmerman, C. (1985). Growing up intellectually: Issues for college women. *Work in progress No. 19.* Wellesley, MA: Stone Center Working Papers Series.

Cohn, C. (1987). *Sex and death in the rational world of defense intellectuals.* Cambridge, MA: Center for Psychological Studies in the Nuclear Age, Cambridge Hospital.

DeAngelis, T. (1987). Therapists who feel as if they're not therapists: The impostor syndrome. *APA Monitor*, July, 14–15.

Dullea, G. (1984, May 24). Birthday celebration: Gloria Steinem at 50. *The New York Times.*

Elbow, P. (1973). *Writing without teachers.* London: Oxford University Press.

Gerzon, M. (1982). *A choice of heroes: The changing faces of American manhood.* Boston: Houghton Mifflin.

Gilbert, S., & Gubar, S. (1979). *The madwoman in the attic: The woman writer and the nineteenth century imagination*. New Haven: Yale University Press.

Gilligan, C. (1982). *In a different voice*. Cambridge: Harvard University Press.

Gilligan, C., & Attanucci, J. (1988). Two moral orientations: Gender differences and similarities. *Merrill-Palmer Quarterly*, 34(3), 223–237.

Kincaid, J. (1984). Girl. *At the bottom of the river*. New York: Farrar, Straus, Giroux.

Kohn, A. (1986). *No contest: The case against competition*. Boston: Houghton Mifflin.

Martin, J. R. (1985). *Reclaiming a conversation: The ideal of the educated woman*. New Haven: Yale University Press.

Martin, J. R. (1986). Redefining the educated person: Rethinking the significance of gender. *Educational Researcher*, June/July, 6–10.

McIntosh, P. (1985). Feeling like a fraud. *Work in progress No. 18*. Wellesley, MA: Stone Center Working Paper Series.

McIntosh, P. (1989). Feeling like a fraud – Part II. *Work in progress No. 37*. Wellesley, MA: Stone Center Working Paper Series.

Miller, J. B. (1987). Foreword to the second edition. *Toward a new psychology of women*. Boston: Beacon Press. First published 1976.

Regan, H. (1987, unpublished). A double helix leadership style. Board of Directors' Seminar, Northeast Coalition of Educational Leaders, MA.

Tillich, P. (1951). *Systematic theology*. Chicago: University of Chicago Press.

Tomlin, L. (1985–1989). *The search for signs of intelligent life in the universe*. Live performances.

Wagner, J. (1986). *The search for signs of intelligent life in the universe*. New York: Harper & Row.

9

SELECTION FROM "FEELING LIKE A FRAUD, PART III: FINDING AUTHENTIC WAYS OF COMING INTO CONFLICT" (2000)[1]

Thank you to the Stone Center for inviting me to do yet another rumination on "Feeling Like a Fraud." This is the third in a series which I began with talks on the same subject in 1985 and 1989.[2]

I want to tell you how I came to this subject. I heard seventeen women in a row apologize as they came to the mike during a general session of a conference. Supposedly we were all educational leaders, and indeed many in the group were college presidents and deans, or were leaders of projects which were considered to be substantial. Yet seventeen women started their remarks with words like "You may not agree with this, but," or "I don't know, but ..." If we were such leaders, where was our confidence? And then, because I was working at a Center for Research on Women, I wondered, "What are these seventeen women really saying with these disclaimers?"

I thought it might be a way of trying to create a relationship with the next person, as if to say, "You are real; I am real; you may not agree with this, but my aim is not to lord it over you with my superior position here at the podium. And we can talk later." It occurred to me that the traditional aim of much public speaking, deriving from Greek rhetorical arts, is that I, the speaker, try to persuade you, the listener, of my point of view. So I thought that in this sense, rhetoric, which Sally Gearhart saw as potentially coercive,[3] can tear the relational fabric. Perhaps what these women were trying to do with their disclaimers was to strengthen the social fabric before it could be torn by rhetoric.

And I came back from that conference and thought that maybe each of these women, standing alone up there, isolated, at the microphone, felt like a fraud. I knew that feeling. Perhaps we didn't want that isolation, and that sense of being above others. So I wrote a little yellow interoffice memo to Jean Baker Miller: "Jean, Do you ever feel like a fraud?" I got back a little yellow memo sheet, including the sentence, "I feel like a fraud all the time." And I thought, OK, if this woman who has mounted the major challenge to Freud in our time, and is loved all over the country already, feels like a fraud all the time, I think there's a topic here.

For the first talk, I made a Moebius strip. I wrote a kind of fight song on one side of the strip. "WE MUST NOT LET THEM MAKE US FEEL LIKE FRAUDS!" That can apply to any "them," or any "us," in cases where some are made to feel less entitled than others to a voice. But then, because I felt it might be deeply wise to feel like a fraud when you are surrounded by fraudulent forms, I presented a different point of view. And on the back of the strip I wrote, "LET US CONTINUE TO SPOT FRAUDULENCE IN THE PUBLIC ROLES WE ARE ASKED TO PLAY," by which I meant the roles of expert, leader, or even competent person. I wanted to show that, for me, both of the exhortations are part of the same analysis. So I configured them as a Moebius strip, following the German mathematician August Moebius, who discovered this marvel: If you pull together the two ends of a strip so that they meet, and then twist one and fasten the ends together, you've created a one-sided strip. You can pull the strip through between the thumb and forefinger; you will cover both messages without changing sides. The rest of that first talk elaborated on the proposition that feelings of fraudulence can be seen as both deplorable and applaudable, in different contexts.

For the second talk five years later, I explored the question, "How come you know you're feeling like a fraud?" I wondered what inner mechanism lets a person know they're feeling fake, or uncomfortable. I tried to identify in myself what I called a "home-self" that is made uncomfortable by being called out of itself into arbitrarily created systems of acclaim or expectations about one's worth.

During that exploration, I had traveled through the house of my psyche. My conclusion to that paper read this way:

My feelings of authenticity came with feeling physically female and being in situations of connection, uncertainty, conversation, solitude, informality, sociability, collaboration, domesticity, repetitive life, spontaneity, expressiveness, and what the world calls madness. I have often felt authentic doing what Jean Baker Miller calls "finding one's development through the development of others," or when entertaining many contradictions and differing people, emotions, and ideas.[4]

That was the second paper. One of my favorite parts in visiting the house of my psyche was dipping into a small greenhouse, in which I breathed in the smell of growing things and realized that to help plants thrive, you reduce competition among them.

Ten years after I wrote the second paper, it came to me more and more that it was difficult to bring what I felt was my home-self into the world of conflict. This is not entirely true. My work in the SEED Project, which I founded fourteen years ago and still co-direct with Emily Style, challenges the world of formal schooling. However, it does so obliquely, by enabling educators to start their own faculty development discussions in their schools. Some probing questions like how well the curriculum is including all students, and what sets of values are being conveyed, are directly provocative, and I experience the SEED

Project as a deeply radical undertaking. But it is not simply conflictual, coming from an attack position. It involves groups of people doing much inner searching based on the premise that we are all part of what we are trying to change. It hopes to heal conflict without self-righteousness or simplicity.

I also have little difficulty in coming into conflict in context of the many public talks I give and the consulting work I do. When I am in a room with other people, I feel less vulnerable to being misunderstood or dismissed or taken for a fool. I can recognize or play with the nuances which keep conflict complicated in a way that feels authentic to me.

But when I am acting on my own and feeling a need to come into conflict, then I have a very hard time. I have been watching my own processes and testing ways of coming into conflict to see which feel more authentic to me. My talk tonight will end with some of the difficulties of coming into conflict when my home-self feels multivariate and complex, whereas conflict is usually staged in a reduced world of this versus that, me versus you, taut, dire, and frightening.

My fears include these thoughts: I can't do it; I'm bad at it; I'm not a warrior, I'm a woman; I'm not courageous; I'm afraid to take sides; I hate to do anything bad to people; I hate it when they do anything bad to me. I was told to avoid playground bullies. Why take them on? And look at the conflict in the world already. Why should I add to it?

While I was writing that, I noticed that the brand name on the very pencil I was using was "Invader." This increased my feelings of fraudulence: I'm hopeless at this contentious world. And of course all of you, who are psychoanalysts or psychotherapists, know that such thoughts come from somebody who is filled with conflict!

In grade school, these are the functions of personality which I was taught were important: being right, being in control, being very exact in our answers, doing our work alone, and turning into a specialist someday. In math, you got it right, or you got it wrong. And in those days, you wouldn't bother to show your work because your train of thought was not what was being graded. In spelling, you got it right, or you got it wrong. Right/wrong; yes/no; success/failure; quick learner/slow learner; either/or. Either you climbed toward the top, or you fell toward the bottom. Your sense of life was polarized, and put into vertical terms. "Win lest you lose," was the hidden ethos. The territory of the losers was much larger than that of the winners, so there had to be competition for the limited space at the "top." There was a nagging sense in lots of us children, male and female, that we were not ever doing quite well enough, ever, to be "top," and that other people would be on top.

Having drawn that psychological picture of vertical functions of personality, I then turned it into a sociological picture of the institutions of the culture, because I realized that my pinnacled psychological structure felt as though it were mapped onto public institutions. I felt these pinnacles had ladder-like structures going up them, and the rungs on the ladders were the markers by which you can answer the question, "How am I doing?" The rungs are pay, promotion, press, praise, prizes, prestige, and all together, power. Then I knew why I had been so anxious in school even though, like many of you, I had "done very well in school." It was so hard to reach the pinnacles; most people would be shouldered off the ladders.

And yet we were in World War II when I was a child, and it seemed at that time, and it was true, that Hitler made the war against him seem morally defensible. So "kill or be killed" did seem like one law of life to me. Yet it seemed to me too terrible to be the only law of life. The war was too simple for my view of things, and I remember feeling sorry for German and Japanese people. I felt frightened on my own behalf, not wanting to kill, or to be killed.

I think what I was divining then was that I was connected within my psyche and in the society to what I was being taught to hate and fear. Traditional conflict implies I am not connected with what I am conflicting with. But I am connected with it. Armies need to train soldiers to break the feeling of connection with those they kill. Soldiers have to be rigorously taught to disconnect with whole groups of people. One lesson I learned by participating in the work of the A.K. Rice Institute for the Study of Social Systems is that when someone in an unguided discussion said something, I was likely to relate to some part of what they had said. That fellow-feeling makes conflict of the either/or kind seem too simple, and I know now better than I did as a child why war terrified me so much, not just for the deaths it brought but for the torn fabrics in every part of the psyche.

When I was a child, the role of killer was not being required of girls directly. We were meant merely to support the boys as heroes. I realized my exemption from their masculine war-training most acutely one day in fourth grade when I got home from school and felt enormous relief that I could go indoors, while my brother had to stay out of doors to play "Guns" with the boys in the neighborhood. If he went indoors he would be considered a sissy.

I remember feeling so grateful that I could go indoors and play with my stuffed animals. What I did with my stuffed animals was ritual and obsessive, and I see it now as highly symbolic: I married my stuffed animals to each other every afternoon. Moreover, I married different animals to different other animals every afternoon. I see that as diversity! I think that as a girl, and indoors, I was trying to make the civilization that was the opposite of the wars outside. I would gather my mother's flowers and put them on the piano: beauty. I would play the piano: harmony. And then I would conduct the wedding ceremonies on the altar of the piano: union. The boys were suffering out of doors in their mode of training for what was (and still is) seen as masculinity. It was through no fault of their own that they obsessively played Guns. It was projected onto them. Making domestic peace was projected onto girls.

I don't use the word "projection" quite as psychologists do. I see a projection as a visiting on to people of an image of what they must be. The projection onto white men that they will thrive in this world of "win lest you lose/kill or be killed" has made them suffer horribly. And I believe that the projection is quite false. I believe we all have in us the capacity to make and live in pecking orders. It shouldn't have been projected racially, ethnically, class-wise, or sex-wise.

Below the fault line in my diagram is the world that is projected onto the rest of us. Above the fault line, the grain of the rock is vertical; below the fault line, horizontal. It's hard to describe the life below the fault line because most of what I have been urged to value involves working toward an apex – developing my best talent, or recovering my most precious memories; in other words, prioritizing.

Below the fault line there is little prioritizing. It is the area of daily upkeep and the making and mending of the world. My most personal metaphor for it is dishwashing. You wash the dishes, you wash the dishes, and you wash the dishes, and you don't win. Or agriculturally, you plant the seed, you water it, perhaps fertilize it, perhaps pray over it, perhaps weed it, and if you're lucky, you harvest, or others do. And if you're lucky, you bring food to your table, or buy food. But you will never have the "mega-meal" and be done with eating. The agricultural cycle must be repeated again and again, or life will not go on. So here is the making and mending of the personal fabric, the agricultural fabric, the kitchen fabric. In the pedagogical fabric: you talk to a student; you talk to the same student the next day about the same thing. The aim is not to win, but to stay in a decent relationship until, say, the end of the semester, or the end of the year, or until graduation, or until death do you part. If you're lucky, the students keep coming back, and you see that the achievement wasn't that you got the better of them, or they got the better of you, for here they are again, sitting on a step saying, "Remember when you said such and such, and I said such and such," and you are still in relation.

And family life at its best is like this. You don't set the children up in a row in the morning and ask which will be the winner and which the loser. You try to work it out so that the growth of the whole family is provided for as well as possible. For parents, it has to do once again with what Jean Baker Miller named as "finding one's development through the development of others." And the development is more through survival than through what the world calls "achievement." The ethos isn't "win lest you lose," but rather, "you work for the decent survival of all, for therein lies your own best chance for survival." When I first began to speak in this way in 1981 and 1982, some listeners concluded that I had been tainted by California New Age thought, or was sentimental or Communist. But with the damage to the ozone layer, and the pollution of so much water and air, this has stopped seeming like such a "pie in the sky" ethos, and people in many places are working for language beyond "either/or" to express an ideal of sustainable balance in the mind and soul and social and biological fabrics.

I believe that beyond the making and the mending of the domestic fabric and the educational fabric are further worlds of necessary relationality. The world of sex doesn't go well when the aim is to win, the world of love doesn't exist when the aim is to win, and the world of friendship is sorely strained when the aim is to win. This world below the fault line includes the enormous globe of the complex, multifaceted soul in each of us, which has in it all the experiences which have moved us and become a part of ourselves. And anybody I meet who is even half-way awake in the late 20th century has a complex, multifaceted, and I would say multicultural soul, comprised of connections and understandings that have had deep, deep positive meanings for us. And these rays which I sketch, emanating from the globe of the multifaceted soul, are the connections to everything in the universe which we cannot see, but which gives meaning to us. And we would be crazy to try to master our divinities.

I see this soul as a site which can enable a blessed solitude, by contrast with the loneliness of the climb up the ladders. Some people have told me that the climbs up the ladders are not as lonely as I think they are. They say that in teamwork, the whole team strives together. It may be called teamwork, but in the long run, does it feel durably supportive? I feel the evidence is mixed. What I notice most is that you are fired from the team alone.

I believe that the sectors above and below the fault line are in all of us by nature. We all have it in us biologically to make and live in pecking orders, and to live in symbiotic relationships within biodiverse habitats. If we were to go out into the grounds of this institution, in any two square yards we would find the land teeming with organisms whose main aim is not to wipe each other out. And except within the human world, there's not a biological effort to create a superpower, a dominator organism for the planet. And in fact, this is not the main human preoccupation. We live symbiotically most of the time. It is the life in which we make our way day by day without doing damage, insofar as we can, making and mending the fabrics. I believe it is also, spiritually, what the theologian Paul Tillich called "the ground of [our] being" (Tillich, 1951).

It was my own world below the fault line which fueled my interest in asking about conflict. Couldn't I reclaim this part of myself as an adjunct, an actual aid in undertaking conflict and fearing it less, maybe even feeling I could do it well? And couldn't it help me to resist feelings of being *reduced* by competition? I wanted to be able to come into conflict using my home-self. And I felt many more resources in me which might be useful than I had been taught I could use, especially as a female of my class and place and race who was not meant to be in conflict to begin with. So – what would it require for me to see what was oversimplified in what I had been taught to develop in myself?

As I watched myself coming into conflict over the last year, I came to this conclusion: the conflict in which I feel most authentic is the conflict in which I oppose the idea that conflict is all there is to life. I learned that I come into conflict authentically with the idea that my "self" has only one identity. I also conflict with the sense that the outer world is about conflict and the inner world is about peace. I have found I can insist on this. In fact, I get angry about this sentimental picture, and harangue people about it. And I feel I can get angry about it without feeling I'm necessarily going to shatter, humiliate myself, or endanger my future. I feel authority, as well as authenticity, in saying conflict is not all there is.

So paradoxically, I use the warring part of me to say that war is not all there is, that there is something larger around it. War is in me, but not the only thing in me or anyone else. This recognition tied many things together for me. This is why I had felt sorry for the losing football team, and for the Germans and Japanese, and for the men who are so damaged by the teaching they receive that they are warriors. They and we bear the burden and the consequences of this.

The world of conflict or war is partially present in all of us, I believe. And why? It is an element of survival, to live in and make pecking orders. But I believe Charles Darwin was misrepresented badly when he was taken to be writing *only* about competition. Social Darwinists who want to use Darwin to justify capitalism have sketched him as a scientist recording only the ways in which organisms compete.[5] Darwin was not about that only. In his home, he kept earthworms, studying them for decades. He was not studying their conflicts, he was studying their lives, observing their behavior. Growth and development are also laws of life.

Walking in the mountains with my family as a child, I liked the first sensation of being together on the trail. But a certain winning streak in certain family members meant that they got ahead on the trail, and had a tendency to make something of it. I identified with the role of our Shetland sheepdog who tried to round us up by running back and forth. My parents told me and I remember that I simply adored the large campgrounds where we would occasionally stay. I liked being all together, with everybody equally needing food, clothing, and tents, and living as my class-conscious parents said, "cheek by jowl." And I remember that when I encountered Jean Baker Miller's book, and read that conflict was essential if we were to move toward our own development, I thought, "I can't bear this." I remember shutting this book, when I found it, at the age of forty-five. I trusted this author, and suspected she was right about most things. What I now think is that that book alerts us to consequences of systems of power that are not good for any of us. She was pointing out how rare the campground is, and telling readers that to have the campground at all we would need to come into conflict with systems that were bad for the recognition of our relationality.

Seen in a Phase I light, my resistance to her words came because I was so firmly trying to stay in the role of good girl, good white girl, and good upper-class girl. I thought then, I can't do this thing that she asks. Now, as it happens, I have on my refrigerator a magnet with an Eleanor Roosevelt quote which reads, "You must do the thing which you think you cannot do." But then, at the age of forty-five, I still hoped to get through life by being nice within the authority systems, and hoped that I could just find the communal and communitarian campgrounds again and again.

As I observed my feelings of fraudulence on coming into conflict this past year, I saw that one aspect is my dislike of trying to "make a case for" my ideas in writing. I feel like a fraud in the conflicts which surround academic and media life in general, the tendency to shoot others down and get shot down. I do not want to get shot down. I do not really fear bringing my ideas into words when I am doing public speaking, public dialogues, or the highly charged work of the SEED Project. What makes me feel like a fraud is writing for faceless audiences. I found I had a variant of this fear in that I feel fraudulent in sending letters to people I do not know, in situations in which committing myself on paper may cost me something and make others see me as angry or stupid.

Through pondering this, I saw I was invested more than I knew in being seen as an intelligent, self-controlled, high-class, undefeated woman. I realized that in the presence of an audience I give some of this impression, and I believe it gives a special protection to my talks, which are unexpectedly issues-oriented, pro-vocative, and original, and yet usually applauded. In print, I am much more vulnerable to the thrashings which authors with even the faintest political awareness may get from anyone who wants to do them in. Yet whenever I do have the courage to go into print, I reach thousands of readers. I decided to go ahead and try to put more of my feelings into print even if this put me in the vulnerable "angry female/feminist" category, open to attack. I wrote more let-ters of protest and support than usual this year, and practiced putting some of my home-self into them rather than being abstractly argumentative.

Here are just a few examples. To the host of a popular call in talk show on NPR, I wrote,

> I am very discouraged to hear you say, quoting Ezra Pound, that, "*The Iliad* is all we need. It has enough drama for a planet." I am discouraged because it appears from time to time when you interview women that you do "get it" about our being left out of the liberal arts curriculum, and out of the main ways of seeing "life" which you and I were raised with. Yet in declaring that, "*The Iliad* is all we need," it is as though you have forgotten all that the feminist women scholars and writers have been saying about most men's and women's daily lives. I'm discouraged that you mistake a war epic and its adorer, Ezra Pound, for a universal and adequate story to cover the experience of us all. Who is this "we," in "It's all we need"?

Instead of agonizing over what tone and words might be more effective than others, I just went ahead and sent the letter. You will have seen that it declares conflict is not all there is, and that I came into conflict with the talk show host over that. This was a letter in which I did not feel that my emotions over-simplified my own multifaceted self, and I let my anger and discouragement show, instead of censoring them.

Just a year ago, I came into conflict in a way that burned some of my bridges. I sent a letter of resignation to the president and board of trustees of Radcliffe College. At the time, I was Second Vice-president of the Alumnae Association, and I was angry that through a series of secret talks the president and board of trustees were arranging to sever their ties to Radcliffe undergraduates and to abdicate their mandated responsibility to advocate for the interests of under-graduate women at Harvard. My action and the protests of others may have delayed the outcome by a year. Radcliffe has now voted not to be a college any longer. I am glad that I took that stand then. It got a lot of publicity, and I felt brave. But I find that the final defeat of what we stood for has made me with-draw into myself somewhat.

Was it worth it? I will never know. But the protest made me feel integrated. I think I was expressing my connection to the institution which Radcliffe was in the 1950s, protecting and also furthering the development of women like me within the patriarchy of Harvard, like a rare mother allowing one to develop a strong "home-self" in the midst of a male-centered ethos of the family. And now I am furious that the mother abandoned the daughters to the "care" of the patriarchal father.

I also wrote a letter to a journalist thanking him for quoting something he had read elsewhere about writers' needs for support at certain times: "This deadening of one's gift by learning not to believe in it is the most dangerous time in the life of an artist." I thought he was also alluding to how hard it is to come into conflict with evaluators who do not believe in one's gift. I wrote to him to say that I saw a parallel in children's learning not to believe in their own gifts.

This was an easier letter to write, serving as an ally piece, and also a mini-conversation, coming off another's thought. It felt relational and I did not feel I was a fraud in writing it, but it was slightly scary at the same time. Will I be misunderstood? I am now trying to write these letters sounding more like a complex, situated human being and less like someone trying to claim abstract authority on a single point or two. But my fear remains that I will be construed as a harridan, an obsessed woman who has nothing better to do than to write crank letters. If I learn that I am seen this way, and feel I haven't been effective, I am likely to forget the long histories of women who have made a difference, and to punish myself as a woman who should have kept her ideas bottled up. Such self-recrimination efficiently continues patriarchy's work.

I will end with two matters, one of which is somebody else's diagram, which has been useful to me in complexifying conflict. And the other is the experience of starting a journal recently called "Gender and Conflict" for a conference I was invited to attend on that subject. The journal-writing experience surprised me.

As you know, I think that our hearts are filled with different voices, and the problem with the war-like either/or is that it over-simplifies the complications of the soul. I am not saying the complications of the issues, but of the heart's many affinities. The men I admire most are those like the writer Donald Murray, who brings tenderly traced mixtures of emotion to his account of his experiences. I am not Gandhi or Martin Luther King Jr., or William James, whose writing on the moral equivalent of war moves me very much. I am interested in moral leadership which discusses how the power relations around us get trained into psyches, and can also be seen and resisted there, and I think this is one thing Jean Baker Miller's work is telling us. But I got a new angle on some dimensions of this when, in preparation for a conference in Virginia on Gender and Conflict, I started to keep a required one-week journal on the conference themes.

The previous Saturday morning, I had decided that while I was thinking about what to write in my Gender and Conflict diary, I would clean up some piles of papers in the kitchen. I was giving myself such grief over my messy habits that finally I couldn't think about gender and conflict at all. Inside me was a noisier conflict, with voices shouting, "Peggy, you are such a mess!" So I asked these voices, "What's wrong with being a mess?" And they said, "We don't do that." And I said, "Who is we?" And suddenly I had a vision of one of the streets in the town in New Jersey where I spent most of my first twelve years. There was a row of houses which seemed to me unbelievable, like a bad mistake. Poor people lived in them, poor people with unfamiliar faces. And my voices said, "We're not like that." I was not being policed for being a messy woman. I was being policed as a person from a well-off, "professional," white family, threatening our family's reputation by crossing over into behaviors which I was taught to project onto poor people, working-class people, and people of color. As a white female, I was being used as a counter and a battleground, being shouted at to keep my identification with whiteness, maleness, and wealth. And I think also to keep my identification with "law and order."

In this fight the classist oppressor was internalized. And as the image of poor people's houses flashed on my mind, I stumbled on the construct of me being divided against myself to save "our" face, projecting problems of mess and everything else onto "them." I was the battleground and the perpetrator, and something that women of color have often pointed out became clearer than usual to me. The female shriekers were trying to get me back into place with the men of my race and class, and away from identification with people in those other houses. And seeing and knowing and coming into conflict with that internal police state became one of the most empowering sensations of this observation.

Meanwhile, I have not cleaned up most of my papers. I am an accumulator of papers. If I do not take my history seriously, who will? I feel on better terms with my papers, now. In fact, the reason I keep them is that they are so interesting; they mean so much to me. Why should I let my history be disappeared?

I want to end with a diagram from a Buddhist, a man who lives in Thailand, whose name is Sulak Sivaraksa.[6] His work on conflict has been very useful to me. He draws a circle and imagines that there are the numbers of a clock face on it. He says that at twelve o'clock, noon, you may feel at peace, perhaps too peaceful. At two o'clock, you have gone out like the Lord Buddha, and noticed the suffering in the world, and at four o'clock, you begin to try to alleviate the suffering. At six o'clock, you are HIT by those who did not want the suffering to end, or did not want you to end it. At eight o'clock, you begin to understand why they hit you. At ten o'clock, you can feel compassion for their suffering, which made them hit you. And at noon you are restored to peace, perhaps too great a peace. One aspect of your life could be at two o'clock, while another aspect of your life is at six o'clock. As one grows in awareness, a cycle can be as short as a minute or as long as a lifetime and, for Sulak, the cycle bears on all areas of your life.

Two years after I saw Sulak draw this diagram, I visited him in Bangkok. I had been "hit" by the *Wall Street Journal* and other right-wing forces. I told him that I was having trouble moving upward from the position of having been hit, at six o'clock on his diagram. I think I expected a little sermon, as my visit occurred at eleven a.m. on a Sunday.

Instead, he answered me simply and gently, in one sentence. He said, "You cannot move off six o'clock into the rest of the cycle until you recognize how angry you are that they hit you."[7] I found this a great antidote to the tendency in me to deny injury, insult, or real defeat. Sulak's statement said I must face injury and pain honestly if I was to get beyond them. I realized that I had a tendency to save face, and also that I had internalized Puritan theological sanctions against any acknowledgment of pain. Yet Sulak's cycle also urged me into relationship with those who had hit me and urged me to feel compassion for their disconnection. Sulak's teachings gave me permission for both the anger and the move toward communication. It felt familiar as well as new, for it corresponded to some of those feelings of empathetic identification with critics which I have already described. Sulak's prescription is useful in talking back to the police-state voices in me which said, "We are not like that." I doubt they enjoy their jobs. I see them trapped in the police state.

Working on this talk has helped me to recognize some of the elements that are present when I avoid conflict, and when on the other hand I feel I am coming into conflict in more authentic ways than before. It seems that I feel best in conflict when I am opposing the tendency toward polarized structures and behaviors inside of my psyche and in the society, and acting on the recognition that my identity contains and knits multitudes, like the campground, and feels at home with the complexities of interrelatedness among all living things.

The Moebius strip derived from this rumination reads on one side "I must not let them make me feel like a fraud when I come into conflict." And on the other side, "Let me continue to spot the fraudulent simplicity of conflict." Colloquially translated, I feel at times, "I am not up to the fray." At the same time, "The fray is not up to me."

Notes

1   This chapter was previously published as McIntosh (2000).
2   See Chapter 7, *Feeling Like A Fraud, Part I,* and Chapter 8, *Feeling Like A Fraud, Part II.*
3   See Gearhart (1979).
4   Jean Baker Miller used this phrase in unpublished personal communication with the author beginning in 1979.
5   For example, Herbert Spencer's body of work.

6 Sulak developed this diagram and presented it at a conference in Bellagio, Italy at The Bellagio Center of the Rockefeller Foundation in 1993.
7 Personal communication with the author between 1995–2000.

References

Gearhart, S. M. (1979). The womanization of rhetoric. *Women's Studies International Quarterly*, 2(2), 195–201.
McIntosh, P. (2000). Feeling like a fraud – Part III: Finding authentic ways of coming into conflict. *Work in progress No. 90.* Wellesley, MA: Stone Center Working Paper Series.
Tillich, P. (1951). *Systematic theology.* Chicago: University of Chicago Press.

10

FEELING LIKE A FRAUD, PART IV: THE PSYCHE AS SINGULAR AND PLURAL (2019)[1]

Multiplicity is a theme of our age, not new but newly obvious. When the noted psychologist Jean Baker Miller said there was no such thing as a self – only a self in relation – she was portraying the relational world of plural connectedness in human relations. I conceive the mind as plural, too. We are multiple inside, and experience the world in so many different ways that it can be hard to think of ourselves as being unitary persons. Our bodies are singular, but I think our psyches are plural, and that seeing the psyches as plural is going to become more accepted as time goes on. We who are white in the United States have been encouraged to see ourselves as individuals, and to recognize and develop our singularity. Now, on every side, a diverse mix of voices, channels, and connections calls into question the feeling that we are singular. For me, the time has come to recognize that my psyche is plural. I suggest that we claim many different identities as part of our internal complexity. The Moebius Strip paradox for this essay is that one side of a strip of paper reads "I am singular;" the other side of the strip reads "I am plural." If you hold one end, twist the other end once, and tape the ends together, both messages will be now on the same side, part of the same analysis. You can pull the strip along between your thumb and forefinger and you will cover both statements without changing sides.

The sensibilities of two revered 19th century Americans, Ralph Waldo Emerson and Walt Whitman, hover encouragingly over this paradox. Emerson urged us toward singularity and Whitman urged us toward pluralness. Both, however, believed in an encompassing Oversoul that includes everything in the universe. Beyond the matter of the Oversoul, they differed. Emerson (1841): "Trust thyself. Every heart vibrates to that iron string." Whitman (1855): "Do I contradict myself? / Very well then I contradict myself, / (I am large, I contain multitudes.)" I believe that the sense of being both singular and plural are in most of us in the U.S. today and that our psyches give us both messages: be yourself, and be part of the ocean of life.

The singularity that Emerson recommends is commitment to what feel like our own multiple thoughts and observations, and no one else's. In recent decades, white U.S. culture has developed so strongly in the Emerson path toward individuality that I think it has given us license to be ignorant of history, unable to see systemically and, in adulthood, to be rather short on empathetic connection. Whitman, in his way, commits to the idea of being immersed in the lives of others as they are enmeshed in his life. He comprises others' lives and holds them all in his psyche. His identity is the identity of the includer. I think he is better than Emerson at seeing history, seeing social systems at work, and seeing commonalities of human effort and suffering. But the two men admired each other and did not see themselves as opposites. On first reading *Leaves of Grass*, fifty-two-year-old Emerson wrote to thirty-six-year-old Whitman,

> I greet you at the beginning of a great career, which yet must have had a long foreground somewhere, for such a start. I rubbed my eyes a little, to see if this sunbeam were no illusion; but the solid sense of the book is a sober certainty. It has the best merits, namely, of fortifying and encouraging.

Leaves of Grass testifies to plural connection.

I feel that our human psyches are mirrored by both Emerson's idea of uniqueness and Whitman's ideal of interconnectedness. These form the paradoxical opposites of the Moebius strip: I am single and I am plural. I feel that the part of us that is singular, and feels unique to us, is as real as the part of us that has plural affinities, and kaleidoscopic variety. Being asked to narrow down our sense of identity too much can distort and damage people.

At a small college in the U.S., I met three African American students who told me that white students do not accept them as American. So they were happy to go on an exchange visit to Ghana where they had high hopes of being embraced for their Africanness. It didn't work out that way. They were deeply upset by being rejected there, too, when they learned the Ghanaians saw them as American, not African. I felt that they had been persuaded by oversimplifications of identity to feel that they were stateless persons, people without a country. They were in great pain. They felt fraudulent. As I saw it,

> You are complex. Part of you relates to America, part of you relates to Africa, and each of you is whole. You all have many other aspects of identity as well. You are not defective variants of anybody else. And you are the way of the future.

But their longing to belong to a nation was poignant. I feel mainstream U.S. culture has visited several problems onto these students. They have been asked to accept others' versions of who they are. They have been led to believe that other people are sure of who and what they are and where their place is. And they are suffering under the cultural imposition that they should settle for simplified senses of their identity. I feel they should be allowed and encouraged to use all of their accumulating experience toward a sense that they are valid, complex people with plural psyches.

Many of the Stone Center papers[2] and *This Changes Everything*, Christina Robb's book about Jean Baker Miller's and Carol Gilligan's relational theories, explore ideas that point towards seeing the psyche as plural (Robb, 2006). Miller's colleague, Jan Surrey, paraphrases therapist Carl Rogers on how a client in psychotherapy "discovers previously unknown parts of him or herself." Surrey writes of the capacity for open, evolving psyches. She writes of flexibility, responsiveness, receptivity, and changing because of making connections. The connections can be with others, but can also be with inner parts of the self (Surrey, 1984). Miller's colleague and successor at Wellesley's Stone Center, Judith Jordan, writes about reconnecting with rejected aspects of ourselves or the "disavowed aspects of the human condition which women often carry" (Jordan, 1989). She defines *self-empathy* as "bringing an empathic attitude to bear on [ourselves]" (Jordan, 1983).

In one of the Stone Center's Working Papers, Maureen Walker refers to Starhawk's statement that there are prisons and battlefields within the self. I feel these too, as a key aspect of pluralness. One of my Phase Theory papers, *Interactive Phases of Curricular and Personal Re-Vision with Regard to Race*, dwells on the poignancy of being made to give up the plural affinities of one's early character. I wrote,

> The multicultural worlds are in us, as well as around us. Early culturally conditioning trained each of us to shut off awareness of certain groups, voices, abilities, and inclinations, including the inclination to be with many kinds of children. Continents we might have known were closed off, were subordinated within us.[3]

I now feel we can reconnect with these lost continents, and that when they do this, we are more whole. I concluded *White Privilege, Color and Crime* by carrying the thought further. Continual dominance can imprison the psyche of the dominator.

> White oblivion about and inculturated denial of white privilege acts as a psychological prison system that costs white people heavily, in terms of preventing human development. Walking obliviously through our own racial experience may perpetuate the imprisonment of the heart and the intelligence in a false law and order of tyrannizing denial about who, what, and where we are. So the societal systems of color and crime may reside also in the psyches of white people where an equivalent of bad race relations or white supremacy damages the civic health and plural balance of the soul.[4]

While systems of racism and privilege subject people of color to external (and internalized) oppression, these same systems force white people also into fraudulent and fractured versions of ourselves. Excluding the parts of ourselves that were once plurally responsive to others creates space for bigotry to take root.

In his writings on pragmatism, the American philosopher William James suggested that the validity of an idea rested in how far it could take one. The idea that the identity is plural takes me to many places. James has been a great model of pluralizing, having himself extended his roles from naturalist to psychologist to philosopher to student of religion. In *The Varieties of Religious Experience* (1936) and in his philosophical work *A Pluralistic Universe* (1909), James repeatedly describes severalness, distinctiveness, and interior differences. For James, the soul has many facets, is never quite pinned down, and never quite sure of itself.

I am not writing about the mental illness called Dissociative Identity Disorder. I am writing about conscious daily pluralness and about *conscious ambivalence*. I completely believe a person who says, "I am of two minds" about something.

Writer Nancy Mairs took ambivalence, which could be felt by any of us about anything, as a positive sign of intelligence and maturity. In Mairs' (1996) book, *Carnal Acts*, she wrote:

> To view your life as blessed does not require you to deny your pain. It simply demands a more complicated vision, one in which a condition or event is not either good or bad, but is, rather, both good and bad, not sequentially, but simultaneously. In my experience, *the more such ambivalences you can hold in your head, the better off you are, intellectually and emotionally* [emphasis added].

Mairs essentially says she believes in our conscious pluralness, our ambivalence. I know that its opposite, unconscious ambivalence, results in many kinds of unfinished business, procrastination, rationalization, denial, dishonesty, apology, and remorse. I feel that Mairs was pioneering when she insisted that what I would call *conscious ambivalence* was for her a key to honest living.

I feel that the pluralities are in us as well as around us in the institutional world. There is understandable political pressure toward seeing singularly, for the sake of the image of national unity. For example, the Latin inscription engraved on the U.S. penny, "E Pluribus Unum," means "Out of Many, One." I feel that to help the U.S. make good on its plural promises, we should make the other side of the coin carry a message of plurality: "Within the One are Many," or "Intra Unum Plures." I feel the United States needs to educate citizens to see our nation as both singular and plural.

At the University of Denver, team teaching in the 1970s, four colleagues and I offered American Studies courses that intentionally gave students differing versions of U.S. culture. The final exam always asked students to "compare the versions of U.S. culture that you got from the first three weeks of the course with the versions that you got in the final eleven weeks." We still get love letters thanking us for teaching that history is versions. I now recognize that when we taught that history is versions, we assumed also that each student already had the capacity, within themselves, to comprehend a plurality of versions. We were teaching them to recognize pluralness in their own experience of the world. I think that what we did is obvious, but is not yet widely accepted or practiced as a form of teaching. This is partly because we as teachers have probably never been encouraged to see ourselves as having plural psyches. And as teachers, we have also been taught we owe it to students to simplify life, clarify complexities, and teach the next generation to argue pointedly in a competitive, win-lose society. Even the most mindful and sensitive teachers serve an educational system that chiefly fosters individualistic, non-plural minds.

As Emily Style pointed out in her well-known essay "Curriculum as Window and Mirror," the United States' liberal arts college curriculum rests on the assumption that human beings are capable of many different mental actions, which are featured in the fields of the humanities, the social sciences, science, math, and technology (Style, 1988). The reason that there are distribution requirements in liberal arts colleges is that the student is asked to become a "well-rounded person" by spreading his or her attention to a number of different fields. The intellectual pluralness that ideally results is not envisioned simply as that of a single self, but rather a self-in-relation to all of the fields it touches and that touch it. The liberal arts curriculum and its distribution requirements postulate that in every student, there is the potential to become competent in many different fields of knowledge. The whole scheme rests on an implicit, though not articulated, model of the mind as potentially plural.

Intellectual history of the 20th century America reveals increasing attention to multiplicity. Anthropologists describe people's use of code-switching, i.e. using differing manners and linguistic modes situationally, as called for. Howard Gardner (1983) describes multiple intelligences. Brain researchers describe multiple regions of the brain with different and overlapping functions, and with mental plasticity developing through age and experience. As a child, I was always thrown off by well-meaning adults' single-minded questions: "What is your favorite color - favorite food - favorite book?" "Who is your best friend?" I respect the pluralist Margaret Mead's coaching of her daughter not to feel that she had to have a favorite color or a favorite book.[5] She told her daughter that one could be equally in love with two people at the same time. This is education in plural thinking and feeling. Wallace Stevens (1917) writes "Thirteen Ways of Looking at a Blackbird," all emanating from him. John Dos Passos (1938) in writing *U.S.A.* conceived the nation as pluralistic mosaic of life. Audre Lorde self-describes as "poet, warrior, woman, lesbian, black, activist, mother, sister." This is plural identity.

In the National SEED Project, we encourage participants to fill in a chart with many circles around a central circle. The chart is entitled "Circles of Our Multicultural Selves." Most people have no trouble filling in multiple circles, naming different aspects of themselves. One thing this exercise has clarified for me is why so many people hesitate to speak in public. Given our complexity, it is not surprising. We would need to censor, evade, neglect, ignore, distort, or exaggerate aspects of our complex selves in saying anything at all.

Once in the National SEED Project's training week in the early 1980s, Emily Style and I created an exercise which was too simple, though we didn't know it at the time. So that they could exchange views with each other, we asked all of the "white people" to line up on one side of the room and all the "people of color" to line up on the other side of the room. Gene Tey Shin, a Korean American man, walked down between the two lines and told us he refused to repudiate his mother, who is white, or his father, who is Korean. Chastened and corrected, we created a third affinity group for people who identify as bicultural, biracial, or multicultural. We are indebted to Gene Tey Shin for staying with the pluralness of his psyche.

When I told a Japanese colleague that because I am not a psychologist, I was fearful about writing that the psyche is plural (I was in fact, feeling like a fraud), my colleague told me, "Well, I am a psychologist and the reason I chose to become a cultural psychologist is that I read a 1991 paper about East/West differences in construing the self." She gave me the research and theory paper by Markus and Kitayama (1991) that spells out some key differences in how the self is construed in East Asian and Western cultures. This paper was instrumental in launching the subfield of cultural psychology. According to the authors, East Asians construe the identity as contingent on relationships, situations, and traditions. The Western, especially American, paradigm of the self is that of an individual, autonomous entity. In the authors' view, the Eastern construal of the self consists of multiple aspects of the self, in contrast to the singular dimension of the Western construal of the self. In this conversation, my colleague told me that when she asks her students in a Japanese university to respond to the question, "Who am I?" they often struggle to come up with ten statements. The American students have no trouble in answering the question, listing their personal attributes and characteristics with ease because they see their attributes transcending relationships and contexts. East Asian students find the question "Who am I?" artificial as it fails to specify a context or relationship to which their sense of self is contingent.

Psychologist Carol Gilligan had interesting things to say about gendered contexts and plural mindedness in her book *In a Different Voice* (1982). Gilligan as a researcher found that women did not conform to Lawrence Kohlberg's typology of moral development. In his studies, Kohlberg had asked a sample of men and women questions regarding moral decision-making, e.g. whether it was ethical to steal a drug if it might save someone's life. In seeing apparently equivocating responses from women, Kohlberg put their responses in the back of a file drawer and built his typology primarily from his male respondents. When Gilligan opened the neglected files, she noticed in the women's responses some patterns that constituted "a different voice." The women in the research sample kept asking for more information before they could make a moral decision. They were not so concerned with the letter of the law as with how a given decision might tear or mend the social fabric. Gilligan later named the tensions in the women and men's decision-making as the difference between what she called the *ethic of care* and the *ethic of justice*. It seemed that the women were revolving many variables in their minds when considering the ethics of a situation.

In some quarters, Gilligan was pilloried for complexifying the simpler model of moral development which Kohlberg had generated. In further studies, she complicated the picture even more by suggesting that one mind could hold both the ethic of care and the ethic of justice. This implied that the dilemma for complex minded people is not to reject but to choose which of their perceptions to deploy in their actions, using situational ethics. The ethic of saying "it all depends" takes into consideration the question of what avenue of action might do the least harm.

In 1976, I was bowled over by reading *Toward a New Psychology of Women* (Miller, 1976). I was impressed by Jean Baker Miller's gutsy, street-wise sarcasm on the subject of the "not too glorious record" of humankind. I loved the way she reconstrued women's "weaknesses" as strengths and was so clear and steady in saying that psychological theory by men about men's experience did not apply to women. I admired the humility of her book's title, not **The** *Psychology of Women* but **Toward a New** *Psychology of Women*. I loved her choice of a humble and tentative word, "toward." This tentativeness presaged her openness to change when women who were not in the economic class or race of her psychiatric sample widened her awareness to the point where she reconceived and renamed the relational model as the relational-cultural theory (Miller, 1987).[6]

Miller's most radical and useful ideas from my point of view are about the "self." There is no such thing as a self; there is only a self-in-relation. Human beings are born into relationship, being literally held by adults, especially mothers. According to Miller, they do not outgrow connection and interdependence with other people as they mature, but well-known psychological theory before her work had posited independence and individuation as mature adult norms and ideals. When Miller made the observations about the self-in-relation, she knew that her theory was far-reaching and could potentially revolutionize thinking about people, policies, and the whole world. "This changes everything," she told her collaborator Christina Robb (2006). It will, however, still be a long time before individualist readings of human psyches stop prevailing in U.S. psychology and economic theory. The dominant political theory of capitalism holds that the *systemic* conditions of people's lives do not much impact *individual* outcomes. Capitalism fosters the myth of mer-itocracy, which as I have defined it has two parts: that the individual is the unit of society and that whatever one ends up with must be what one individually wanted, worked for, earned, and deserved.

If we are to see the psyche itself is plural, we can take Jean Baker Miller's entire relational paradigm and turn it inward. In that case, we could say that the relationships and the connectedness that she stressed in the social world are obviously found within the content of the mind and heart. In this reading, the relational world of one's interior is filled with multiplicity. And then the psyche itself can be understood to be plural. For many readers, examples will probably present themselves. Who doesn't know the feeling of being "of two minds" about something, or having many interior voices on a given dilemma? Or, as poet Mary Oliver, wrote, "I am, myself, three selves, at least" (1995, p. 2). She was referring to the child, the social being, and the creative being in her.

In *The Mind's I*, by psychologists Douglas R. Hofstadter and Daniel Dennett, Hofstadter writes, "It is a common myth that each person is a unity, a kind of unitary organization with a will of its own. Quite the contrary, a person is an amalgamation of many subpersons, all with *wills of their own* [emphasis added]" (Hofstadter and Dennett, 1981, p. 342). His co-author, Dennett, writes,

> So far there is no good theory of consciousness ... The mere fact of such a familiar feature of our lives has resisted for so long all attempts to characterize it ... suggests that our conception of it is at fault ... What is needed ... is a careful rethinking of the assumptions that lead us to suppose that there is a single and familiar phenomenon, consciousness ... Might a human being harbor more than one conscious subject or ego or agent within one brain?
>
> *(Hofstadter and Dennett, 1981, p. 8)*

If you go back to founding of Psychology, you will find both Freud and Jung had pluralness in their models of the psyche. They simply could not figure out the psyche without seeing separate elements in it. For Freud: there are the superego, the ego, and the id. For Jung: there are the four psychological types, as well as the anima and animus, and many archetypes. Both men lacked awareness of how overarching systems of power affected their clients' lives. As the field of Psychology developed under the influence of Freud and Jung, many kinds of privilege were ignored in their writings: patriarchy, white-European colonial privilege, and privilege related to sexuality, class, religion, nation, geography, age, and ability. It is odd to me that both founders of Psychology as a field lacked an understanding or willingness to notice the crucial role of circumstances of birth in affecting a human life within systems of power. They lacked the systemic insights of Miller and her colleagues at the Stone Center, and of Carol Gilligan, which came from putting women at the center. Nevertheless, Freud and Jung, in context of their time, were quite plural-minded.

The American assumption that the identity is singular is crucial to individualism, capitalism, and the myth of the independent male adult. In the plural self, there are important and useful irreconcilables; the effort to get them all together may be the same old singularity error - the manufactured ideal. My case for seeing identity plurally corresponds to Freud, to Jung, to Miller, and to my own experience of what feel like interdependent actors in my psyche. The singular identity probably is accompanied by an existential sense of isolation, whereas a pluralized sense of identity comes from a relational, contingent sense of existing within multiple communities.

My liberal arts education was partially successful in pluralizing my mind, though its contents were all framed by white European and American males. My talk about Rugged Individualism at University of Denver in 1976 performed pluralism through its twenty chairs labeled with parts of my psyche.[7] My second Fraud paper rejected the academic genre of the outline and substituted instead a list, a tour of the plural rooms of my psyche. The Madwoman's poem is about four different elements of creation. Working toward a new definition of consciousness as plural has been a relief to me, validating my sense of multiplicity within myself and giving me more curiosity about other people's minds.

I believe that Jean Baker Miller was right: we are born into relationship and we stay there. So to me it makes sense to conceive ourselves as plural. We never outgrow relationality, though we may think we do. Relationality in our outer lives has created relationality and variability in our inner lives, just as external institutions, like family life, school, and employment, have created relationality and variability in our minds. We may as well go ahead and posit that the psyche is as plural as social life itself. Physically, we are singular; in our hearts and souls, we are plural. When teachers urge a student to follow the Delphic teaching "Know thyself," I think it would be more useful to urge, "Know thyselves."

To students I say: Trust your complexities. You are the only authority in the world on your own complex experiences. Nobody knows more about them than you do. Track your complexities, sort them, study them, and honor them as sources of your knowledge and actions in the world. You are singular; no one else in the world is like you. At the same time, your experiences hold countless different threads, themes, patterns, sensations and mixes of feeling and thought that constitute your plural soul. I define the soul as everything that has ever deeply touched you regardless of its source. No one else's soul has your particular set of complexities. Your plural soul and your singular self are both unique in the history of the evolving world. Trust their complexities, take an interest in them, and be curious about them. Study your own inner and outer worlds, how they are hurt and what would be good for their healing. You may be better respected by others as well if you have done a lot of work toward plural self-knowledge and compassion for your own complexities. Others may see you as helpful because in taking yourself seriously you have given them confidence in doing so themselves. This is not the false leadership of self infatuation that loves only those who grovel at its feet, but leadership of the many faceted soul, trying to act in ways that are in harmony with its own complexity, and puzzling out what might be the greatest good for the greatest number.

I get brought up short in trying to express this, for in the matter of words and communications I have limited faith. You can answer the question of who you are, who any person is, in a thousand different ways. Some people do this confidently in words. But I do not think that reality comes in words. I feel that words and sentences are blunt instruments invented to communicate some senses of reality but not finely successful in accomplishing understanding. Music, art, color, and motion may be able to take over where words leave off.

It may seem odd that a person who earned three degrees in the field of "English" and taught English for three decades is so skeptical about the effectiveness of language. I am writing the words I want to read and they were not in all the hundreds of thousands of lines I have read in "English." I wish the next generations of students well in bringing language around more satisfactorily to their experiences of their lived lives.

I am left wondering whether feeling that the psyche is plural helps in matters of social justice. I think so. It increases compassion, honors ambivalence, encourages generosity, and rewards vicarious experience. Seeing plurally widens the heart. Plural thinking makes ego boundaries less rigid. It makes empathy and modesty and self-awareness more possible. It strengthens courage by removing the idea that courage is straightforward and that bravery consists in being sure that you are right, and in the right. The soul that knows its own pluralness is more modest than the soul that does not; it has let more influences and experiences touch it.

Along these lines, a very notable TED Talk in the U.S. by brain researcher Jill Bolte Taylor (2008) underscores pluralness of the psyche. She discovers her right brain after a stroke. It had been there all along, a place of halcyon peace, hidden behind the activity of the left brain. After the stroke, her right brain became as real to her as her left brain, but it was absolutely Other. Which person is Jill? The left or the right brained person? Answer: Both. Though she was a brain researcher, this was the first time she actually experienced the double nature of her psyche.

Pluralness is so much a part of the life of young people today in the 21st century that I will not attempt to describe in any detail the glimpses I see. There is fluidity of many kinds - gender fluidity, technological fluidity, fluidity in language, manners, and in all of the arts. There is willingness to explore new paths, invent new ways of being in the world, and seek out information from multiple sources simultaneously.

I cannot speak for young people, but will simply end with a quote from one. Zoe Madonna, of the *Boston Globe*, interviewed Emi Ferguson, a young musician, about her bluegrass and jazz-inspired Bach arrangements and her involvement with the daring, deliberate arts collective American Modern Opera Company (Madonna, 2018). Madonna asked, "If you could change something about the music world, what would it be?" Ferguson responded,

> The first thing that comes to mind are these boxes! Classical music is one thing, pop music is another thing. Things should be fluid to encourage listeners to continue to explore ... To try and break down some of those imaginary marketing walls that we've built, to have a lot more fluidity ... "You play the flute and you sing, but the singing is pop and the flute is classical? And what genre do we put you in!?" I don't know what a better

way is. How to better address the minutiae of the metadata, to encompass a human being who is not one thing ever, but many things all the time?

Notes

1 McIntosh delivered this essay first as a keynote address for the American Psychological Association on August 5, 2017 and has refined it since. This is the first publication of *Feeling Like A Fraud, Part IV* as an essay.
2 The main mode of the Stone Center was discussion among therapists and with the Wellesley Centers for Women community. Many things were said that were not formally recorded, though they were part of the working terminology and conceptualizations at the Stone Center.
3 See Chapter 13, *Interactive Phases of Curricular and Personal Re-Vision with Regard to Race*.
4 See Chapter 4, *White Privilege, Color, and Crime: A Personal Account*.
5 Talk by Mary Catherine Bateson at a Radcliffe reunion. See Bateson (2001) for more about her relationship with her parents.
6 See also Jordan (2001).
7 See Chapter 8, *Feeling Like a Fraud, Part II*, for more on this talk.

References

Bateson, M. C. (2001). *With a daughters eye: A memoir of Margaret Mead and Gregory Bateson*. New York: Perennial.

Dos Passos, J. (1938). *USA*. New York: Harcourt Brace.

Emerson, R.W. (1841, 07). Self reliance. *The Journal of Belles Lettres (1832–1842)*, 1.

Gardner, H. (1983). *Frames of mind: The theory of multiple intelligences*. New York: Basic Books.

Gilligan, C. (1982). *In a different voice: Psychological theory and women's development*. Cambridge: Harvard University Press.

Hofstadter, D. R., & Dennett, D. C. (1981). *The mind's I: Fantasies and reflections on self and soul*. Toronto: Basic Books.

James, W. (1909). *A pluralistic universe: Hibbert lectures to Manchester College on the present situation in philosophy*. New York: Longmans, Green, and Co.

James, W. (1936). *The varieties of religious experience: A study in human nature*. New York: The Modern Library.

Jordan, J. V. (1983). Women and empathy. *Work in progress No. 2*. Wellesley, MA: Stone Center Working Papers Series, Wellesley College.

Jordan, J. V. (1989). Relational development: Therapeutic implications of empathy and shame. *Work in progress No. 39*. Wellesley, MA: Stone Center Working Papers Series, Wellesley College.

Jordan, J. V. (2001). A relational-cultural model: Healing through mutual empathy. *Bulletin of the Menninger Clinic*, 65(1), 92–103.

Madonna, Z. (2018, December 14). Venturing outside the box with American Modern Opera Company's flutist. *Boston Globe*.

Mairs, N. (1996). *Carnal acts: Essays*. Boston: Beacon Press.

Markus, H. R., & Kitayama, S. (1991). Culture and the self: Implications for cognition, emotion, and motivation. *Psychological Review*, 98(2), 224–253.

Miller, J. B. (1976). *Toward a new psychology of women*. Boston: Beacon Press.

Miller, J. B. (1987). *Toward a new psychology of women* (2nd ed.). Boston: Beacon Press.

Oliver, M. (1995). *Blue pastures*. New York: Harcourt Brace.

Robb, C., 1946. (2006). *This changes everything: The relational revolution in psychology* (1st ed.). New York: Farrar, Straus and Giroux.

Stevens, W. (1917). Thirteen ways of looking at a blackbird. In Kreymborg, A. (Ed.). *Others: An anthology of the new verse* (109). New York: A. A. Knopf.

Style, E. (1988). Curriculum as window and mirror. In *Listening for all voices: Gender balancing the school curriculum*. Summit, N.J.: Oak Knoll School.

Surrey, J. (1984). The "self-in-relation": A theory of women's development. *Work in progress No. 13*. Wellesley, MA: Stone Center Working Papers Series.

Taylor, J. B. (2008, February). *Jill Bolte Taylor: My stroke of insight*. [Video file] TED Talk.

Whitman, W. (1855). Song of myself. *Leaves of grass*. Brooklyn, New York.

PART III
The Phase Theory Papers

A LETTER ABOUT PHASE THEORY

Dear Reader,

After the first Women's Studies Department began in 1970 at San Diego State University, there was an immediate feeling from many women that they wanted not only to study women separately from men, but also to study both together. On the other side of the continent, Carolyn Elliott launched a seminar series for Wellesley College professors on bringing materials on women into college courses generally. She said to me, "Women belong in every subject – Women and the Railroad!" I thought at the time she was going too far. But since she hired me in 1979 to lead the seminar, I began to facilitate as though I agreed with her, and, sure enough, I came to feel she was right.

Those of us who had moral, intellectual, or financial support began to ask questions about every academic discipline – Where are the women? What are the framing dimensions of the subjects I teach? Who made these frames? Who was served by these frames? And my own question was, "What would change in any classroom if women were included as half the world's population and were seen as having had half the world's lived experience?"

About this time, philosopher Elizabeth Minnich said in a talk about curriculum transformation, "You don't just add the idea that the world is round to the idea that the world is flat. You go back and rethink the whole thing." She was quoting from what was to become her own book *Transforming Knowledge*. [1]

But just how to get women's half of experience into academic courses raised complicated questions that surfaced all over the country, in classrooms, departments, journals, and at professional meetings. Several of us at the same time realized that there would probably be a phased-in understanding of how to include women and to reconstrue the bodies of knowledge into which they were being introduced. We who undertook this kind of transformative thinking were never the same again. We would never see ourselves, Knowledge, men, marriage, labor, childhood, power, poverty, or empire in the same way again.

There were many discussions of how the "phased-in understanding" could develop. I feared suggestions of linear phases that proceeded in order, as if one phase replaced the previous one entirely. I wanted to see them all together and turned to Joan Gundersen's phrase "interactive phases" to carry the sense that I can be simultaneously in all of the various phases I have recognized and described.[2] My Interactive Phase Theory became one of several models of change in bringing women into the liberal arts curriculum. The interactive phases I outlined can be seen, in brief, as I: domination, II: assimilation, III: resistance, IV: inclusion, and V: wholeness. The chapters in this part of the book will show you my first publication on the idea of curricular expansion in 1981 and then my subsequent 1983 and 1990 descriptions of what the five phases can look like.

At the time when I published my first Interactive Phase Theory paper in 1983, I did not expect that it would last, so I just used numbers for the five frames of mind I designated. I now think readers could have benefited from having some names in the typology, describing the political nature of these outer structures in the world and inner frames of mind that they form in people.

When I developed my Phase Theory in 1981–3, many other women were simultaneously developing their own phase theories. We were all wondering how to bring women into the liberal arts curriculum and had agreed with the words of Charlotte Bunch that you can't just "add women and stir." You will find others' phase theories both like and unlike my own. I notice that what I dwelt on somewhat more than other writers was the domestic, repetitive work of "making and mending the fabric" – agricultural, domestic, social, emotional, intellectual, religious, spiritual, artistic, educational, and political fabric. Making the fabric was projected onto and required of people of color and all women.

I benefited from the many other women who were at the same time working on bringing women into the curriculum and into knowledge-making itself. Since we were making our own theoretical frameworks, it was a great time for feminist imagination and reconsideration of the curriculum. Florence Howe published a directory of thirty-two colleges and universities that were bringing women into the main curriculum in 1983 (McIntosh, Stanis, and Kneubuhl, 1983). This feminist work has benefited many who have followed us and has produced marked changes, especially in the humanities and social sciences.

Mary Kay Tetreault wrote her own Phase Theory and gave an excellent description of Phase Theories generated by a number of feminist scholars in the 1986 Volume 15 Number 2 issue of *Comment* (Tetreault, 1986). Chicano scholar and poet Gloria Anzaldúa first described a Phase Theory in her 1987 book *Borderlands/La Frontera*. It traces her own shift from thinking colonially to becoming spiritually active. She further developed her theory in "Seven Stages of Concocimiento" (Anzaldúa, 2015):

1.   *el arrebato… rupture, fragmentation… an ending, a beginning*
2.   *nepantla…torn between ways*

3.   *the Coatlicue state... desconocimiento and the cost of knowing*
4.   *the call... el compromiso... the crossing and conversion*
5.   *putting Coyolxauhqui together... new personal and collective "stories"*
6.   *the blow-up... a clash of realities*
7.   *shifting realities... acting out the vision or spiritual activism.*

All of the phase theories have value, and perhaps you as a reader will want to create your own model, your sense of the sequence in your own expanding development as a student or perhaps teacher. You can make Phase Theory for any part of your life in which you feel you want to bring in new perspectives or re-orient yourself.

Growing up as a student or teacher, I would have appreciated multiple typologies, not single models. Nobody gave me anything like a phase theory. Raised in a white male-dominated tradition of education, I found that visualizing phases of curricular expansion offered escapes from top-down constructions of the excellence I was meant to be striving for or supporting in other people.

Though my first essay on Phase Theory included a number of references to people of color and fictional black students Maya and Angela, I imagine that my African American colleagues sometimes wondered, "When will Peggy wake up to the whiteness of her Phase Theory?" It took me seven years, between 1983 and 1990. I had published my White Privilege paper in 1988 and its Knapsack version in 1989. Given my growing awareness of how corrosive a male and white curriculum must be for the minds of all of us, I set out to re-engage with my Phase Theory as it applied to race in 1990.

I decided to keep the same phases but with different examples of its effect on students' lives. I kept the same phases because I thought there was such a clear parallel between what male dominance and white dominance did to the curriculum and to students' minds. This second Phase Theory paper captured many white attitudes that I had seen while working with faculty to expand the curriculum along the lines of race.

For years I felt accountable to a black student at the University of Denver who had approached me after an American Literature class I taught on Jean Toomer. The student told me she had waited all semester for this class because finally she saw a black writer on a syllabus at the University. But she said I had given a negative slant on Toomer and implied that he didn't know what he was doing as a writer. Perhaps I had done that unconsciously for all black writers I had ever encountered, being so ignorant of Black culture. It is a reverse example of what I now need to do – learn from those I was taught to look down on; learn more about and from them, and learn more about how my top-down assumptions can damage me and a whole class of students.

Now I would describe the Phases this way: in Phase I, white patriarchy rules. In Phase II, I can aspire to be an exceptional white woman. In Phase III, I get angry at and resist the whole vertical power structure. In Phase IV, I inhabit my many selves and feel all of us are human beings, though not given just chances at being so. Phase V is nowhere near conception or realization. We get glimpses of it when the strengths of all five phases are creatively aligned and when our humanity seems whole and strong.

After I conceived Phase Theory as a description of five ways of seeing history in college curricula, I expanded it to become a description of five ways of teaching in college courses generally. Then it expanded further to be a description of many problems in our society and in my psyche. I now see phases everywhere, for example in how people receive and conceive medical care, food, language, public politics, journalism, sports, clothing, money, race, sexual orientation, gender identity, ethnicity, and religion. I also see think that the phases relate to the five myths that keep racism in place: meritocracy, manifest destiny, monoculturalism, white racelessness, and white moral and managerial superiority.[3]

In making Phase Theory, I thought that I was describing both psychological and sociological structures. But now I think that I was also doing political science, and describing capitalism and colonialism with their win-lest-you-lose mentalities and structures. The Phases may be seen as alternative strategies for survival and are not necessarily warring or competing or mutually exclusive.

Gradually over the years, readers began to apply my and others' phase theories to community climates, business enterprises, foreign policy, and every single one of the academic disciplines of the United States. It became clear that the whole country had a win-lest-you-lose mentality among those who held the most power. As I see it, beneath the geologic structure of the peaks are the alluvial plains drawing on a very different set of functions which are essential to empowering those in the vertical structures. In this lateral world, the hidden mantras are not kill-or-be-killed nor win-lest-you-lose. The hidden mantra is "you work for the decent survival of all, for therein lies your own best chance for survival."

In the years since phase theories emerged, colleges and universities have made some progress in Phase IV lateral teaching, in which everyone is seen as a teacher and learner. Frances Maher and Mary Kay Tetreault wrote about implications for feminist teaching of phase theory in their book, *The Feminist Classroom* (Maher and Tetreault, 1994). College and university classrooms also pay more attention than in 1980 to sources of knowledge that do not appear in textbooks or journals. Perhaps the greatest gains in freedom have been made in progressive teaching methods, where the line between the teacher and the taught had always been less clear. And the rise of technology, in some ways, has propelled teachers' acceptance of the idea that a student's experiences are wide and valid. Still, I think we need to attend to the human heart of students, regardless of how they appear to be placed in a stronger position. I feel them thirsty for connection with caring and listening elders.

If you as a teacher have few coherent memories of how you were taught, examples from Interactive Phase Theory may bring back some of your memories. I have used all five of the styles of teaching that I describe, when teaching grades 6, 7, 8, 9, 10, and undergraduate and graduate students. I don't want to pressure readers to discount any part of their previous development. Change your style, change your content, change your perceptions of education, but do not punish yourself for what you were taught and what you did. You were probably doing what you'd been taught to do, and doing the best you knew how. My Phase Theory may help you to recognize some different types of teaching and the different results I feel they produce.

If you start with your own experience and view it minutely, you will find in the power relations keys to the major problems of our time locally and globally, and you will see depression and anxiety and fear fueling violent repression and trampling on humanistic values. What values our curriculum and teaching methods convey to students has a large bearing on the futures of all of us.

Encouragingly yours,

Peggy

Notes

1 Minnich writes, "Because the dominant few were not only taken to be the inclusive term, the norm, and the ideal, but were defined and came to know themselves in *contradistinction* to all others, we cannot just add equalized 'others' on to established systems. Our cure requires reconfiguring, transforming, so that the devalued and excluded can be included not within the same systems that cast them out and down a scale of worth, but on their own, differing terms. The idea that the world is round cannot be added onto the idea that the world is flat; the idea that the sun is the center of the solar system cannot be added onto the idea that the earth is the center – and 'lower,' 'deviant' 'kinds' of humans, and other animals, and all of nature, cannot be added onto systems that took one 'kind' of man to be the center, pinnacle, and master of creation" (Minnich, 2005, pp. 266–267).
2 Prior to publishing her 1986 paper using the phrase "interactive phases," Gundersen used the phrase in personal conversation with the author.
3 See Chapter 6, *White People Facing Race: Uncovering the Myths that Keep Racism in Place.*

References

Anzaldúa, G. (1987). *Borderlands/La frontera: The new mestiza.* (1st ed.). San Francisco: Spinsters/Aunt Lute.
Anzaldúa, G. & Keating, A. (Ed.) (2015). *Light in the dark/Luz en lo oscuro: Rewriting identity, spirituality, reality.* Durham, NC: Duke University Press.
Gundersen, J. R. (1986). Re-visioning the past: Toward a more inclusive telling of history. *The History Teacher, 20*(1), 51.
Maher, F. A., & Tetreault, M. K. (1994). *The feminist classroom.* New York: Basic Books.
McIntosh, P., Stanis, K., & Kneubuhl, B. (1983). Transforming the liberal arts curriculum through incorporation of the new scholarship on women. *Women's Studies Quarterly, 11*(2), 23–29.
Minnich, E. K. (2005). *Transforming knowledge.* Philadelphia: Temple University Press.
Tetreault, M. K. (1986). Women in the curriculum. *Comment on conferences and research about women, 15*(2), 1–2.

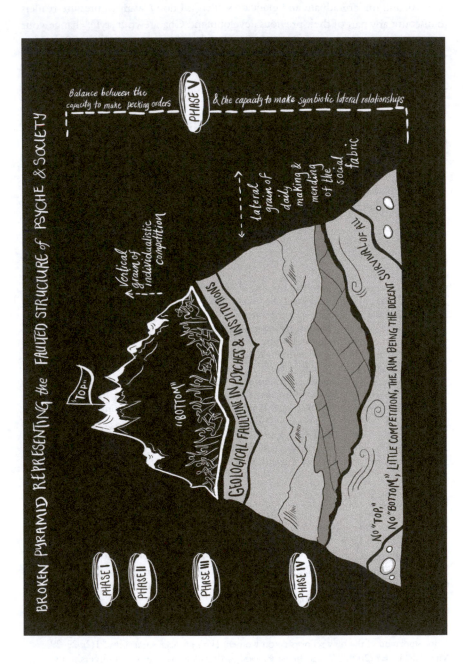

11

THE STUDY OF WOMEN: IMPLICATIONS FOR RECONSTRUCTING THE LIBERAL ARTS DISCIPLINES (1981)[1]

Research on women – the study not only of the women we are allowed to call "notable" but of women as half the world's population – poses challenging questions for scholars and teachers in each of the academic disciplines. As we come to see the comparative absence of women's experience from the account of reality which is passed on to students by our present curriculum, we may ask two clarifying questions which will help us, as scholars, to fill in the overlooked record of the "other" half of the human race. First: What is the basic content and methodology of my discipline? and second: How would my discipline need to change in order to reflect the fact that women are half the world's population?

The initial answers vary from discipline to discipline and thus appear at first to reinforce our sense of the differences between disciplines. But in the end, the answers lead us to perceive that some of the boundaries between disciplines result from the same compartmentalizing tendency that kept women's experience from being construed as a part of social reality in the first place. Therefore, research on women has come to pose a challenge not only to the epistemological ground rules within disciplines but to the very distancing between disciplines which our present modes of finding and passing on knowledge enforce and reinforce.

The traditional curriculum has stressed the public sphere: laws, wars, cultural change, public events, individual accomplishment, and the activities of "the makers and shapers of civilization," or of those who survived fairly well within cultural systems. But society has been held together by groups of people who are not distinguished by public achievement, public power, or recognized cultural innovation, but who weave and maintain the social fabric, living out of the limelight except in times of violence and social disruption. Some of the valuable work that such people have done has been the taking care of people and systems, and the maintaining of production and reproduction. Many have barely survived; some have prospered; all have lived within worlds we have been taught to overlook, those "lower worlds" including that of the "women's sphere." The richness and complexity of their lives, the facts about their existence, "achievement," and "genius" have yet to be recognized within our academic disciplines.

If we balanced the curriculum, we would diminish the emphasis on those who attained power, "importance," or "excellence" as we have been taught to define them, and increase the attention given to those men and women previously invisible in the curriculum whose lives are equally important, interesting, and revealing for us to study, if we are claiming to "know" about human life and history.

If transformed, the field of religion would become less centered on theology and public religious institutions and would cover the *effects* of religious belief or observance on the daily lives of ordinary people. Intellectual history would balance attention to the thought of recognized individuals and "movements" with the study of platitudes, truisms, and the givens which most people live by most of the time, and which may not have the "intellectual purity" of the thought of the individuals who we are told shaped history. History itself, if it reflected the fact that women are half the world's population, would concern itself less with laws and wars and more with the social fabric of most people's lives. A course called "History of France" which omitted women would have to change its name. Historians would attempt to answer more questions like "What was it like to live, to be a human being, in given ages of the world's history, and in a variety of statuses and places?" Though women's studies scholars sometimes ask "What was it like for those 'at the bottom'?" they also begin to ask whether what we defined as "top" and "bottom" are in fact representative of the best and the worst in human life, and who wrote those definitions, and whom the definitions serve.

The study of music, art, and architecture are transformed if one studies not only those works which were made for public use, display, or performance and which required the money of buyers or aristocratic or institutional patrons. One starts to study quilts and breadloaf shapes, clothing, pots, and kitchens, and songs and dances which people who had no musical literacy or training took for granted. Architecture becomes less the study of the architect's place in a tradition of designers and more the study of the effects of buildings on those who inhabit them – the effects on daily lives of the dwellings and buildings which help to shape those lives. One looks at the same time for the influence which women did have in shaping – or resisting – their environments, and in bringing about architectural and environmental change.

Economics, changed to reflect the fact that women are half the world's population, would put more emphasis on unpaid labor, but to consider unpaid labor as part of the economic picture would transform economics. In political science, the meaning of "politics" is being extended to cover private relationships which do involve power but which are not often explored by scholars in political science: the politics of neighborhoods, of schools, of families, of classes and races and ethnic and religious groups within institutions, and of those who do not exercise authority. To add the family to the political sphere is both to make women visible and to reconstrue "politics."

A freshman English curriculum reflecting the fact that women have been half of the world's population might give academic credit for the development of skill in written conversation, rather than simply stressing the art of writing monologue, which is a genre derived from the rhetorical patterns of persuasion in which one single leader persuaded a group of listeners of his point of view. Women, like most people we do not often study, have chiefly used language to make connections between people, to elicit information, and to carry on daily work. We might devise ways to give academic credit for the mental pluralism which exists but does not lend itself to the monologue of the expository essay. In literature itself, we need far more descriptive work on writing by women, whatever its genre. How does it happen that the genres most used by women – the journal and letter – are considered sub-literary? Or how does it happen that the thousands of novels by women have so disappeared from accounts of America's literary history?

We move, then, from simple answers to complex answers in addressing the question "How would my discipline need to change in order to reflect the fact that women are half the world's population?" In general, the simple answer involves getting the "women's sphere" added to the subject matter of the discipline. But then the discipline itself is not simply enlarged but also challenged in its essential terminology and methodology by the addition.

The new developments in scholarship and teaching about women call into question Matthew Arnold's (1875) prescription that we study "the best that has been thought and said in the world." Research on women both enlarges the definition of "best" and asks who defined what was best, whom the definitions benefited most, and why the student must be called upon to look "up" rather than "down," *around*, and *within*, in being taught about the world. Hierarchies and canon-making in the academy were corollary to hierarchies and canon-making in social life, and so it is no surprise that a thorough study of women also makes visible many men who were not previously featured in the curriculum. In fact, about nine-tenths of the world's population suddenly becomes visible when one takes the emphasis off the public lives of white Western men, who are seen as cultural leaders, and includes those who for reasons of sex, race, class, national, or religious background were defined as lower-caste. One sees that the record of knowledge was not only incomplete but that it was also *incorrect*, and that its errors perpetuated the past balances of power in our society. In the words of Professor Marilyn Schuster of Smith College, "At first, you study women to fill in the gaps. But then you see that the gaps were there for a reason."[2] Our curriculum and our other societal structures were products of the same social and political construction of reality.

The new scholarship on women has unearthed such tremendous amounts of material that this development of new knowledge can probably never, in retrospect, be seen merely as a fad. It promises to widen the account of reality which institutions of higher learning pass on to their students, to broaden or challenge the definitions of the "best that has been thought and said in the world," and to increase students' awareness of the world they live in. The traditional curriculum was designed for the education of white male Western leaders in a time of Western dominance and economic expansion. A revised curriculum would give both our male students (now a minority) and our women a better preparation for a world in which non-Western women of color are the world majority, the life of Western dominance and expansion is no longer taken for granted, and caretaking roles assigned previously to women and other lower-caste people will be needed on a global scale for human survival. In our present situation, men and women, though told they have equal access to higher education, sit in courses which day in and day out deliver the message that the "women's sphere" never really existed. Such courses tend to make students male-identified and contribute to a society in which most people are persuaded that only "men's work" and value systems developed by men really count as valuable.

Notes

1 This essay originally appeared as McIntosh (1981).
2 Professor Schuster said these words at a conference in Princeton, NJ in 1981. See Schuster and Van Dyne (1985) for more of her work on transforming the liberal arts curriculum to include women.

References

Arnold, M. (1875). Preface. In *Culture and anarchy* (p. viii). London: Smith, Elder and Co.
McIntosh, P. (1981). The study of women in the liberal arts curriculum. *Forum for Liberal Education*, 4(1).
Schuster, M. R., & Van Dyne, S. R. (1985). *Women's place in the academy: Transforming the liberal arts curriculum*. Totowa, NJ: Rowman & Allanheld.

12

INTERACTIVE PHASES OF CURRICULAR RE-VISION: A FEMINIST PERSPECTIVE (1983)[1]

I want to speculate here about a theory of five interactive phases of personal and curriculum change which occur when new perspectives and new materials from Women's Studies are brought into a traditional curriculum or a traditional consciousness. After a number of years of work in curriculum revision involving Women's Studies, I found that my colleagues and I were frequently making judgments without having made the grounds of our judgments explicit. That is, we were seeing some efforts of curriculum revision as better than others, more advanced along a spectrum of curricular possibilities which had not yet been described. My theory is an attempt to describe the spectrum.

Such theories have their dangers. Typologies scare me because abstract schemas have so often left out most people, including me. Stage theories in particular are dangerous because they can so easily reinforce present hierarchies of power and value. Nevertheless, I want to speak in terms of curricular phases here, partly because colleagues in Women's Studies on many campuses are making similar analyses, speaking and writing about the process of curriculum change as if we could see in it identifiable varieties and types of change. "Such and such a course still has a long way to go," we say. A long way toward what? This is what I will try to spell out here. I like the tentativeness with which others interested in stage of phase theories in this field have drawn their pictures. D'Ann Campbell, Gerda Lerner, Catherine Stimpson, Marcia Westkott and the faculty development team of Arch, Tetreault,[2] and Kirschner at Lewis and Clark College have developed theories that do not entail ranking and labeling of a sort which perpetuates oppression and exclusion. I take them as models.

For my own analysis, I have adopted, instead of the word "stages," the phrase suggested by Prof. Joan Gundersen of St. Olaf College: "interactive phases."[3] Initial phases of perception do not disappear, but can be felt continually in the mind of the discipline, as one moves toward or away from a more inclusive body of knowledge, a more active process of learning, and a greater ability to see the dominant modes of thought and behavior which we wish to challenge or change.

I begin also with a sense of indebtedness to many other colleagues, including especially the women and men who have taken part over the last four years in the Mellon Seminars at the Wellesley College Center for Research on Women. These seminars are focused on liberal arts curriculum re-vision in two senses: re-seeing and re-making of the liberal arts curriculum. Each year, the Mellon Seminar participants meet together once a month for five hours to consider each of their academic areas or disciplines in turn. The questions we ask in that seminar for each discipline are the same: "What are the present content and scope and methodology of the discipline?" (Or, to use a phrase of Elizabeth Minnich's: "What are the shaping dimensions of the discipline at present?")[4] And then, "How would the discipline need to change to reflect the fact that women are half the world's population and have had, in one sense, half the world's experience?"

The phases in curricular revision which I will describe owe their conceptualization in part to the work of the seminar. Sometimes after a presentation, a member of this group will say, "We really can't get any further in my field on this question." Or "I think you can get further ahead in Religion than we can in Philosophy; we can't make most women's experience visible, given the self-definition of the field." There is a sense among the seminar members that degrees of change do exist in the process of curriculum transformation. I will trace here what I think are the types of curriculum corresponding to five phases of perception.

In naming the five phases I will use history as the first example. I call Phase I: Womanless History; Phase II: Women in History; Phase III: Women as a Problem, Anomaly, or Absence in History; Phase IV: Women As History; and Phase V: History Redefined or Reconstructed to Include Us All.

Analogously, we can have Womanless Political Science, then Women in Politics, then Women as an Absence, Anomaly, or Problem for Political Science (or in Politics); next, Women as Political, (the study of women's lives in all their political dimensions, or, to use a phrase from Elizabeth Janeway (1981) "the powers of the weak" – the politics of the family, the school, the neighborhood, and the curriculum; the politics of culture, class, race, and sex); and finally, Politics Redefined or Reconstructed to include multiple spheres of power, inner and outer.

Or we can have Womanless Biology, followed by (great) Women in Biology. Here, Phase II tends to be about a few of the few who had access to lab equipment, a handful of women still remembered for their work. In Phase III we have Women as Problems or Absences or Anomalies in Biology, for example as analyzed in the collection of essays called *Women Look at Biology Looking at Women* (Hubbard, Henifin, and Fried, 1979). In Phase IV we have women taking the initiative to do science in a new way, on a differing base of assumptions, and finally, we can imagine Biology Reconstructed to Include Us All.

The Phase I syllabus is very exclusive; Phase IV and V syllabi are very inclusive. Individuals and courses do not, as I have said, exist in fixity in given phases, but will show points of dynamic interaction among several of the phases, if the teacher or researcher is conscious of the magnitude of the problem of women's invisibility, and of the many forms of the problem. I think that superficial curriculum change gets arrested in what I have called Phases II and III.

In proposing these phases of curriculum change, I may seem to be creating yet another ladder of values and arranging things so that Phase I is the bottom and Phase V is the top. This is not quite so; in one respect it is the reverse of what I intend, and what I see in my mind's eye. For Phase I thinking reinforces what we have been taught is the "top" and Phase IV corresponds to what we have been taught is the "bottom" according to present hierarchies of knowledge, power, and validity. Phase IV, however, is not "the bottom" but rather the foundation of life. Phase V puts what we were taught to devalue and to value into a new revolutionary relation to each other.

For me, the varieties of curriculum change in order to be accurately understood need to be set against models of the large society and should be overlaid on an image of a broken pyramid. This image has come for me to stand for our culture as a whole. In my imagination it represents our institutions and also our individual psyches. I want to spend some time now developing this image of the broken pyramid and setting what I see as phases or types of curriculum development against the background of that image.

The upper part of the broken pyramid consists of peaks and pinnacles, peaks and pinnacles particularly in the public institutional life of nations, of governments, of militia, universities, churches, and corporations. Survival in this world is presented to us as a matter of winning lest you lose. We are taught to see both our institutions and ourselves within this framework: either you are a winner or you are among the losers. The winners are few, and high up on narrow bits of land which are the peaks; the losers are many and are low down, closer to the bottom. Institutions, groups, and individuals are seen as being on their way to the bottom if they are not on their way to the top.

The mountainous and pyramidal form of our society and of our psyches is a social construct invented by us. The shape of the pyramid was not necessarily inherent in the human materials but developed in our minds, and has now become reified, not only in our minds but in our institutions and in our behavior. We are taught that civilization has a clear top and a clear bottom. The liberal arts curriculum has been particularly concerned with passing on to students the image of what the "top" has been.

Both our public institutions and collective as well as innermost psyches have taken on the hierarchical structure of this winning-versus-losing kind of paradigm. Those who climb up get power; we are taught that there is not power for the many but there is power at the top for those few who can reach the peaks and pinnacles. College liberal arts catalogues, which package liberal arts education for sale to incoming students and to parents of students, make the claim that colleges help students to realize themselves, to discover their individual uniqueness and to develop confidence which will lead to achievement, accomplishment, and success in the world outside the university. Most of this language masks, I think, the actual liberal arts function which is, at present, to train a few students to climb up to pinnacles and to seize them so as to have a position from which power can be felt, enjoyed, exercised, and imposed on others. Images of upward mobility for the individual pervade the admissions literature of most of our colleges and universities today. We are taught that the purpose of education is to assist us in climbing up those peaks and pinnacles to enjoy the "fulfillment of our potential," which I take to mean the increased ability to have and use power for our individual selves.

As I have said, we are taught that only a few will be able to wield power from the summits. Behind the talk about scholarly excellence and teaching is hidden a voice that says: "The territory of excellence is very small. Only a few will be allowed to gain the peaks, having had access to excellent teaching and having earned excellent grades." A few will be "winners," perhaps featured in the subject matter of future courses, as winners in the history of the world – those worthy of the limelight. A few will be tenured and promoted in the pyramid of the college or of the university on in the pyramids of legal, medical, financial, and governmental institutions, but the rest in some sense or other are made to be or feel like losers. The words "success," "achievement," and "accomplishment" have been defined in such a way as to leave most people and most types of life out of the picture.

Now, Womanless History is characteristic of thinking which reflects the society's pyramidal winning-vs-losing mentality. Phase I curriculum in the United States reflects only the highest levels of the existing pyramids of power and value. Womanless History specializes in telling about those who had most public power and whose lives were involved with laws, wars, acquisition of territory, and management of power. History is usually constructed, in other words, to exclude those who didn't possess a good deal of public power. This kind of history perfectly reinforces the dominant political and social systems in that nonwhite males and women, the vast majority of the world's population, are construed as not worth studying in a serious and sustained way, and not worth including in the version of reality passed on to students.

Womanless History, in other words, is about "winning" and has been written by the "winners." Feminist analysts of that version of reality have come to realize that a privileged class of men in Western culture has defined what power is and what constitutes knowledge. Excluded from these definitions and hence from consideration in the traditional History curriculum are types of power and versions of knowledge that this privileged class of men does not share. Hence a corrective is called for if the definitions of power and knowledge are to become more complete.

At first glance, the Phase II corrective, Women in History, appears to be an improvement over Phase I, but Phase II History is very problematical for me and for many of my colleagues. I have come to think that it is worse than the traditional curriculum, and worse than Womanless History, in that it pretends to show us "women" but really shows us only a famous few, or makes a place for a newly declared or a newly resurrected famous few. It is problematical to argue against Phase II history at a time when many are concerned that young women have something up there on the pinnacles for them to look at and when many others want to restore to women of the past a historical record which has been taken from them. But Phase II is all too often like affirmative action program which implies that institutions are model places which need only to help a few of the "inferior" Others to have the opportunity to climb onto these pinnacles with their "superiors." Affirmative action programs rarely acknowledge that the dominant group can and should learn from the Other. Phase II curricular policies, like most affirmative action programs, assume that our disciplines are basically functioning well, and that all that women or Blacks or Chicanos could need or want is to be put into higher slots on the reading list. In other words, the World Civilization course just needs a little attention to Africa, as a disadvantaged culture, giving Africa the time of day but from a position of "noblesse oblige."

In Phase II History the historians' spotlight is simply trained a little lower than usual on the pinnacles, so that we see people like Susan B. Anthony trying to scramble up the rocks. Anthony is featured as a hero in that she tried to make it into men's territory and succeeded. And she gets on the silver dollar. But there were all the other women on behalf of whom she was speaking whose lives remain completely invisible to us. That's the trouble with Phase II History. It conveys to the student the impression that women don't really exist unless they are exceptional by men's standards. Women don't really exist unless we "make something of ourselves" in the public world. Phase II History or Literature or Science or Economics repeatedly featured the famous or "notable" or salaried women. In the American Literature course on 19th century America, Emerson's friend Margaret Fuller may get added to the syllabus, but all the women of Emerson's family, as representative of the women whose unseen labor made possible that transcendental obliviousness to daily life, get left out. You never see in English courses anything about all the women who were preparing Emerson's meals while he wrote "Self Reliance." In Phase II History we particularly see consorts featured. Sometimes they are neutered consorts like Betsy Ross who is seen as a sort of asexual "forefather." Sometimes you see a woman who is both a public figure and a consort, like Cleopatra, or a consort manquée, like Queen Elizabeth I. But very rarely do you get a sense of all that substructure of the culture composed of women who didn't "make it" into the spheres of power, and who did not furnish material for myths. And almost always (or quite often) the women who did "make it" are devalued in the historical record by being portrayed chiefly in terms of sexual relationships. Phase II thinking never recognizes "ordinary" life, unpaid labor, or "unproductive" phenomena like human friendship.

Phase III takes us further down from the pinnacles of power toward the valleys. It brings us in touch with most women, and makes us realize that curriculum change which addresses only discrimination against women or "barriers" to women hardly begins to get at the major problems we have face and the major experiences we have had. Phase III introduces us to the politics of the curriculum. We can't simply "include" those who were left out, who were "denied opportunity" to be studied. It's not an accident we were left out.

Phase III curriculum work involves getting angry at the fact that we have been seen only as an absence, an anomaly, or a problem for History, for English, for Biology, rather than as part of the world, part of whatever people have chosen to value. There is anger at the way women have been treated throughout history. We are angry that instead of being seen as part of the norm, we have been seen, if at all, as a "problem" for the scholar, the society, or the world of the powerful. People doing scholarship in Women's Studies get particularly angry at the fact that the terms of academic discourse and of research are loaded in such a way that we are likely to come out looking like "losers" or looking like pathological cases. A teacher at one of the Claremont Colleges has eloquently asked, "How can we alter the making and the finding of knowledge in such a way that difference needn't be perceived as deprivation?" Phase III work makes us angry that women are seen either as deprived or as exceptional. I think that the anger in Phase III work is absolutely vital to us. Disillusionment is also a feature of Phase III realizations, for many teachers. It is traumatically shocking to white women teachers in particular to realize that we were not only trained but were as teachers unwittingly training others to overlook, reject, exploit, disregard, or be at war with most people in the world. One feels hoodwinked and also sick at heart at having been such a vehicle for racism, misogyny, upper class power, and militarism.

Phase III challenges the literary canon. We ask who defined greatness in literature, and who is best served by the definitions? We ask the same in Religion — who defined "major" theology, and "important" church history? In Music and Art, who defined greatness and who do the definitions best serve? Both the definers and those best served by the definitions were Western white men who had positions of cultural power or who fared fairly well within cultural systems.

In Phase III, scholars rankle against statements like this which as freshmen they might have taken for granted: "The quest for knowledge is a universal human undertaking." "Economic behavior is a matter of choice." "Man has mastered the environment and harnessed the resources of the planet." We may laugh today, but as freshmen, we didn't laugh. We just absorbed these ideas.

Once when I was a freshman, the present personality in me, then a hidden part of the psyche, below the winning and losing part, spoke up — just once, six weeks into a freshman social science course on the History of the Church in Western Civilization. I suddenly blurted out something I hadn't meant to say at all. It was that voice which is now speaking to you directly today,[5] briefly speaking then, twenty-six years ago. I was in a small discussion section which accompanied one of the Harvard lecture courses. The "section man," who was a graduate student, was running a discussion on fine points of theology, and on the governance of bishops and kings. Joined with him in this conversation were two dazzling freshmen; one was the son of a famous theologian, who knew all the fine points of theology; the other was from Pasadena, a tall, god-like man, with a tan, carrying a tennis racket; I remember him as wearing a cream-colored V-neck cable sweater with two blue and red stripes, and knowing all the fine points of theology, too. I couldn't understand what was going on in any of this course. I had not even begun to learn about the medieval feudal system until I took this course. Then suddenly one day, in the middle of a discussion, I blurted out: "I don't see why the serfs stood for it."

We hadn't even been talking about the serfs. You can imagine the dilemma of the teacher, hearing this utterly irrelevant freshman comment coming from someone who hadn't said anything for six weeks. He said gently, but in a very somber voice, "I think you had better see me in office hours." I was of course too scared to go see him in office hours; as one who had not yet noticed how the pyramids of power work, I was afraid of those in authority, and I always hoped that the professors wouldn't notice me. I was humiliated by my comment. I assumed that the others in the class understood how the feudal system worked, and that I was the only one who didn't understand "why the serfs stood for it."

I went through four years at Harvard thinking that everyone else had understood medieval social systems, but then in later years, after I had done some teaching, I began to see further dimensions in that uncontrolled comment. It was coming from a "serf," a freshman girl who was asking not only "Where am I in this picture? but also, why am I standing for this picture that leaves me out, and this discussion which leaves me out?" Years later I began to see that, uncontrolled though the comment was, it was based on very important material which hadn't been covered in that course about the pinnacles. We never studied the peasant woman on her knees in Chartres; we only studied Abelard in the streets of Paris and discussed what various intellectual geniuses or power-holders were saying. And the class discussion itself was only among the power-holders.

It seems to me now, in retrospect, that if my teacher had really been able to do the kind of systemic teaching which Women's Studies encourages and enables one to do, he could have quickly filled me in on a number of points which would have shed light on the stability of the pyramidal feudal system. He could have mentioned the psychological theory of identification with authority; there was more in it for the serfs to identify upward with the apparent protector than to identify laterally with people who couldn't help them. He could have reminded me that before the Industrial Revolution serfs didn't have telephones, newsletters, or political movements to allow them to work for revolution. He could have mentioned the serfs' identification with the Kingdom of Heaven. Years later, I began to realize that all teachers are trained to isolate bits of knowledge and that this very training keeps their students in turn oblivious of the larger systems which hold pyramids of power in place. I was obediently oblivious; having been raised on the American myth of individuality, I thought that there were no social systems anywhere, and then couldn't imagine why a serf wouldn't assert that God-given gift of individuality and make his way out of what I considered to be "the bottom," in the first social system I had ever noticed.

This autobiographical vignette is important to me now, though it shamed me and gnawed at me for years at Harvard. For a long time I thought it was "the stupidest thing I ever said in college," but now that I have flip-flopped the values, I think it was one of the smarter things I said in college. This inchoate and uncontrolled outburst of the serf against a Harvard education came from a voice which spoke for people and functions of personality which we are trained to disregard.

Phase III gives way to Phase IV at the moment when all of those who were assigned to specialize in the functions of life below the fault-line refuse to see ourselves only as a problem and begin to think of ourselves as valid human beings. Phase IV vision construes the life below the break in the pyramid as the real though unacknowledged base of life and civilization. In the fourth phase we women say: "On our own ground, we are not losers; we have had half of human experience. The fact that we are different from men and diverse within our own group doesn't necessarily mean we are deprived." Those who embark on Phase IV thinking find the accepted pyramidal modes of seeing and evaluating to be inappropriate to our sense of worth. For within the pyramidal images we can be seen only as being "at the bottom." All of the first three phases of curricular revision which I have described omit that positive look at us which is the crucial healing ingredient of the fourth phase and the chief revolutionary ingredient of the fifth phase. In other words, I see Phase I, II, and III in varying degrees as misogynist. In Phase I, we weren't in history; Phase II allows that only a few exceptional women were in history; and Phase III says we were in history problematically, messing up the purity of the historical model, or making demands and being victimized. Women or men who say only these things have internalized the view of women as problems, or as deviant people with "issues." Such people can demonstrate persistent internalized misogyny in the midst of their righteous and legitimate anger on behalf of wronged women.

Phase IV is the development in which we see Women As History, and explore all the life existing below the public world of winning and losing. Now I want to go back to the image of the broken pyramid and say that in the top part of the pyramid I drew, the only two alternatives are to win or to lose. But there is another whole domain of the psyche and of the public and private life that works on a different value system or ethical perception altogether. These are a value system and an ethical system which operate laterally on the principle that you work for the decent survival of all, and that this effort conduces to your own survival and your humanity as well. This value system is approved in the spheres we have called private, invisible, and domestic. I cannot claim that families actually work on a lateral model. But mothers are not specifically trained to do with their children something that would involve, for example, marking the children and grading them to see which will win and which will lose. The publicly sanctioned behavior of mothers, though it is partly to make the children adjust to the pyramids in the public spheres, is partly to work for the decent survival of all the children at once. Moreover, the idea of the decent survival of all lies behind our friendships and our conversations and much of our daily life as we go about our ordinary business. Most of what we do is on this lateral plane of working for our own decent survival rather than "getting ahead."

Now, the assigned work of women in every culture has chiefly been in this unacknowledged, lateral network of life below the fault-line, supporting the rest of the pyramid but really opposed to it, because lateral consciousness is at odds with the value system of winning versus losing. The two systems have been pitted against each other through projection onto two "opposite" sexes. The value system of winning and losing has particularly been projected onto white Western man, and men in power in all cultures, and the value system and the work of the part below the break, involving the decent survival of all, has been particularly projected onto women and other lower caste people. However, in the pyramidal configuration, one system is subordinated to the other. The contest is not equal. In Phase IV thinking, whether in daily life or in curriculum revision, you call into question whether all that work behind the scenes is the work of losers. You ask if it isn't the real work of civilization. And you may also ask whether it isn't the work of the "haves" rather than the "have-nots." That's the moment at which the pyramid as a social construct begins to be seen as the creation of a special interest group. The work of taking care of ourselves and other people can be seen as a role assignment in our society, carrying many rewards and gratifications as well as punishments. If it is seen only as the work of victims, then it is still seen, I believe, in a misogynist way. We who were assigned the work of domestic upkeep and maintenance for the human race and the making of ties and relationships have done in many ways a reasonably good job of it. The race hasn't blown itself up yet. We most need continued work for the decent survival of all in a nuclear age. The collaborative values coming out of the base of the pyramid are the ones we desperately need in public policymakers.

We cannot, by wishing, dismantle the upper parts of the pyramid, or bring the unseen base into compatibility with the upper part. The two types of existence are presently at enmity with each other, as two differing value systems of "mastery" and "decency" (or compliance) projected onto powerful men and onto lower caste people respectively. But we desperately need for the future to try to carry the values from the undervalued sphere into the public spheres, in order to change the behavior and the sense of reality in all of our public institutions and the people who control them. The study of women, like women themselves, can help to supply the vision, the information, and the courage needed for this task, and can thus increase our chances of global and personal survival. I hope you realize that I am not claiming that women are morally superior to men by birth, and hence able to save the world. It is just that we were assigned the task which Jean Baker Miller calls "developing ourselves through the development of others." And that has meant that we have developed skills in keeping the human race alive which are the basic indispensable skills in an age of nuclear weapons.

Curriculum work in Phase IV, when you have begun to construe women as the world majority and see women in some respect as the "haves," not simply the "have nots," breaks all the rules of ordinary research or teaching. One studies American literature of the 19th century not by asking, "Did the women write anything good?" but by asking "What did the women write?" One asks not "What great work by a woman can I include in my reading list?" but "How have women used the written word?" In Phase IV one asks, "How have women of color in many cultures told their stories?" not "Is there any good Third World literature?" Phase IV looks not at Abelard but at that peasant woman in Chartres who didn't have any "pure" theology or even understand the heresies, but who rather had an overlay of platitudes and "Old Wives' Tales" and riddles and superstitions and theological scraps from here and there and kitchen or farm wisdom in her mind.

In Phase IV, one looks at the mix of life, and instead of being scared by the impurity of the mix, notices that the impurities reflect the fact that we have been terribly diverse in our lives. Biology taught from a Phase IV perspective does not define life in terms of the smallest possible units that may be isolated and then examined in isolation. When you are doing Phase IV Biology, it seems to me you particularly teach reverence for the organism, identification with it, and you see in terms of large, interlocking and relational systems which need to be acknowledged and preserved, or whose balance needs to be observed and appreciated (Keller, 1983).

Many of civilization's present emergencies suggest that we need wider constructions of knowledge in all fields than our present investigators have developed, with their exclusive methods of study, whether empirical or otherwise. All of Phase IV work is highly speculative and experimental in its epistemology, for we have not yet learned to name unnamed experiences of the plural, the common, the lateral, and the "ordinary" life. In Phase IV curriculum development, it feels as though we are all making it up together. Teachers can look at each other's bibliographies, but this work is so new that we need people to invent their own ways of describing what they are finding, to invent new categories for experience, new ways of doing research, and new ways of teaching (Belenky, Bond, and Weinstock, 1997; Belenky et al., 1986).

In Phase IV, most of the teaching materials are non-traditional. Moreover, the boundaries between disciplines start to break down, for scholars doing feminist work come to realize that boundaries between disciplines serve to keep our present political, economic, and social arrangements in place. There are a number of other boundaries that break down also. The relationship between the teacher and the material changes in Phase IV because the material is so non-traditional and includes so much that we have never studied before that the teacher becomes less of an expert. The relationship between the teacher and the student changes because the teacher now seems less "high" and the student less "low" in knowledge about the areas of life being studied. Then, in addition, there is less of a distinction between the "observer" and the "observed," and often the "subject" of study is treated, in Phase IV work, as a primary authority on her own experience. That is, economists doing really good work on women will listen very seriously to what a housewife wants to say about spending and then borrow from Psychology and Religion and Sociology to analyze her spending patterns and perceptions, rather than trying to fit her into an intricate economic model already built, which could account for her behavior in terms of a number of variables which have already been identified but not by her.

The pinnacles of fragmented and isolated knowledge seem more and more abstract and irrelevant as you try to learn from within women's experience what women's experience has been like. Phase I reinforces vertical value systems; Phase IV reveals systems of lateral values and relationships. One key hallmark of Phase IV consciousness and curriculum is that the Other stops being considered something lesser to be dissected, deplored, devalued, or corrected. The Other becomes, as it were, organically connected to one's self. Realities, like people, seem plural but unified. That fragmentation of knowledge which characterizes our disciplines at present begins to end if you descend to the valleys of civilization in Phase IV and you start to study commonality, plural experience, and the work of daily survival. You also come to realize that the valleys are in fact more suitable places to locate civilization than are the deoxygenated summits of the mountains. The heights of specialization, like the concentration of economic power in the hands of a few, are seen to have questionable usefulness to our continued survival.

One danger of Phase III and IV work is that scholars trying to alter the structures of knowledge or society make the mistake of thinking that all women are alike, so that the study of a few will suffice to fill in the picture. Minority women in particular have often stated that Women's Studies tends to fall into some of the same traps as the traditional curriculum in describing chiefly the elites and the worlds they control, or in polarizing the elites and non-elites along bi-polar lines.

When well done, Phase IV work honors particularity at the same time it identifies common denominators of experience. It stresses diversity and plurality, and for many people doing work on women in Phase IV, William James's *The Varieties of Religious Experience* seems like a model book (1936). It takes the pluralistic view that there are many varieties of religious life, and that one needn't rank and judge them. It shows a cast of mind which also accompanies serious work on women.

Now, Phase V curriculum revision is the hardest to conceive. I said it was the phase in which History (or Knowledge) gets redefined, reconstructed to include us all. But how can this be done? At a conference in 1981 for college deans and presidents held at the Johnson Foundation's Wingspread Center in Wisconsin, Gerda Lerner gave a keynote address on "Liberal Education and the New Scholarship on Women." After her talk, I asked, "On the basis of all the work you have now done on American women's history and on the experience of Black Americans, how would you organize a basic text called *American History?*" She answered, "I couldn't begin to do that; it is too early. It would take a team of us, fully funded, two years just to get the table of contents organized – just to imagine how we would categorize it." And then she said, "But don't worry, we were 6,000 years carefully building a patriarchal structure of knowledge, and we've had only twelve years to try to correct it, and twelve years is nothing" (Lerner, 1981).

As Elizabeth Minnich has pointed out, there have been important movements to do and to institutionalize women's scholarship in earlier decades, so this isn't only a twelve-year effort.[6] But Lerner's larger point is important. We have had only a little time to correct major paradigms. We don't know yet what reconstructed History would look like. In my view, the reconstructed curriculum not only draws a line around the vertical and lateral functions, examining all of human life and perception. It also puts these horizontal and vertical elements in a revolutionary new relation to one another, so that the pyramidal shapes of the psyche, the society, the world are discarded, seen as inaccurate and also incompatible with the decent, balanced survival of human psyches, institutions, and nations. Global shapes replace the pyramids. Human collaborative potential is explored and competitive potential subjected to a sustained critique. A genuinely inclusive curriculum, based on global imagery of self and society, would reflect and reinforce the common human abilities and inclinations to cultivate the soil of the valleys and to collaborate for survival.

A teacher doing work in Phase V develops inclusive rather than exclusive vision and realizes that many things hang together. A Phase V curriculum would help us to produce students who can see patterns of life in terms of systems of race, culture, caste, class, gender, religion, national origin, geographical location, and other influences on life which we haven't begun to name. At the same time, Phase V curriculum promises to produce students who can carry with them into public life the values of the private sphere, because inclusive learning allows them to value lateral functions rather that discredit them in the context of paid or public life. Right now, Phase II thinking tends to work only for the promotion of individual values; it tends to advance a few women who can "make it in the public world." But I think that putting women's bodies into high places does little for people in the aggregate and little or nothing for women in the aggregate. It makes life nice for, or brings power to, a few women but it doesn't necessarily bring about social change. At present our so-called "leaders," women included, are mostly working from that misguided worldview that says either you win or you lose. It's not true, and women in the aggregate know it's not true. And the conviction that you either win or lose is, as I have said, a very dangerous ethic and prescription to carry into public life and into leadership positions at a time when nuclear weapons are what you have to test the idea with.

We can't afford to have leaders who think only in terms of winning or losing. And so it seems to me critically important for us to develop a Phase V curriculum. But lest you think I am forgetting the educational world in my interest in world peace, let me say that the development of Phase V curriculum is also important to colleges and universities because of their own educational claims. The university claims to develop and to pass on to students and to the wider society an accurate and comprehensive body of knowledge. And in the words of Ruth Schmidt, the Provost of Wheaton College, and now President of Agnes Scott College, "If you claim to teach about the human race, and you don't know anything about half the human race, you really can't claim to know or teach much about the human race." The main argument for curriculum change is that it will help universities to fulfill their acknowledged primary responsibility: to develop and pass on the society and to students accurate bodies of knowledge. Since women are now left out, those bodies of knowledge are grossly inaccurate.

I want now to illustrate these five interactive phases of curriculum development in five specific disciplines. While I was writing this part of my talk, discipline by discipline, abstractly analyzing Psychology, English, and so on, I heard the voice of Florence Howe asking her familiar question, "Where are the women?"[7] So I stopped organizing my ideas according to those fragmented peaks and pinnacles called "disciplines," and began mentally to follow a group of women like ourselves studying in a variety of curricula from the most exclusive to the most inclusive I could imagine, and then I watched the effects on their minds and their lives. These women are named Meg, Amy, and Jo, and Jo's children: Maya and Angela and Adrienne.

Meg feels extremely privileged to go to college and to sit at the feet of her professors. Her Phase I freshman English class is called "Man's Quest for Knowledge." She studies *Huckleberry Finn, Moby Dick,* Walt Whitman's poetry, Emerson on *Self Reliance*, Thoreau's *Walden*, a Hemingway novel, and Norman Mailer. Meg thinks it really is amazing when you think about it, how man has quested for knowledge; it's a universal trait! The expository essays are very difficult for Meg to write, and she cannot remember after she's handed them in what any of them were about. She gets middling grades. Her professors find her indecisive. In Medieval History she studies bishops and kings. She wonders once or twice, but doesn't ask, why the serfs stood for the feudal system. Mostly she hopes that she will marry a strong man who will take care of her just as a bishop or a king must have taken care of the serfs.

In Psychology, Meg learns of a number of interesting complexes, and she feels particularly glad that she has studied the Oedipus Complex because it will help her as a parent, someday, to understand her sons. In Freud's model of the personality she identifies strongly with the superego. She is very relieved that there is a part of the personality with which she can identify as a beautiful soul, one who has transcended the moiling, toiling world and the need to compete. She overlooks the fact that Freud did not think women had highly developed superegos. She is vulnerable, deluded, and ignorant about what Freud really said, since she has received no training in looking for herself in the curriculum.

In Biology, having been told that man has mastered nature and that knowledge is mastery, Meg dissects a frog. She finds this repulsive, but necessary for Science. After all, Scientists would have to take life apart in order to understand it, wouldn't they? Mostly she dreams of security, and will succeed in marrying, at the end of her junior year, her lab partner. In Art History, which is Meg's favorite course, she moves away from that bewildering world which really hasn't made much sense to her and looks at beautiful things. She really respects her art professor, a kindly man who is teaching her what to admire in the great masters' work. She hopes that when she and her husband have raised their children and have some extra money, they can themselves collect some beautiful works of art for the walls of their house. She would, however, not want to collect second-rate art, so that may be a problem.

Amy goes to college a few years after Meg. Amy talks a lot about role models. Amy intends to Make It. She says things like "My mother never did anything." Amy's freshman English course is called "The Individual versus Society." She studies *Huckleberry Finn, Moby Dick,* Walt Whitman's poetry, Emerson's "Self Reliance," Thoreau's *Walden, The Autobiography of Frederick Douglass,* Hemingway, Kerouac, and Sylvia Plath. This is a Phase II course; there is one black writer and one woman on the reading list. The curriculum has started to change to include a few "exceptional" members of minority groups who are considered capable of "making it" in the syllabus. Amy gets a lot of "ammunition" for her life from Sylvia Plath's (1971) character in *The Bell Jar* who says, "I didn't want to be the platform that the man shoots off from; I wanted to be the rocket myself and shoot off in all directions." Amy is fueled by Esther Greenwood's words to drive herself to exceptional heights. She doesn't notice that the speaker, like Plath herself, was suicidal. She is identifying upward, and she likes the Medieval/Renaissance course best when it moves from the static feudal system into the development of guilds, and the middle class, and upward mobility. She is psychologically tuned into the theme of individual autonomy that is running through that part of the course.

In her Women in Psychology course, Phase II, she learns about women who "made it" in Psychology. She learns nothing of their struggles nor of the women psychologists who have remained invisible to us. "They did it, I can too," Amy believes. "Women can do whatever they want, if they want anything enough to really work for it. *Of course,* Biology isn't destiny." Amy is, however, very little interested in the psychology of women, and her courses don't give her anything to make her interested in her own psychology, or make her ask why she has switched from pre-law to art or wonder about any inner life in women which psychological research hasn't named.

In her Biology course, she is interested in Darwin's theories about competition and the "survival of the fittest." She thinks of herself as one of the "fittest." The losers will lose, but she, Amy, is going to make it in a man's world. She thinks of herself as a Frederick Douglass, "smart enough to get away," and as an organism ready to adapt to a particular niche in the environment, her niche; she intends to fight for her niche.

Amy's Art History work further demonstrates to her that women have now "arrived," because her Impressionist Painters course includes Mary Cassatt and Berthe Morisot. Amy does not notice that they are called "Mary" and "Berthe" throughout the course, whereas the men are "Monet" and "Degas." All of Amy's eloquent papers in her freshman year in every course are variations on the theme of "The Individual versus Society." She never sees herself as "Society." Amy has been given the Phase II vision of herself as the unique woman rising up in history and leaving her mother behind where mothers really always were.

Jo comes to college later than Amy, tired and rather battered by certain personal episodes in her life. She comes reluctantly to college for further training; she is a "re-entry" woman. She finds to her surprise that college speaks to her condition. She comes alive in class. Other students like to be with Jo and Jo likes to be with them. She is somewhat older than most around her. In her freshman English course she reads Dale Spender's *Man Made Language* and she reads Nancy Henley and Barrie Thorne, and then she reads Emily Dickinson and is invited to take an interdisciplinary look at Emily Dickinson after having read five feminist critics. She writes a paper she will never forget, on Emily Dickinson as a person working on many rebellions at the same time – against the social mores and axioms of her community, against patriarchal, public "authorities," against intellectual certainty, against the theology of her church, and against conventions of the sentence and of language itself. She will never forget this paper; it actually possesses her while she writes it. Somewhere in the curriculum she is finding something that speaks to her personally and directly about her own life.

In Medieval History, Jo's teacher introduces her to the essay by Joan Kelly-Gadol (1977): "Did Women Have a Renaissance?" She gets mad, particularly when learning the answer is "No, not in the Renaissance," and she determines to mistrust periodization of history from then on. She has found something that fits with her sense of not having fitted in. She is being given the "doubled vision" which Joan Kelly-Gadol refers to in one of her last works, of both fitting in and being alien and apart from a dominant culture. She is being given the enabling doubled vision that explains her life to her.

Then in Psychology Jo reads Naomi Weisstein (1971) on "How Psychology Constructs the Female," and Carol Gilligan. In a time warp, Jo has just received Gilligan's (1977) latest book, *In a Different Voice*. She reads that women don't fit the existing models of moral development and that they really seem to test out differently. She learns that Lawrence Kohlberg's "Six Universal Phases" are not after all universal but were based on a small white male sample. But because Jo is in a Phase III curriculum, she is also told that Gilligan's sample has its limits too. She learns that women are probably more diverse than most of the existing research shows. She reads Berger and Luckmann's (1967) *The Social Construction of Reality* and learns that the world of "knowledge" was constructed by cultural authority figures. She finds herself almost insouciant in starting to write a paper now.

In Biology, she reads Ruth Hubbard's (1983) essay, "Have Only Men Evolved?" She is shocked to learn that scientific knowledge is permeated with politics. She learns that accounts of evolution and of human propensities which she had taken as objective are completely androcentric. She learns that all forms of female life have been seen as defective or incapacitated versions of male life. She can hardly bear to think that even Science is not objective, but as her distress grows she find herself grateful to Ruth Hubbard for a metaphor which explains her distress to her: she looks out the back window of a bus and sees that she is herself pushing the bus in which she is riding.

And then in her Art History course Jo, in another time warp, goes to New York City and sees Mary Beth Edelman's work, filled with anger and expressiveness and female nudity. Jo is shaken but not revolted. She invites Amy who lives in New York, to join her at the show. Amy is patronizing; Jo has nothing much to say but is moved by the show in ways she cannot express.

Sometime later, Jo's children come to college. They are twins. She has named them Maya and Angela, not by accident. Their freshman English course isn't in English at all. It is in Spanish. They need Spanish for an oral history project they are doing. In my fantasy they are at college at Humboldt State University. They are spending a great deal of time becoming proficient in Spanish, and moreover, their final exams in the Spanish Language and Composition course are not only on the way they read and write the language but also on their ability to elicit information from others in Spanish, their ability to understand what they have heard, and their ability to carry on a conversation in Spanish, linking on to previous things said rather than directing the talk or making statements.

In the History component of their curriculum, these twins have a project in which they are doing oral history research with six Spanish-speaking women. It started to be the history of migrant labor in a certain part of northern California but the students persuaded the professor not to label it a history of migrant labor before they had interviewed these women, lest they narrow the canvas too much. The students have decided that right now it will be an open-ended series of interviews and the topic will not be named. They will ask the women about their lives rather than asking them about migrant labor history; then they'll see where the women start.

In Psychology, Maya and Angela read Jean Baker Miller's (1976) *Toward a New Psychology of Women* and they feel they have been invited on an exploration with her, to try to name all of that women's experience in us that doesn't come under the public spotlight and hasn't yet been focused on or seen to exist. They also read Caroll Smith-Rosenberg's (1975) essay, "The Female World of Love and Ritual: Relations Between Women in Nineteenth Century America," and see what a rich world is revealed when you look at women's lives starting from women's own ground. They begin to care about their mother's letters and their mother's past in a new way, and begin to understand why their mother named their sister Adrienne.

In Biology, Maya and Angela take a course called "A Feeling for the Organism: Science Without Mastery." They read Evelyn Fox Keller's (1983) book of this title on Barbara McClintock's work on genetics in a field of corn. The course syllabus opens with a remark of McClintock's on receiving the Nobel Prize: "It might seem unfair to reward a person for having so much pleasure over the years, asking the maize plant to solve specific problems and then watching its responses."

Last of all, in Art, Maya and Angela have a terrific project and they are having a lot of fun doing it. They have two assignments in Art. Humboldt State, in my fantasy, has a big art building whose front hall is decorated by a long mural made by art students. Every year each student replaces a part of the mural. Maya and Angela each have to replace a previous year's painting with a tempera painting of their own. But what are they to replace? This is where their teaching assignment comes in. In this Phase IV curriculum every student is also a teacher. Therefore Maya and Angela have to spend part of every day teaching some young children in a subject which they are themselves "taking." Maya and Angela have a group of ten children working with them to decide whose work from the previous year's mural will be taken down and whose work will be replaced by Maya's and Angela's new work. How will the judgments be made? The children are doing a number of things, both talking and writing about the paintings that are to be replaced and also copying them with their own paints. Maya and Angela are teaching art at the same time they are studying art because this revised Phase IV curriculum not only lowers the usual wall between the teacher and the taught but also alters the relationship radically. Moreover, art is construed in my fantastic Humboldt State as including decoration of the entire environment beyond walls and canvases and pieces of paper. Therefore the second art assignment which Maya and Angela and their students have is to take care of one of thirty gardens assigned to their art class and they are allowed to plant it as they like but they must then maintain it throughout the year. The children dislike this assignment very much. Maya and Angela have chosen succulents, and shrubs which need pruning and cleaning up; those plants thrive in the climate of the campus. The children wish there were flowers. Maya and Angela explain why this isn't a flower garden. The children watch the flowers wilting in other people's beds and gradually learn that there is a reason to plant shrubs which strike them nevertheless as unpromising, unpretty, and unromantic.

Maya and Angela have an ambition for the years after college. Their father lives in New Hampshire. Whenever they visit him in the summers they are galled by the New Hampshire license plate. It has a slogan which reads "Live Free or Die." The more they read it, the more it annoys them. So they are going to spend their time after college working for a few years in New

Hampshire. They'll earn a living, but their aim is to change that slogan. They have a slogan they are going to try to get put in its place: "Share Life or Perish." They'll learn the political ropes, work through the legislature, or lobby, or work through the state's committee system, or campaign, or run for office; this is partly a lark but they're in dead earnest, and they'll give it a good try for ten years or so, as they make a living in New Hampshire. They imagine they'll have several public and professional and perhaps several private lives as well, before they're through.

Now these phases of curriculum have socialized each woman differently. Meg has been socialized to "fit in," oblivious to and therefore very vulnerable to the forces at work on and around her. Amy has been socialized to kill herself trying to be, and dreaming that she is, exceptional, different from other women, and dreaming that she will be seen as different from other women. Jo has been socialized to understand the interlocking systems that work to produce Meg's illusions, Amy's internalized misogyny, and the dangers to all of learning systems that exclude them. Maya and Angela have been educated to be quite happy with the diversity of life and canny about systems; they are able to use their anger in a way that gives them pleasure. They are real to themselves and may well become to larger groups: a legislature, or drivers on the roads of New Hampshire. Well, what of Adrienne? Phase V remains for her. I dream we invent for her a circular, multicultural, inclusive curriculum which socializes people to be whole, balanced, and undamaged, which includes rather than excluding most parts of life, and which both fosters a pluralistic understanding and fulfills the dream of a common language. This is the Phase V curriculum.

Ten years after graduation Meg, deserted, divorced, and still not knowing what hit her, re-enters college as a Continuing Education student and now again reads the Masterworks of Western Civilization. She finds them not so great. She has learned that the bishops and kings do not take care of the serfs. She is bewildered, amazed by Jo's girls, Maya and Angela. She is in one course with them. They say things she couldn't have imagined at their age. She admires them, she likes them, and to her amazement, she is learning from them.

Amy does all right in New York as an artist; she is tough as nails, lonely, and scornful of the women's groups. She hasn't joined any collective. She's furious that she hasn't had her own show yet. She thinks if you're good enough you'll get recognized and that if women would only pull "their" act together and stop bitching, her chances for recognition would improve. Jo feels more and more whole and effective as her life goes on. She is past her first self-directed anger and her years from forty onward are her best; she has herself learned to see systemically and become a force for personal and for aggregate change.

Maya and Angela – will they change the New Hampshire license plate? But wait – they haven't yet gone to college. We haven't yet got the Phase IV curriculum. And the Phase V curriculum has not yet been invented for Adrienne. So the answer about what Maya and Angela and Adrienne will be able to do lies in us, and in the work we do now for their future and for ours.

Notes

1 Originally published as McIntosh (1983).
2 See Tetreault (1985).
3 See Gundersen (1986).
4 From 1985 to 1990, Minnich and McIntosh spoke together at a number of events regarding bringing people of color and women into the curriculum. It was during these consultations that Minnich would ask this question.
5 I first delivered this talk at The Claremont Colleges in February, 1983.
6 See earlier comment about McIntosh and Minnich speaking at academic events.
7 Howe often asked this unpublished question of her colleagues at the Wellesley Center for Research on Women and in her talks in the late 1970s and 1980s.

References

Belenky, M. F., Bond, L. A., & Weinstock, J. S. (1997). *A tradition that has no name: Nurturing the development of people, families, and communities.* New York: Basic Books.

Belenky, M., Clinchy, B., Goldberger, N., & Tarule, J. (1986). *Women's ways of knowing: The development of self, voice, and mind.* New York: Basic Books.

Berger, P. L., & Luckmann, T. (1967). *The social construction of reality: A treatise in the sociology of knowledge.* New York: Doubleday.

Gilligan, C. (1977). *In a different voice: Women's conception of the self and of morality.* Cambridge: Harvard Educational Review.

Gundersen, J. R. (1986). Re-visioning the past: Toward a more inclusive telling of history. *The History Teacher,* 20(1), 51.

Hubbard, R. (1983). Have only men evolved? In Harding, S. G., & Hintikka, M. B. (Eds.), *Discovering reality: Feminist perspectives on epistemology, metaphysics, methodology, and philosophy of science* (pp. 45–69). New York: Kluwer Academic Publishers.

Hubbard, R., 1924-2016, Henifin, M. S., 1953, & Fried, B., 1951. (1979). *Women look at biology looking at women: A collection of feminist critiques.* Boston: G. K. Hall.

James, W. (1936). *The varieties of religious experience: A study in human nature.* New York: The Modern Library.

Janeway, E. (1981). *Powers of the weak.* New York: Morrow Quill Paperbacks.

Keller, E. F. (1983). *A feeling for the organism: The life and work of Barbara McClintock.* San Francisco: W.H. Freeman.

Kelly-Gadol, J. (1977). Did women have a renaissance? In Bridenthal, R. & Koonz, C. (Eds.), *Becoming visible: Women in European history.* Boston: Houghton Mifflin Co.

Lerner, G. (1981, 10). *Liberal education and the new scholarship on women: Issues and constraints in institutional change.* Keynote presented at the Wingspread Conference, Racine, WI.

McIntosh, P. (1983). Interactive phases of curricular re-vision: A feminist perspective. *Working paper No. 124.* Wellesley, MA: Wellesley College Center for Research on Women.

Miller, J. B. (1976). *Toward a new psychology of women.* Boston: Beacon Press.

Plath, S. (1971). *The bell jar* (1st U.S. ed.). New York: Harper & Row.

Smith-Rosenberg, C. (1975). The female world of love and ritual: Relations between women in nineteenth-century America. *Signs: Journal of Women in Culture and Society,* 1 (1), 1–29.

Tetreault, M. K. (1985). Feminist phase theory. *The Journal of Higher Education,* 56(4), 363–384.

Weisstein, N. (1971). Psychology constructs the female; or the fantasy life of the male psychologist. *Feminism & Psychology,* 3(2), 194–210.

13

SELECTION FROM "INTERACTIVE PHASES OF CURRICULAR AND PERSONAL RE-VISION WITH REGARD TO RACE" (1990)[1]

Nearly twenty years ago, one afternoon in 1972, a friend on the faculty of the University of Denver was standing in the door of my office. We were talking about some aspect of race relations. My colleague said, with gentle offhandedness, "I wouldn't want to be white if you paid me five million dollars." I was startled to hear that she would not want to trade her racial identity for mine. In the previous three years, I had seen my African American friend survive many problems caused by systemic and personal racism. My dim awareness of, and paltry education in, just about everything pertaining to our lives made me think that hers was a racial identity not to be desired. Now I learned that I had a racial identity that she wouldn't think of wanting.[2]

My friend's candor was a gift. Her comment opened doors into areas whose distinctness I had been taught not to see: her culture and my culture. Like many people of my race and economic class, I had been taught that there was only one culture, and that we were both in it. Looking toward hers for the first time, I began to see what I had missed. I learned that my colleague would want to change her circumstances in a racist society, but not her cultural identity. I had been led to assume that her circumstances relative to mine were her cultural identity, which I thought must consist mostly of burdens. Her strong words made things more complicated, pluralized the picture, and started me doing what felt and still feels like essential Ethnic Studies homework on the elements of my friend's culture that sustained her and the elements in mine which made the idea of being "white" anathema to her.

I tell this story as a description of an awakening from what I now see as a generic state of mind trained into middle-class white Americans: monoculturalism, or single-system seeing. Racial or ethnic monoculturalism is the assumption that we are all in the same cultural system together, and that its outlines are those which have been recognized by people who have the most ethnic and racial power.

Single-system seeing with regard to gender takes a related form. I see it especially when men, and many women, assume that we who work in feminist movements toward alternative ways of organizing life and using power must want to do what men have done. I know a number of men who think that when we women get together, we must talk about them, or conspire against them. But if one listens plurally instead of monoculturally, one will hear that women want to survive with dignity, and agency, but in general do not want to do what white Western men have done, or been asked to do.

Monoculturalism, like all forms of single-system seeing, is blind to its own cultural specificity. It cannot see itself. It mistakes its "givens" for neutral, pre-conceptual ground rather than for distinctive cultural grounding. People who have been granted the most public or economic power, when thinking mono-culturally about "others," often imagine that these others' lives must be con-stituted of "issues," "problems," and deficits relative to themselves. But in fact, the politically "lesser" are, or can be, culturally central to themselves. Most will see much that is positive about their lives, through strength inherited with their traditions. Most will have learned despite and through the conditions of their lives how to behave in ways that sustain and stabilize themselves and the cultural fabrics of the world.

I write about monoculturalism and single-system seeing both as a financially secure white person in the United States who has been, within those dimensions of my identity, seen as fitting a monocultural norm, and as a woman who has been seen, in my gender identity, as culturally lesser, in Anglo-European male terms. I now know that with regard to my sex I do not simply have a deficit identity, i.e. a defective variant of male identity. Moreover, though my chosen place of work is located at the very edge of a College, we who work here call this marginal place devoted to research on women the Center.[3] So it is with people in all cultures, I now think; we can be culturally real or central to our-selves, knowing that no one center is entitled to arbitrary dominance. And if we do not challenge the single-system seeing which projects deficit identities onto us, we will continue to be seen only as defective variants of ideal types within ruling but unacknowledged monoculture.

One great gift of my colleague's comment nearly twenty years ago was that she located herself in a position of strength and made it clear that she saw my racial group as something she would under no circumstances want to join. Within white monoculture, her position was unfamiliar; she was locating herself outside what I imagined was her status within the "one system." Her words made me begin to see my own culture as ethno-particular, ethno-specific, and in fact ethno-peculiar.

It took me some years to revise my understanding to the point at which my colleague's words came to bear very directly on the ways I taught. For like most traditionally trained white teachers, I needed a long time to reconceive myself before I could ground teaching in cultural pluralism. While coming around to seeing both my culture and hers in their distinctness and their interrelations, I experienced with regard to race the same slow interactive processes of re-vision which I have traced with regard to teaching about women. This is the process I described in my 1983 paper "Interactive Phases of Curricular Re-Vision: A Feminist Perspective."[4]

I restate here that typology of Interactive Phases of Curricular Re-Vision, this time with a focus on race, and on processes of making curricula and personal perception more multicultural. Once again, a group of hypothetical seventeen-year-old students appears at the end of the paper, and in this case, I write about the various kinds of understanding the "Little Women" are given with regard to Native American women and men.

Typologies are rather blunt instruments, easily misused and misunderstood. In the case of this typology, a key adjective is "interactive." Interactive ways of seeing coexist in dynamic interrelation. Varieties of awareness are within us; we are not fixed within them. For this reason, it is a mistake to use the typology of Interactive Phases to label, type, or critique individuals, as though they were fixed forever in one or another form of awareness, or as though we could pass from one to another form of awareness forever. But when we widen our ways of knowing or thinking, we can become aware of the cultural particularity and the societal consequences of ways of knowing, seeing, or being that we were taught or took for granted.

My 1983 theory of Interactive Phases of Curricular and Personal Re-Vision derived from my work with college faculty members to bring into the liberal arts curriculum new materials and perspectives from Women's Studies. I saw that in the early 1980s, traditionally trained white faculty members in History, for example, were likely to move from Phase I: Womanless History, to Phase II: Women in History, on Phase I terms. Both kinds of thinking are challenged by what I identified as Phase III: Women as a Problem, Anomaly, or Absence in History. I meant "in History" in two senses: in the past, and in History's telling of the past. Phase III involves and requires more anger and critique than either of the first two, but can get arrested in victim-studies. It can also lead con-structively to a potent wordlessness and to a daring plunge into the moving, grounded, humble, and plural inquiry of Phase IV: Women's Lives As History, looking toward Phase V: History Reconstructed and Redefined to Include Us All, which I said would take us 100 years to conceive.

After observing traditionally trained faculty in all academic fields over the last eleven years, I think that the schema can be applied to the processes of faculty growth and development in all of them, even the so-called hard sciences. Tea-chers are likely to begin teaching chiefly in what I termed Phase I: Womanless Science, with perhaps a little attention to Phase II: Notable Women in Science, but only on the existing terms. There may follow, if the faculty member has been keeping up with scholarship on women, and is not too defensive about what it reveals, some teaching along lines of Phase III: Women as a Problem,

Anomaly, Absence, or Victim in Science. Phase IV teaching and inquiry dares put what was neglected or marginal at the center, to see what new insight or theory can be developed from hitherto excluded or overlooked sources whose absence helped to determine the shape of each field. It can be called Experienced-based Science; it goes far beyond the exceptional achievements allowed in Phase II and the discussion of "issues" allowed in Phase III. Always the dynamic interactions among the phases suggest the making of new knowledge, the making of Phase V: Science Redefined and Reconstructed to Include Us All.

As I have said, no one person or course exists in complete fixity in a given phase, and the phases I describe do not always occur in the chronological order given. Some of those who are born either within or outside of dominant groups may have been immersed since childhood in awareness of the "issues" of Phase III, or in the relational alertness and the plural consciousness which I attribute to Phase IV. Most traditionally trained white faculty members, however, started teaching within the framework of Phase I monoculturalism, oblivious of the racial and gender elements they were immersed in. Some have moved on to think in rather predictable Phase II ways about how to get more overlooked individuals (for at first it is seen only as a matter of overlooked individuals) into the essentially single-system version of reality which is handed on to students and is not, within monoculture, acknowledge as a version at all. One sees often in sequence the dawning realizations and syllabus changes which I identify as belonging to Phases II, III, and IV of consciousness.

When one considers Interactive Phase Theory with regard to race, an obvious curricular example is the U.S. History course required of most students in middle or high school, or both. Most secondary school history textbooks are stuck in Phases I and II.

Phase I: All-White History may be followed by Phase II: Exceptional Minority Individuals in U.S. History, which leads to Phase III: "Minority" Issues or "Minority" Groups as Problems, Anomalies, Absences, or Victims in U.S. History. Then may come a rare and important conceptual shift to Phase IV: The Lives and Cultures of People of Color Everywhere As History. I think such courses, if they survive at all, will move toward an eventual Phase V: History Redefined and Reconstructed to Include Us All.

My original analysis of Interactive Phases Of Curricular Re-Vision was diagrammatically overlaid upon my theoretical model of double structures within both psyche and society in the industrialized West: overvalued, overdeveloped, "vertical," competitive functions at odds with undervalued, underrecognized, "lateral" collaborative functions. The shape of the whole is that of a faulted pyramid or mountain range with a vertical "grain" in the higher rocks and a horizontal "grain" in the rock of the substructure.

Racially speaking, Phase I consciousness involves identification with publicly powerful white Western males. In this phase, whites neither study people of color nor notice that they have not. The obliviousness of single-system seeing is a hallmark of this phase. The Phase II remedy admits a few "minorities" to History, but only on

History's terms, still without any reflectiveness on the racial history of those traditional terms and definitions. Phase III goes into "race issues." It identifies "race" mono-culturally, ascribing race only to people of color, and sees people of color only in the category of Problem, identifying whole groups of people chiefly with losers' "issues" rather than with human life experienced fully. Doing work only in Phase III can be inadvertently racist or sexist, for it is a cultural insult to any group to imply that its main feature is what I have called above a deficit identity. Phase III never does a full analysis of the psyche or peculiarity of the oppressor. The oppressed group is set up to look powerless and defective by contrast with the more powerful group, which is seen as the norm, and not examined for its cultural specificity, peculiarity, or pathol-ogy. Still, Phase III at least encourages students to recognize the existence of invisible systems of power and disadvantage.

Phase IV comes out of and recognizes the lateral, connected, and diverse func-tions of psyche and society; it is about creativity, integrity, wholeness, ordinariness, and multiple forms of power and talent unrecognized in vertical systems of apprai-sal. It honors both/and thinking about who exists and what counts. Without it, we will not be able to make sense of the world nor policy for our survival. Phase IV reveals us, in LeRoy Moore's language, as "bodies in the body of the world."

Phase IV can be healing. But Phase IV unattached to the issues-awareness of Phase III can be sentimental. It may be a celebration of diversity as if there were no politics which had prevented, and keeps working against, such celebration. If teachers lapse into Phase IV while forgetting about vertical power structures, they may become romantic, and not face the pain which systems of subjection inflict. For example, while honoring the strengths of African American culture as Toni Morrison may describe them, I need to keep in mind the contexts that produced these strengths. My ancestors on one side were slave-owners. This fact bears on the conventions and particularities of many aspects of Morrison's cul-ture and of mine. Only it bears differently on each.

Though Phase IV without Phase III awareness can be naive, Phase IV has potential reconstitutive power for all students and teachers. For an enormous shift in the con-sciousness occurs when people of color are understood as the world's majority, and the ordinary lives of people are seen to constitute the main human For an enormous shift in the consciousness occurs when people of color are understood as the world's majority, and the ordinary lives of people are seen to constitute the main human story. Then history is defined as all of those elements of the past in the multiplicities of our heritages which can take each of us feel fully real in the context of education or life. history is defined as all of those elements of the past in the multiplicities of our heritages which can make each of us feel fully real in the context of education or life. In Phase IV, the question of "How was it for people?" opens the study of History to every kind of humble detail. All voices count. Pedagogy shifts so that the teacher's forms of knowing are not necessarily superior to the students' forms of knowing. The elements of Phase I are not obliterated, but take a new place in the picture. Someone has said that if you study the experience of an escaped slave woman in Boston in the 1850s you will find Lincoln, but if you start with Lincoln, you will not necessarily get to the experience of any slave. Phase IV stays very close to the ground of daily human experience, and asks many questions of people about their lives, listening for many human voices, and examining the cultural and political specificity of frameworks for collecting and evaluating information. All experience is seen as a source of knowledge.

With regard to race in the undergraduate curriculum, most of our universities still feature Phase I introductory courses in virtually all departments and disciplines. If readers doubt this, they should examine the introductory-level course reading lists of their own institutions. White teachers should imagine themselves as students of color, for example as Asian American students, trying to find their people reflected as valid in basic readings. Most courses are still monocultural, even Anthropology, in which teachers focus on the thinking of white, mostly male, anthropologists. This gives white students the impression that there is one main piece of cultural turf and it is their turf. The students of color, like the white women, are implicitly shown they have not been necessary to knowledge, enterprise, and past culture-making, nor are they essential to future cultural invention or reclamation. In such courses, oral traditions are seen to count for nothing at all; argumentative written traditions, though very culture and gender-specific in origin, inform most of the "objective" texts and all of the assignments. Historiography courses, much touted for their plural, comparative sophistication, focus on white men.

Phase II courses bring in a few famous or notable people of color but do not challenge the traditional outlines and definitions of what is worth studying. Therefore the emphasis continues to be on "firsts," laws, wars, winners, talented individuals, fighters, and those who nearly matched what is taken to be "white" male achievement. People of color who succeeded in getting and holding onto some kinds of social, political, or artistic territory are seen as "possibly worth studying." But often those who are noticed in Phase II courses are represented as having gone far but not irrationally far in challenging existing "white," male, or colonial frameworks, and therefore are seen as being worth noticing: Sacajawea, Sequoyah, Black Elk, Frederick Douglass, James Baldwin, Martin Luther King Jr., Alice Walker, Toni Morrison. Usually, Latinos and Asian Americans do not get into Phase II courses at all; recent and rare exceptions are Maxine Hong Kingston, Yoko Ono, and Cesar Chavez. Those who most strongly rebelled against white dominance are usually annihilated in the telling of history as they were in life. Those who accommodated or assimilated somewhat may become cultural heroes, especially in retrospect; they may come to be seen as almost within the "mainstream."

In Phase II, teaching about people of color as exceptional and therefore worthy of notice, can create psychological problems. Many teachers think that in holding up "exceptions," they are providing role models for students of color, and demonstrating to white students that people of color should be taken seriously. The impulse can be genuine, and a fairly wealthy white person like myself should take care not to dismiss models of "success" for students who may be feeling desperate and continually put down. It is easy to critique prevailing definitions of success from a position of economic security. Still, the Phase II–Famous Few curriculum can be damaging, as it may deliver to students of color the message that most of their people are not worth studying, and that if they become unlike their people, they may be worthy of notice. It may serve as a bribe: leave your people and you may rise up the "real life" ladders from the bottom to become an American hero. Phase II can put students at psychological risk, encouraging them to make their way not as members of their ethnic group but as soloists.

Elizabeth Minnich has pointed out that this loner status makes a person from a nondominant group vulnerable to every setback.[5] Once the loner goes through the gates alone, refusing to identify with her or his stigmatized group, then every setback must seem like something which has been caused by personal behavior or is at some level merited.

A second psychological danger to students of Phase II–Famous Few teaching is the implication by whites that if you are "really good," you will not be seen as African American, Latino, Asian American, or Native American, but only "as a person," and that this will be good for you. We women are sometimes taught that we will be seen as persons, if we will just forget that we are women. No; we will be seen as having sex and race and ethnic identity, especially if we are female or dark-skinned, or have features identified with a cultural sub-group. It is mere illusion to imagine that American adults see anyone as "just a person"; our "educational" and media training in typecasting, hierarchical ranking, and mistrust has been too strong. Phase II success stories of "achievers" imply to students that all they need to do to get out of their debilitating circumstances is to work a little harder and "make it on their own," without complaint, and without ties to their (impaired) people.

One further problem with Phase II teaching is that the singling out of cultural heroes misrepresents the values of cultures in which the making of the individual hero is not thought of as possible or desirable. Sojourner Truth and Harriet Tubman were working for and with their people, yet are featured as outstanding individuals. Often collaborative group work is not seen to exist. The chief poster for the UN Decade for Women 1985 conference in Nairobi features a single woman weaving a basket. Women weave baskets together in Kenya; it is a group activity. In order to create the poster the designer had to misrepresent the culture. Phase II courses featuring a famous few who stand out "above the crowd" can grossly misrepresent Asian American, Native American, and Latino cultures in which the star system is not the norm.

The shift to Phase III usually comes when teachers realize that Phase II is politically naive: it features a few who survived in society but gives little attention to the structures of power in society. An important emotional shift occurs when teachers look past individual lives and experiences to invisible hierarchical systems which have very strong predictive power for the general outlines of any given life. Most teachers in the United States were not educated in school to see these systems at work, but were taught that the individual is the main unit of society and that the U.S. is a meritocracy for individual advancement or failure. It is a sign of personal growth when teachers begin to pass on to students systemic awareness of social inequities in resources, opportunities, and access to public power.

Phase III, then, focuses on racism, classism, sexism, struggle, overt violence, persecution, persistence, protest, and work toward new policies and laws. Especially in the field of social history, the emphasis is on those who fought for change which would benefit oppressed people. Phase III usefully focuses on interlocking oppressions, and at its best it links the study of power within the United States to power world-wide, so that students can see how patterns of colonialism, imperialism, and genocide outside of the U.S. match patterns of domination, militarism, and genocide at home. All teachers and students in the United States need this experience of asking who has the most power, and why and how it is used, and what is going on.

But Phase III has its weaknesses. Many white social historians think they are studying multiculturally when in fact they are merely studying the energy in protest movements monoculturally. All the protesters look more or less the same. Phase III scholarship never asks "ordinary" people about their lives, never takes children, women, or servants as authorities, and never listens to voices which the academic world has not yet respected.

Phase III, then, like Phase II, opens some doors and keeps others shut. Its main conceptual fault is that it keeps the powers of definition and evaluation in the hands of the present white authorities, within a single system of meaning and value defined monoculturally. We will never make most people's experience seem either real or valid if our teaching and research still rest on the kinds of credentialing and vertical appraisal derived from the experience of those who have had the most power. Just as Phase II analyses of "Black achievement" rarely encompass one chief achievement of African Americans, which is to have survived and endured, Phase III tends to focus on visible political deficits without acknowledging any political dimension in focusing on "deficits" to begin with. The analysis of others' "issues" does not prepare Caucasian people to look at their own psyches, or to learn from "others."

I have noticed that many or most of us in the white academic world are more comfortable discussing issues of disempowerment than taking seriously those lives which do not center on, depend on, or resist "white" male governance, and which embody alternative forms of power. Phase III attributes to whole groups deficit identities, while denying their cultural identities, and in doing so it maintains control for the dominant group. It sets up a dominant paradigm in the mind of the student and then allows the underdog to be seen only as challenging it. It says to students of color, "You can be a fighter," not "You are a maker of culture and of life." It says to white students, "You are high; others are low." Such monocultural teaching about racism may ironically increase arrogance or ignorance in "white" students. It may teach them to sympathize with, or even admire the struggles of people of color but it will not teach that "winners" have anything to learn from "losers," except perhaps how to fight. Its lenses are useless for clarifying my colleague's comment that she would not want to be white.

Phase IV, on the other hand, illuminates her comment. For Phase IV makes a crucial shift to a lateral, plural frame of reference beyond winning and losing. It produces courses in which we are all seen to be in it together, all having ethnic and racial identity, all having culture, all placed by birth in particular social and political circumstances, all with some power to say no, and yes, and "This I create"; all with voices to be heard, all damaged, and all in need of healing, all real, very distinctively ourselves, potential makers of new theories and new understandings of life. When I say "all damaged," I am thinking of the fact that my slave-holding ancestors were damaged. They were not damaged in the same ways that their slaves were, but they were made cruel and sick by their roles. Phase IV, being a frame of mind that goes beyond monoculturalism to cultural pluralism, allows me to see this. It opens the doors that my friend opened for me, onto my own culture newly realized by me as a culture, and onto hers, formed on a different base of experience. Phase IV suggests multiple worlds, or in the words of the Pueblo Indian scholar Gregory Cajete, it suggests Multiversal Realities, rather than a single Universe.[6]

Phase IV reading lists in any discipline often contain multiple short works or types of material, including work by students, and provide multiple insights on any situation, in several media, with a de-emphasis on "issues" of disempowerment and a more unusual emphasis on cultural detail, and voices from daily life. Phase IV classes can be wondrous in their energy, interest, and healing power. Students feel co ownership of them, and sometimes experience such courses as life-lines. It is true that competitiveness, anxiety, and vertical stereotyping from the conventional types of teaching carry over into the work of Phase IV classes, but teachers creating laterally expanded and culturally explicit syllabi usually try to redistribute power more evenly than usual in a classroom, and to weaken privilege systems which interfere with listening to many voices, and respecting testimony from many sources.

Whereas Phase III emphasizes differences from an assumed but unexamined norm, and Phase IV recognizes distinctiveness without accepting any norm; it recognizes in experience the equivalent of what Gerard Manley Hopkins named as the "inscape" of created things – particular, vivid internal distinctness.[7]

Some time ago I wrote a paper which lists forty-six ways in which I daily experience having white privilege relative to my African American colleagues in the same building.[8] This is a Phase IV analysis. The paper rests on my sense of ethno-particularity, ethno-specificity, and ethno-pecularity with regard to unearned advantage in my workplace. White privilege is invisible in the Phase III monocultural focus on issues and deficits of "others." I could see the cultural circumstance of having unearned advantage and its attendant cultural deformities only within the multicultural framework of Phase IV, in which my racial group is not assumed to embody a neutral or desirable norm.

Phase IV understandings take some blame out of the description of dominant groups; all people are seen as born into circumstances they did not ask for and systems they did not invent. The processes at work in Phase IV include listening, observing, making connections, respecting many kinds of life, power, and thought, including one's own, and imagining how to institutionalize the protection of diverse forms of life including distinct forms of human community.

Phase V is needed to help us to an as-yet-unthinkable reconciliation between our competitive, hierarchical propensities and our contingent and relational propensities. Phase IV education helps to develop and reward the capacity for being in relation to others; Phase V will need to help us also to rethink organizational structures in complex worlds where distribution of resources, services, and basic supports requires balanced uses of vertical and lateral abilities.

For this reason, as I imagine Phase V, my diagrammatic model of psychic and societal structures turns into a large, three-dimensional globe. The faulted pyramids, with their bedrock lateral functions underlying the vertical functions, become simply one element in the topology of each continent, in a world like our own in which mountain ranges are one of the forms of geography. Each continent, each group of cultures, has its ranges, its "peaks," its dynasties, but mountain climbing is understood to be one particular human activity, not the only human activity. Sending expeditions to climb very high mountains requires preparation, equipment, technologically preserved food, support systems, maps, base camps, porters, sponsorship, and people who can bow out of other life-sustaining activities or responsibilities. Certain maps can be drawn from high summits only. Many useful maps can never be drawn from summits at all. In any case, high summits do not support many forms of life. They are deoxygenated, and it is well known that most people on too little oxygen do not make very wise decisions about the welfare of themselves or others.

It is the foothills, valleys, and alluvial plains which support life best, with rainfall, fertile soil, and concentrations of human knowledge about growing and harvesting. This is the geography of Phase IV awareness. And at the edge of the water we can learn to farm the sea as well. For the last forty years, we in the U.S. have, figuratively speaking, taught that mountain climbing is the worthiest activity, the mark of ambition and of success. To shift to metaphors of making and mending the fabrics of culture and environment seems to me to make more sense now. We can also usefully teach metaphors of journeying. Many of our students in the U.S. are free to travel, metaphorically speaking, to many sites in the topology, to experience many varieties of life, on many figurative continents. Some will stay in single locations throughout a lifetime. But we will continue to suffer if educators keep teaching that mountain climbing and peak experience are the best activities, and that the resources of the society are well spent operating base camps which help only a few people or nations to stand briefly on summits and feel they have prevailed over life or each other.

The metaphysical shift from a faulted pyramid to a globe in which peaks and valleys are parts of cultural topology is accompanied by a further conceptual shift. The multicultural globe is interior as well as exterior; the multicultural worlds are in us as well as around us. Early cultural conditioning trained each of us as children to shut off awareness of certain groups, voices, abilities, and inclinations, including the inclination to be with many kinds of children. Continents we might have known were closed off or subordinated within us. The domains of personality that remain can and do fill the conceptual space like colonizing powers. But a potential for pluralized understanding remains in us; the moves toward reflective consciousness come in part from almostsilenced continents within ourselves. Greater diversity of curriculum reflects not just the exterior multicultural world but the interior self which in early childhood was aware of, and attuned to, many varieties of experience.

Readers of my 1983 paper on phase theory will know that I matched the phases with the sensibilities of hypothetical first-year college students called Meg, Amy, Jo, and Jo's twin daughters, Maya and Angela, and their younger sister Adrienne. I wished to indicate that what and how we teach in each of these frames of reference actually has life outcomes for students. This is true for the various ways Ethnic Studies is taught. I cannot guess about the effects on students of color of instruction in Phases I, II, and III, but I will sketch some portraits of the ways in which I have seen instruction in these phases affect the development of Anglo-European American students, and then suggest the consonance between Maya and Angela's lives and Phase IV curriculum. My focus here is on the various kinds of understanding which the "little women" are given with regard to Native American culture.

Meg, who is a casualty of a Phase I curriculum, is a white girl who tries very hard to be good. She wants to be "sugar and spice," and also to be kind. When she is growing up, her brother plays "Cowboys and Indians" every afternoon with his friends in the neighborhood. She watches shows on cowboys and Indians. She learns in elementary school that the "settlers" had to contend with many "dangers of the wilderness," which included Indians and wild animals. She learns in high school that the settlers had to protect their families from Indians, who took scalps. In four years of college, she reads one chapter on "The North American Indian," which cites twelve white male anthropologists, refers to nearly 300 tribes and hundreds of language groups, yet does not make Indians seem the slightest bit real to her. This is Phase I Ethnic Studies in which "white" people neither study people of color nor notice that they haven't. Meg has studied "white" anthropologists. During her years in college, Meg will never start a conversation with a student of color. The way they "band together" makes her nervous. She seeks her friends, for safety. Meg will marry young, feeling a need of protection from many perceived dangers. She will marry a "white" man who turns out later to be neither a settler nor a protector. Many years later, as a Continuing Education student, Meg will find herself in another college course, reading for the very first time the words of a Native American. She reads *Black Elk Speaks*, and she is in tears.[9] The sacred hoop is broken. Meg is devastated to discover the wholeness of Indian worlds just at the same time that she learns of their near destruction.

Amy, the ambitious art student schooled in Phase II, appraises Indian work casually, as well as competitively. She knows it is only "craft," not Art, but feels the need to find grounds for putting it down. She finds it repetitive, primitive, inexpressive, and of course merely functional. Amy thinks some of the rugs and pots are handsome, and she is sure that she would recognize the work of a first-rate Indian artist, if only these people would put away their talk about broken treaties, and transcend their "cause." Amy cannot understand why they keep repeating old stories of their traditions, instead of joining what she thinks of as the cultural mainstream. She feels no curiosity about Indians, but gives a silent cheer when she hears that Wilma Mankiller has become Principal Chief of the Cherokee Nation. "That's the way it should be done," she thinks. "Just go for it and don't let anything get in your way." The idea that Wilma Mankiller was chosen because of her consonance with, rather than her competition against, others in her nation does not occur to Amy, who has been deeply dyed in the tradition of "the individual versus society." Amy takes a passing interest in Curtis's photographs of Indians, for their strong and striking faces. She feels, however, that if these people were "really good," they would have prevailed. She cannot imagine a culture in which the aim is not to prevail. As a gallery owner in middle age, Amy is criticized for her failure to show works by artists of color. She says that she would show some if she could find a truly outstanding artist. Her mind is as open as the "exceptions" curriculum of Phase II can make it.

Jo, the older "white" woman who comes to college out of a failed marriage at the age of forty, is appalled by what she learns in her course on Gender, Race, and Class in American society. She had never understood why the Indians disappeared; she had known nothing of the slaughter of the buffalo, which took away the Plains Indians' means of existence, the Trail of Tears which killed tens of thousands of Cherokees and deprived most of the Nation of its native habitat, or the outlawing of Indian languages, laws, and rituals. She sees in the silencing and crippling and betrayal of the Indians the same kinds of systemic oppression she has felt as a woman, silenced, dispossessed, beaten, and battered in a marriage which now feels to her like a broken treaty. She is outraged that the books in which white anthropologists speak about Indian demographics do not make Indians' sufferings come alive. She writes a history paper on the way in which whites have named as great Indians only those who "met Europeans halfway," but she does not know what to say about the corrective except that the American historians should recognize the fiercest fighters more honestly, and make the betrayals by European Americans clearer. Jo is distressed by this paper as she hands it in; something is missing, but she does not know what.

After the class ends, Jo starts a correspondence with an Indian woman in prison whose name she has found in an anthology of writing by North American Indians. As this correspondence goes on, she begins a support group for imprisoned Indian women, in order to raise money for their legal expenses and their families, and to provide them with reading and writing materials. Jo feels that she is at the edge of a vast territory about which she is wholly ignorant, and is angered to see in retrospect that the book she read on United States Women's History in a Women's Studies course did not contain a single mention of Native American women. She wonders whether she shouldn't have majored in Ethnic Studies rather than having to find out about Indians in this roundabout way. She can't seem to get people in her field, Women's Studies, interested in Native Americans. She persuades the Student Union Committee to show the film "Broken Treaty at Battle Mountain."[10] She thinks of her work for Indians as being for them, but not for herself.

Maya and Angela, Jo's twin children, are attached both through schooling and through life outside of school to both their Anglo-American and their African American cultural roots. Whereas the white feminists they meet often talk about inventing new forms beyond patriarchy, they think of their "black" culture as both prepatriarchal and nonpatriarchal, and assume that it is these cultural traditions which need to be reclaimed in order to make the world a saner place. They own a cassette of the television interview in which Bill Moyers asks Louise Erdrich how Indian values can survive in this world of individuality, competition, and technology.[11] Erdrich asks how the world can possible survive without Indian values, saying that it has come to the brink of ecological crisis without them. The twins also like Michael Dorris's account of the mailman who came to his door asking him how to run an all-Iroquois week for a group of Cub Scouts in the woods. Dorris laughs and says that the most important thing was to take these boys' mothers, because Iroquois boys wouldn't possibly know how to get along in the woods without their mothers to teach them.

Maya and Angela are of course aware of Indian persecution, but they share Mohawk writer Beth Brant's (1988) feeling that they are not victims; they are "organizers, freedom fighters, feminists, healers, and ... none of this is new; it has been true for centuries." They like their own laughter, their powers of spirit, and their identities. They would not like to trade their identities for anyone else's. They feel affinities with Native Americans, with many other men and women of color, and with the few white feminist women and men who have made common cause with them. Their mother wants to talk about Indian Issues with the Cherokee friend whom they bring home for a meal. Maya and Angela have to explain why their friend did not make eye contact and did not respond warmly to this subject. They explain that her lack of eye contact is a mark of respect, and that her manner reflects Tsalagi cultural values of patience, respect for age, personal caution, listening and observing, making criticism indirectly, and keeping the emphasis on the whole group.

Maya and Angela see themselves as coming from different Nations than Indians, with heritages of different stories, but feel that they are similarly guided by spirits, and they have deep affinities with the Black community. In their identification with darkness, they find nurturance. They do not study Indians so much as to derive strength from them; Carol Lee Sanchez, Joy Harjo, Beth Brant, Marilou Awiakta, Bea Medicine, Brenda Collins, Linda Hogan. They feel connected to their ancestors, to the invisible world, and to birds, trees, earth and sky.

Maya and Angela write on Native American cultures in college term papers; Maya writes on Mother Earth and Grandmother Earth, describing the distinction between Mother Earth, who brings forth trees and corn and Grandmother Earth, who appears in some Indian cosmologies as the growing principle itself.[12] She contrasts Plato's view of the defects of the accidental or merely actual, as against the pureness of pure Form, with the Indian view that Mother Earth's products are not defective reductions of any purer principle. Angela, in a Phase IV Education course, writes a primer for grade school children, explaining that the Indians were the settlers, and illustrating elements of the wholeness and integrity of their lives, before the European invaders arrived. It is no surprise when several years after their leaving college, these women are adopted into one of the clans of the Cherokee Nation, and continue various forms of teaching and learning on the Cherokee theme that we are *all* part of the human circle.

Adrienne, their younger sister, is trying to help work on the curriculum toward survival. She dreams of balance between the creatures of the earth and their habitats, and she dreams of balance among nations and individuals so that all may survive with dignity. She is rather abstracted and preoccupied, and is working toward metaphors for the new texts which might sustain us.

Maya, Angela, and Adrienne have refused to accept the projections onto them of deficit identity by the dominant culture. Though my description of them may sound simple and even halcyon, they are doing heroic work in refusing monocultural messages about what they are. Their affirmation of their wholeness and their will to connect rather than sever themselves from others is a hard-won sanity which could cost them very heavily. They may *be seen as* unnatural, neurotic, unambitious, devious, secretive, out of touch with the "realities" of modern civilization, non-professional, unable to "progress." They may be seen as enemies of the government, and vilified both subtly and obviously by those who have the most cultural power. Ethnic Studies and Women's Studies can strengthen their hand if taught not only with a focus on aspiration (Phase II) or understanding of systemic oppressions (Phase III), but also with respect for and reinforcement for their personal and cultural integrity. Mending the sacred hoop is dangerous political work, but it is work toward survival. When Women's Studies makes common cause with the Ethnic Studies to put human dignity and integrity at the center, then both will be doing their most dangerous and healing work.

It is significant that Meg, Amy, and Jo never receive a version of curriculum that goes much beyond the boundaries of the United States. Maya and Angela, on the other hand, have been supported to think beyond national boundaries, recognizing people everywhere, and seeing the earth and the sky as more basic organizers of human life than local or colonial governments. They have cross-cultural curiosity and commitment, trusting their own daily experience to lead to questions about larger world patterns. It is as though they have mentally signed a treaty of peace with others across national boundaries, regardless of what national leaders allow or want. They think of people in cultures other than their own as having cultural complexity and integrity, and as being unknown to them, but potentially in conversation with them. They feel a strong need to find common bonds and make some common policy amidst the diversities. Differences in governing bodies and strategies are not to them any indicator of final separateness; instead, they feel they belong in contingent affiliation with life everywhere. To citizens like this, we could entrust policy-making. Our choices about education will determine whether we will have such citizens.

Notes

1 This essay originally appeared as McIntosh (1990).
2 My colleague was Gwendolyn Thomas, who in 1972 was Assistant Professor of English at the University of Denver, in Colorado. She later became Assistant Vice President of Student Affairs at Metropolitan State College in Denver.
3 Wellesley College founded the Center for Research on Women (CRW) in 1974 and the Stone Center for Developmental Services and Studies (SCDSS) in 1981. From 1974 until 1995, researchers and staff referred to the CRW as "the Center" and the SCDSS as "the Stone Center." In 1995, the two centers came together to form the Wellesley Centers for Women, commonly referred to as "the Centers" or WCW.
4 See Chapter 12, *Interactive Phases of Curricular Re-Vision: A Feminist Perspective.*
5 From 1985 to 1990, Minnich and McIntosh spoke together at a number of colleges and universities regarding bringing people of color and women into the curriculum. It was during one of these consultations that Minnich made this observation.
6 Cajete consulted with the National SEED Project in 1990 and shared this observation with the author, that the universe is actually a multiverse. See Cajete (1994) for more on Pueblo multiverse understandings.
7 See Allsopp and Sundermeier (1989).
8 See Chapter 1, *White Privilege and Male Privilege: A Personal Account of Coming to See Correspondences Through Work in Women's Studies*, and Chapter 2, *White Privilege: Unpacking the Invisible Knapsack.*
9 See Elk and Neihardt (1988).
10 See Freedman (1974).
11 See Moyer (1988).
12 In response to my question about Grandmother Earth, Brenda Flyswithhawks told me that the soil itself can be seen as Grandmother Earth.

References

Allsopp, M. E., & Sundermeier, M. W. (1989). *Gerard Manley Hopkins: New essays on his life, writing, and place in English literature.* Lewiston, NY: E. Mellen Press.
Brant, B. (Ed.) (1988). *A gathering of spirit: A collection by North American Indian women.* Ithaca, NY: Firebrand Books.

Cajete, G. (1994). *Look to the mountain: An ecology of Indigenous education*. Durango, CO: Kivaki Press.

Freedman, J. L. (Producer). (1974). *Broken treaty at battle mountain*. [Videotape]. Westport, CT: Cinnamon Productions.

Elk, B., & Neihardt, J. G. (1988). *Black Elk speaks: Being the life story of a holy man of the Oglala Sioux*. Lincoln: University of Nebraska Press.

McIntosh, P. (1990). Interactive phases of curricular and personal re-vision with regard to race. *Working Paper No. 219*. Wellesley, MA: Wellesley Centers for Women.

Moyers, B. (1988). *A world of ideas with Bill Moyers: Louise Erdrich and Michael Dorris on the real Columbus*. [Videotape]. Arlington, VA: Public Broadcasting Service.

PART IV
The SEED Project Papers

A LETTER ABOUT THE NATIONAL SEED PROJECT

Dear Reader,

  You may be wondering, with all of these theories I've described, what do they mean in practice? For me, it meant starting an experiment in 1986 to see whether teachers might be the leaders of their own professional development. This experiment became the National SEED Project on Inclusive Curriculum (Seeking Educational Equity and Diversity).

  School teachers had begun to ask for seminars like the ones that I had led for seven years, from 1978 to 1985, on bringing women into the curriculum of college courses.

  So in 1986, I proposed regional seminars to be held in the next four years for K-12 teachers on bringing women into the content of school courses. Scott McVay of the Dodge Foundation had read Carol Gilligan, and he believed in this proposal. It was wonderful to have Dodge Foundation funding, but winter weather made traveling to New York, New Jersey, or Philadelphia each month chancy and nerve wracking. There were postponements, telephone calls, and urgent changes of plan for twenty people at once, before the advent of cellphones. As I avoided the thought of going through another wintry trip to another city, my mind was half way toward the idea that I needn't go to each seminar myself. When I did go and we used methods that included everybody in every conversation, I learned paradoxically that I need not have gone at all. When we used methods that insured that time would be shared, anxiety in the seminar room about who was "in charge" disappeared. I began to realize that in this equitable atmosphere, anybody could be facilitating the conversation. So if I could just prepare leaders, anyone could lead a seminar anywhere in the US. The idea expanded like an airbag and the National SEED Project was born.

From my point of view, the greatest gift from the Dodge Seminars was that Emily Style, a public high school English teacher with many years of experience in schools and colleges, joined the program and became an invaluable colleague, collaborator, and lifelong friend. She is a relational teacher, scholar, poet, essayist, anthologist, compassionate and gregarious shepherd of people in their growth and development. She taught me about the importance of small group processes, and lateral inclusiveness in every kind of curriculum design. She and I co-authored two of the articles on SEED which are in this book. Together, we co-directed the first twenty-five years of the SEED Project, Emily from her base in New Jersey and I from my base in Massachusetts.

I assumed several things about teachers that have proved to be durable over the life of the project. I assumed that teachers, like all citizens, have been wounded by inequitable systems, and that understanding of the wounds will help us to create teaching and learning spaces where all students feel they belong and can learn. We could address power dynamics explicitly as they appeared in the curriculum and in ourselves. I felt that teachers had the capacity to lead this work on educational equity and diversity as long as they had had an experience of sharing discussion time quite consciously. I thought that if we could recall and examine inequitable experiences in our lives, especially in our school years, any of us could lessen inequities within our practices of education. This is something we could do for each other and with each other.

I felt pretty sure that teachers could become their own counselors and equity leaders if they could be immersed in a carefully designed, multicultural, residential program with other educators for a week. I thought that then they could return to their schools and provide for school colleagues over an academic year the same kind of structure for discussion of difficult equity subjects that they had experienced in the one-week training.

What began as an experiment thirty-three years ago has evolved into a solid working model that is deliberately refined year after year by a diverse group of veteran and devoted SEED staff members. The basic structure remains a week-long residential training called the New Leaders Week, followed by participants' facilitation of monthly, school-based seminars in the following academic year for up to twenty of their colleagues.

Starting with the first New Leaders Week in Claremont, CA, Brenda Flyswithhawks of Santa Rosa Junior College joined us and took part in all of the first twenty-five years, initially as a speaker, then as a consultant, staff member, and ultimately as Co-Director with Emily and me. Brenda's presence became indispensable to SEED. Many participants know her as the principal guide of their own transformative work in both education and in life.

The conceptualizations of the three of us were SEED's underpinnings. Emily's 1988 essay "Curriculum as Window and Mirror" and her perception that we should attend as closely to "the scholarship in the selves" as we attend to "the scholarship on the shelves" was critically important to SEED's development. SEED focuses on studying oneself as a key to re-seeing the experience of students in our schools who are rarely encouraged or allowed to study themselves. My Phase Theory was another foundational element of SEED, together with my ideas about fraudulence and my writings on privilege, starting in 1988.

Brenda clarified and strengthened SEED's practices by bringing her indigenous world views into each New Leaders Week. She would share her Cherokee spiritual and social philosophies, drawing parallels between them and the diagrams I and others presented. Our SEED colleague from the Philippines, Raquel David-Ching, presented the mandala as another way of seeing holistically. Brenda and Raquel saw the training week as a spiritual holding container[1] for people in many phases of their life journeys. By building a culture at SEED in which leaders are carefully "held" by mentoring adults in their understanding of difficult power dynamics, we fostered leaders' abilities to be "holding containers" for the development of other adults, and young people. SEED leaders understand that people develop at their own speeds. Neither leaders nor participants can be expected to be at the same places in their awareness or effectiveness. The process accommodates many kinds of learners with many degrees of openness, as schooling itself should do, while holding out the belief that all people have some capacity to learn and grow from the revealed humanity of others.

SEED seminars do not treat teachers like neutral pass-throughs who simply need to learn new skills to "apply" in the classroom. They reorient educators to the social worlds of schools and their own psyches. Greater professional and personal coherence results through the balance of inner-directed and outer-focused discussion. The Project encourages educators to become more committed to education as growth and development rather than education as gatekeeping.

The National SEED Project is thriving and expanding. National SEED is based at the Wellesley College Centers for Women with Emmy Howe, Gail Cruise-Roberson, and Jondou Chase Chen as Co-Directors and Motoko Maegawa and Ruth Mendoza as Associate Directors. The Project's remarkable staff is comprised of a wide range of people, most of whom have been with the Project for five years or more. They work intensively to create and offer resources, activities, and continuing connections for an ever growing network of more than 2,700 educators, parents, community leaders, and other professionals from forty-two U.S. states, Washington D.C., and fifteen other countries. SEED currently trains approximately 150 New Leaders every year.

In these hard times, many teachers wonder whether they should keep teaching. SEED can solace and support participants. The staff see the deep goodness in all people and understand that this goodness thrives when it is seen, held, respected, and elicited through interactions and interactivities in and outside of school. For many of us, the SEED work has felt like a rescue or like a revelation. It has permitted a change of course to many who had found schools discouraging. What pleases me most at present is hearing from teacher participants like the one who said, "SEED is the one meeting everyone wants to go to," or reading the words of the school district superintendent who wrote, "Nobody puts it all together like SEED." SEED says to teachers in a strengthening way,

> You are all right as a person despite these harsh times. You can be more whole than the fractured world that causes the problems that you face in school and in class. SEED can help lessen your isolation and frustration and give you some companionship and some new perspectives on yourself and your life. SEED ideas and connections can help to sustain you.

The two essays in this book that Emily Style and I co-authored in 1994 and 1999 describe how teachers can do their own professional development work with each other and increase the prevalence of what Jane Martin (1985) called the three C's needed in education: care, concern, and connection. In these two essays, we lay out some of the guiding observations of SEED with an emphasis on subtleties of power and uses of autobiographical testimony to put teachers at the center of their own development.

We want the United States to do better by all of the youth in our country and by all the knowledge-making in our culture. We want to know: What are students learning and what is it doing to them? How can parents, relatives, and friends affirm and stabilize the next generations? Will they use their power to make things better for everyone? Will they have a sense of devising the greatest good for the greatest number? I fear that those students we have educated unthinkingly to win, in a win/lose culture, will not be interested in figuring out what could be the greatest good for the greatest number. How will they use their power? Will they care about creating equalizing policies that spread the resources of the society? I think if we educate the next generations to a broader range of values, they may well be the best caretakers and custodians of the planet that we could hope for. Meanwhile, I wish you as a reader well on your own journey to put sustaining ideas into practice.

In the words of Pat Badger of Racine, WI and the SEED Project:

Arms 'round,

Peggy

Note

1 The phrase "holding container" comes from Tavistock Group Relations Theory and conferences.

References

Martin, J. R. (1985). *Reclaiming a conversation: The ideal of the educated woman*. New Haven: Yale University Press.

Style, E. (1988). Curriculum as window and mirror. In *Listening for all voices: Gender balancing the school curriculum*. Summit, NJ: Oak Knoll School.

14

SELECTION FROM "FACULTY-CENTERED FACULTY DEVELOPMENT" (1994) BY PEGGY MCINTOSH AND EMILY STYLE[1]

It is increasingly clear to us in the National SEED Project that what works for teachers is a staff development process that mirrors teachers' own lives and offers windows into new areas that have not, up until now, been part of their schooling or life experience. It is our belief that unless teachers experience themselves at the center of new learning (which draws upon both university scholarship and what Emily Style calls "the textbooks of their lives" as scholarship (Style, 1981)) they cannot provide curricula for students which, in turn, puts students' balanced growth and development as cultural beings at the center.

Emily Style found that the standard curriculum offered no windows into her mother's life or mirrors for her as a young girl who might be a mother someday. One of the reasons that Style became a teacher was to "do something" with her life, and be unlike her mother who "never worked." Her mother "just" gave birth to and cared for seven children. As a young person in a culture and in school, Style was not in a position to question the silence covering up mothers in the curriculum. She simply received it as a given, oblivious to the damage that it did to her intellectual relation to her mother and to the aspect of herself that would play a caretaking role in culture.

The faculty-centered faculty development process put Style at the center and took what she calls her life-text seriously. Over time, through reading in women's studies and engaging in monthly conversation with other teachers, Style noticed that school silence had taught her to dismiss her mother intellectually. Eventually, Style interviewed her mother, treating her belatedly the way that school taught her to treat "important people," and subsequently compiling *Mom's History Book* to honor her mother and to balance the record in her own head and for her own daughters.

That document, which makes a textbook of her mother's life, created a respectful window and a validating mirror unlike any other text. The SEED process gave Style permission to take her mother and herself seriously, discovering in the process that (family) life and her own existence were far more complex, multiple, problematic, and profound than she had been led to believe.

Fashioning a more inclusive curriculum is inner and outer work, hard work, and heart work that makes rigorous demands on memory and intellect. Experienced teachers need professional space to engage with their own life-texts as a fundamental resource. Some teachers have been engaged in just such thinking all along, but in isolation. Most school reform efforts completely ignore teacher and staff (auto)biographies. Becoming part of a community of learners that values autobiographical reflection is a key SEED experience. As Minnesota SEED leader teacher Cathy Nelson explained in an article which appeared in the December 1991/January 1992 issue of *Educational Leadership*:

> [At the SEED Summer Workshop] I became part of a SEED community of thirty-five learners who teach. Looking at the textbooks of our lives was essential before imagining school climate and curriculums that would more accurately reflect our diverse world. During our first moments together as a community of scholars/learners, we read aloud our personal versions of Caribbean writer Jamaica Kincaid's (1978) "Girl," drawing upon the gendered and remembered voices from our own pasts. The first voices we heard were our own. Immediately, we recognized the authenticity and power of our own lived experience.

SEED seminars are led by teachers for their colleagues. They offer both window-views out into areas that have not, until now, been part of teachers' formal schooling or their life-texts, and mirrors of their own lives' complexity. They include numerous, brief narratives by participants, told as we go around what becomes "a talking circle." In the conversational nature of this practice, a story told by one participant might become for one listener a window of revelation and, for another, a mirror recognition of a once-known landscape, the dim memory of which brightens in the course of the circle conversation.

There are significant dimensions of the personality and the past that are never invited into "professional" conversation in staff development. Due to private reflection, some teachers are aware of the "windows" and "mirrors" of their own learning and teaching process, but most staff development efforts build in no process for either recovering or sharing life-forming knowledge with one's colleagues. SEED seminars are the richer for tapping onto this vein of insight and cultural information which is contained within all people and in all school staffs.

At the same time, the SEED process offers avenues into the last twenty years of university-based scholarship on gender, race, class, culture, and many other diversities of experience. This scholarship illuminates many aspects of cultural power relations. Those of us teaching today are "products" of schooling which embedded in us deep imbalances or obliviousness in regard to matters of cultural positioning and power. Teachers today face a daunting task in dealing with all sorts of matters surfacing in schools which our own schooling evaded. Many explosive and political matters assert themselves in today's schools regardless of whether or not teachers are dealing with a student population primarily composed of "their own kind."

The American Association of University Women report entitled "How Schools Shortchange Girls" (Bailey et al., 1992) uses the term "evaded curriculum" to label the subjects covered only by powerful silences which, in turn, perpetuate particular positions of gender dominance or mask huge matters of cultural change. In the National SEED Project, we have found that breaking silence about evaded subjects is best done with eminent respect for what is already embedded in the texts of teachers' lives and trusting teachers' ability to talk about these matters as adult learners who are also, in the process, equipping themselves to handle students' life experiences as a central text in schooling. Participating in such a "modeling" experience, in a year-long SEED seminar, enables teachers to do less evading and more educating for real life in their own classrooms than was done for them in their K-12 schooling time.

In a SEED seminar that Emily Style facilitated at Madison High School in New Jersey, where she was on the staff for a decade, a white teacher revealed that a significant dimension of his identity was being a parent of four children including his thirteen-year-old son who was autistic. Up until then, in his teaching career of over twenty years, no one had ever asked him to speak about his own life-text as the white, male parent of an autistic child. In his own experience of schooling, there had been no windows regarding such a life, nor were there any mirrors in the faculty in-services[2] that he had experienced before the SEED seminar. Isolation and invention characterized his existence.

After this teacher talked from the textbook of his life in the SEED seminar, Style invited him, the following fall, to speak to her American literature classes during their reading of Steinbeck's (1937) novel *Of Mice and Men* whose character Lennie could be labeled autistic. This teacher broke more than one silence in Style's classroom in speaking out of the authority of his experience in handling his son's condition and his own experience of parenting. This added (multicultural) dimensions to the curriculum that cost nothing in terms of dollars and cents and benefitted all. In the National SEED Project, we have found that the development of teachers as "interior resources" for others in their school buildings (as SEED leader Verdelle Freeman of Piscataway, New Jersey, phrases it) is a critical first step in creating a multicultural curriculum that provides integrity and balance for all staff and all students.

In the SEED Project, we try to model respect for teachers' complexities with the hope that teachers will then show the same kinds of respect for their students' complexities. Teachers are not empty vessels any more than students are. Faculty development that ignores a teacher's own complexities and life-contexts repeats the same old errors of what Paulo Freire (1970) named the "banking model" education, which has failed so many students. If we aspire to student-centered learning, we need also to be thinking in terms of faculty-centered learning by teachers. The SEED Project promotes faculty-centered faculty development.

Using her model of "Interactive Phases of Personal and Curricular Re-Vision,"[3] McIntosh describes five interactive phases of professional development of teachers which she has come to see through work on gender and culture in the curriculum. They range from the most obliviously authoritative to the most respectful and inclusive. They also constitute a repertoire of ways of working with faculty, which have different degrees of appropriateness depending on the task at hand. Her Phase Theory is adapted here to describe a variety of ways of doing faculty development or professional development of teachers.

Phase I. Teacherless Faculty Development. "Outside" presenters, "expert" in their subject matter, neither notice teachers nor notice that they haven't.

Phase II. Exceptional Teachers. Exceptional teachers are featured in faculty development, seen as unusual for their kind (teacher), capable, for example, of "doing multiculturalism" for/in their institution and therefore, worth drawing attention to, rewarding and spotlighting. Such exceptional teachers are set apart as examples of what most teachers are not.

Phase III. Teachers as a Problem, Anomaly, Absence, or Victim. The administrators let the faculty air their "issues," permitting them to rebel/gripe against school norms and/or "fads" such as multiculturalism. Teachers are expected to attend faculty development events, oblivious of how they are being positioned as problems and/or victims. Faculty development in-service seems to be aimed at "fixing" defective or recalcitrant teachers.

Phase IV. Faculty Lives as Faculty Development. All teachers are seen as having complex lives, encouraged to resort to memory to "make textbooks of their lives" by narrating their own experiences. Faculty development provides both "windows and mirrors" for all participants: windows out to the realities of others, and mirrors of one's own reality and validity. Faculty development processes respect memory and a range of emotions in teachers; tap into deep knowledge of inner and outer schooling; enable the recovery of lost worlds. Faculty development work filled with intellectual and emotional respect leads to individual healing and institutional vigor. Phase IV is the first phase in which teachers' own stories count as curriculum for faculty development and are not seen "simply" as opinion, complaint, or mere anecdote.

Phase V. Faculty Development Redefined and Reconstructed to Include All of Our Complexities of Self. Phase V recognizes and uses all of our human modes of development, both the vertically oriented ones identified with "improvement" and the laterally oriented one identified with connection and (re) construction of self and society.

With regard to faculty development in multicultural and gender study, Phase I is obviously identified with authority and its functions. In Phase II, the lines are clearly drawn between the aspiring soloistic self (a possible "winner") and the great undifferentiated mass of "losers." Phase III, though "issues-oriented" and systemic in its awareness, is not conducive to nurturing deep reflection or the memory of the self-in-construction; Phase IV recognizes the self-in-relation[4] to others, and the self in relation to systems of power, respecting each teacher's response-ability. In Phase IV, the self becomes re-known as a microcosm of a complex world, with the promise of more perceived connection and coherence than at present.

SEED Summer Leaders' Workshops are designed to prepare leaders of SEED seminars to travel, emotionally and intellectually, between Phase II, III, and IV of the consciousness, providing an exhilarating sense of development and reconstitution in teachers. Respectful faculty development is deeply rewarding. Re-construing and re-situating the self as complex transforms thinking and allows for authentic multicultural connections which formal education and society have discouraged in both students and teachers. These interactive processes result in a powerful, grounded impulse toward curriculum re-vision.

Please note that we are not claiming that all cultural differences are contained in any of us, only that we have been, since early childhood, more complex than we have been taken to be, and shaped to be. Since it is impossible to "cover" all types of diversity in the curriculum, it makes sense to start with the inner and outer complexities that the learners in any situation carry within them. For when deep learning, unlearning, and relearning occur with one's own life-texts, they yield powerful illumination and educational energy. Such energy gets passed on to students whose life-texts are respected as well.

Notes

1 This essay originally appeared as McIntosh and Style (1994).
2 The word "in-service" refers to trainings that are given for teachers who have already embarked on teaching. Education for those who have not yet begun to teach are called "pre-service."
3 See Chapter 12, *Interactive Phases of Curricular Re-Vision: A Feminist Perspective* (1983), and Chapter 13, *Interactive Phases of Curricular and Personal Re-Vision with Regard to Race* (1990).
4 See Miller (1976) for more on the concept self-in-relation.

References

Bailey, S. M., Wellesley College Center for Research on Women, & American Association of University Women Educational Foundation. (1992). *How schools shortchange girls: The AAUW report: A study of major findings on girls and education.* Washington, DC: American Association of University Women, Educational Foundation.

Freire, P. (1970). *Pedagogy of the oppressed.* New York: Herder and Herder.

Kincaid, J. (1978, June 26). Girl. *The New Yorker.*

McIntosh, P. & Style, E. (1994). Faculty-centered faculty development. In Bassett, P. & Crosier, L. M. (Eds.), *Looking ahead: Independent school issues and answers.* Washington, D.C.: Avocus Publishing, Inc.

Miller, J. B. (1976). *Toward a new psychology of women*. Boston: Beacon Press.

Nelson, C. (1991, December/1992, January). The National SEED Project. *Educational Leadership*, 49, 66–67.

Steinbeck, J. (1937). *Of mice and men*. New York: Covici-Friede.

Style, E. (1981). *Multicultural education & me: The philosophy and the process, putting product in its place*. Madison: University of Wisconsin Teacher Corps Associates.

15

SELECTION FROM "SOCIAL, EMOTIONAL, AND POLITICAL LEARNING" (1999)[1] BY PEGGY MCINTOSH AND EMILY STYLE[2]

We the authors have never experienced any school learning that is not social, emotional, and political in its implications and consequences. The process of being schooled delivers social and emotional messages to a student in everything from the route of a school bus through end-of-the-day glimpses of school custodians cleaning up the building. Classroom decorations, student behavior in corridors, homework assignments, textbooks, and the minute-by-minute body language of teachers and students carry embedded and various social and emotional messages. Tracking, grading, and counseling make visible and audible the socializing judgments of elders about the comparative standing of young people. How could students not pick up social and emotional lessons from the charged atmospheres of assemblies and athletic programs? The fact that many students do not relish much about school has social and emotional causes and explanations. Parents' and communities' relation to and demands on schools also have social and emotional dynamics.

If there is no such thing as education that does not have social and emotional dimensions, why isn't this more commonly understood? Education generally is not seen, and does not present itself, as doing social and emotional teaching, when in fact it does so. Moreover, social and emotional relations between people exist within matrices of power relations that are a taboo subject in most K-12 schooling and in the majority culture of the United States. Power relations are therefore little understood, either individually or systemically. We feel that nevertheless students learn about power by watching, by imitating, by avoidance of what they fear. Their experience of the school bus, the custodian-servants, the tracking and grading systems socializes them to suppress most emotional responses to the stratified political and psychological structures within which their socialization takes place.

Teachers have trouble teaching about power intentionally or, as McIntosh says, *advertently*. Teachers have absorbed social, emotional, and political learning as part of their own schooling in which matters of power were, for the most part, evaded. At times, teachers teach about power when a blowup occurs on the playground, in the cafeteria, or in a classroom and a school crisis occurs. At such a time, some social, emotional, and political learning may take place within special forums, though they often have a muting, rather than clarifying, effect. For example, acts of routine violence may be renamed as "isolated incidents."

For the most part, our inadvertent teaching about power, social relations, and emotions in school delivers a message that these matters really cannot and should not be handled in school: they are beyond the pale of education. Most schools will leave children no better off, no more knowledgeable about power systems, than they were when they entered. While offering a socially desired commodity called education, schools deliver the message that any attempt to fathom students' social, emotional, and political locations within power systems must be left outside, at the schoolhouse door, and that the school cannot help students to understand themselves or others in certain ways that powerfully affect their daily well-being, security, and chance for development (McIntosh, 1983; McIntosh, 1990).

We the authors of this chapter are involved in helping teachers to do more effective and *advertent* emotional and social education. To do so requires that teachers pay attention to their own past (political) schooling, within power structures that socialized each to be this, not that; to do this, not that; to see this, not that; to act like this, not that; to believe this, not that; to feel this, not that. We cannot foster teachers' capacity to do better and more self-aware social and emotional education within a political vacuum. Most traditional and current schooling restrains both teachers and students within existing power structures, through (unacknowledged) social and emotional denial that power structures exist in the society and the psyche.

To talk with teachers about social and emotional learning (SEL) without addressing their own experience of the political dimensions seems to us to be both sentimental and disempowering. To learn why one feels like an outsider or an insider, or why groups can't get along, or why bullying and teasing and sexual harassment exist and are often overlooked by adults in a school, or how often teenage violence is fostered by schools, requires teachers to look at themselves. It requires that we look at what was done to us in school and how we lived then and live now politically, in institutions, families, and in our own self-appraisals. It also requires that we look at the powers we have in our hands to see if we want to use them to change education so that it promotes the growth and development of all, including ourselves.

The SEED Project

SEED seminars invite teachers' conscious attention to social, emotional, and political education. We feel that unless teachers can do for themselves what was not done for them in the way of breaking silence and isolation around social, emotional, and political learning, they will continue in the patterns of denial they have grown accustomed to living within and (inadvertently) enforcing.

For the SEED Leaders' training process, we have developed many exercises that help us to reflect on the social, emotional, and political educations we received through inadvertent instruction on taboo subjects of power, especially with regard to gender, ethnicity, sexuality, class, race, group dynamics, community relations, commonalities, differences, jobs, roles, authority, and inter-group relations. The aim of these exercises is to foster *advertent* growth and development in social, emotional, and political learning in all who are touched by the SEED Project, whether they are the new seminar leaders each year, the hundreds of teachers in their seminars, or the thousands of students whom those teachers teach.

We describe here just two out of some fifty interactivities, which is our term for activities in which everyone participates, with no one simply functioning as an observer.

Interactive Exercise #1

In the words of Emily Style (1981), we "make textbooks" of the lives in the room, by going around the circle, writing and reading aloud Girl/Boy pieces using the discipline of the circle.

Before the week-long summer New Leaders workshop, we send the forty teachers who are preparing to lead seminars Jamaica Kincaid's (1978) short autobiographical piece called "Girl." We ask participants to write their own version of voices in their heads from early childhood telling them how to be a boy or a girl. We tell them that at the opening meeting of the workshop they may read all, some, or none of their piece.

For the opening circle on the first afternoon of the residential week, no one wears a name tag. It is not clear to new leaders which of the sixty people in the room are staff members and which are new leaders like themselves. There is no formal welcome. Sitting in a circle, we read, or occasionally say, the words we have brought in response to the Kincaid assignment. McIntosh repeats the statement that participants may read all or none or part of what they have brought. They may choose to listen rather than read. The point, she says, is to hear each other around the circle. She reads part or all of her own "Girl" piece and turns to the person to her left. Reading around the circle usually takes two hours.

For many people, this activity draws up deeply buried, influential teachings from childhood. The listening circle enables all sixty participants to respond (mostly in silence, sometimes with empathic sounds or laughter) to what others call up, to hear commonalities and differences, to sort and sift and connect. This assignment, including what Style has come to call "the discipline of the circle," is a *political* arrangement that invites and regards intense listening to others' stories and forecloses the possibility of issues-oriented discourse on gender in the abstract. Hearing about the personal (and political) teachings given to others deepens one's awareness of one's own early teachings as well.

Many participants' voices and body language show the impact of the training they received with regard to gender and also (often) race, class, sexuality, fear, avoidance, self-censorship, self-doubt, self-denial, and silence. Themes surface and recede. Messages that have worn well take on stark contrast beside the many that have not. There is laughter at familiar prescriptions and at particularly pungent formulations. Sometimes, there are tears. Kincaid's piece is written in the imperative voice, so we encourage the speakers to use the imperative voice in their pieces. The effect is that they transmit decades-old messages coming directly through them, now offered to a circle of listeners in the present.

"Becoming" a boy or a girl for most people in the circle required a lot of training and repetition and warning. One was not automatically, easily, or naturally a boy or girl but needed to have one's gender socially constructed, artificially channeled, so as not to encroach on the territory of the other, some-times called "opposite," sex. Those who escaped such conditioning within their families and cultures stand out by contrast with those who remember emphatic teaching about shaping themselves to fit a gender norm. Leaving the circle, most if not all have a heart and head full of others' cultural constraints, obligations, and coping strategies in relation to those they themselves received.

In this interactivity, we answer Style's invitation to make "textbooks of our lives" and balance our attention to both the "scholarship on the shelves and scholarship in the selves" (Style, 1981). Kincaid's piece is the (published) scho-larship on the shelf to which we respond. The Girl/Boy activity is orchestrated to include every person in the circle as the authority on his or her own experi-ence, invited to speak in personal terms and not to comment on others' words, except by muted responsive exclamations and facial expressions in the course of the serial testimony process.

This exercise, which McIntosh devised in 1985, teaches about "gender" dif-ferently than an abstract discussion on gender would, by tapping into everyone's own deep internal development in a gendered world. We find that abstract discussions of gender (or any other complex matter with systemic dimensions) invite familiar conflicts and impasses. They result in an often polarizing, unsa-tisfactory pattern, in which everyone talks at the same time from stubborn, unexamined positions. This pattern operates in classes with students as well as in faculty meetings, and does not advance awareness; abstract discussion usually keeps most faculty or students "stuck" in familiar locations, most being silent observers of others and all but a few wishing to be elsewhere.

Interactive Exercise #2

We use Style's 1988 essay "Curriculum as Window and Mirror" to respond to the art of Carmen Lomas Garza. Style devised this exercise.

On any available surface, Style spreads out photographs of paintings by Carmen Lomas Garza that are found in the collection published by The New Press entitled *A Piece of My Heart/Pedacito de mi Corazon* (1991). She asks each participant to choose a picture and to pair up with any other person to discuss their chosen pictures. She states her idea that at its best, curriculum can serve as both window and mirror. In Style's 1988 essay, she imagines the curriculum as an architectural structure that schools build around students. Ideally, for each student, this structure will provide both windows out to the experiences of others and mirrors of the student's own reality and validity. Style points out that the Garza pictures may seem to serve some people as windows only, as one did for her when she first saw it, a man with a flaming cone of paper stuck in his ear. However, upon reading that the title of the picture was *The Earache*, she came to remember the hot salt bag used for earaches in her family, that she had forgotten years ago. Suddenly, the picture became a mirror as well.

Style asks participants to study a Garza picture silently in order to identify some window and mirror elements relative to their own experiences. Then she asks each participant to tell his or her partner for three minutes about how the painting serves as both a window and a mirror. The second partner is invited to speak as though the first has not spoken. The task is not to respond but to start fresh. If a partner runs out of words in the allotted time, both discussants can remain silent.

In a debriefing, Style asks, "How was this activity for you?" The responses palpably refute the charge that multicultural curriculum is "divisive." All participants find some self-mirroring elements in the pictures they have chosen. In other words, they find some familiar ground in their identification with the scenes and people of the pictures. Most *also* find elements strange to them. Many find differences in depiction of activities that they do not know (but did not necessarily know that they did not know). Garza's illustrations carry a lot of cultural specificity about Texan Latino/a daily life, behavior, customs, dress, food, families, celebrations, and living arrangements. In each picture, it is clear that something is going on, though the nature of the event may be quite opaque to some observers.

By way of teaching about acculturated social behavior, Style asks for a show of hands from those who had trouble filling their three minutes. She invites all to ponder what these responses show them about themselves. The ripple of response in the room indicates that these questions in themselves open up significant windows and mirrors about speaking and listening behavior. It has been our experience that the three-minute time frame invites people to get into a second and even third layer of rumination about a picture and to be heard out, while they embark on wording thoughts about a picture about which they may have thought they had little to say.

The Garza illustrations are colorful, detailed scenes of rural or village life in Texas in the 1950s. Most feature at least four people engaging in activity that one could describe to a curious five-year-old child, allowing a strong sense of common ground in the midst of cultural specificities. Often Latino/a participants upon finding some culturally familiar and intimate details have a very strong positive reaction to this activity. Their pleasure in it points up how few mirrors have existed in curricula and staff development projects for this population of teachers and students and, likewise, how few curriculum materials serve as "windows" for non-Spanish-speaking teachers and students.

Conclusion

The activities we sketch out here can be effectively used with students at a number of different grade levels. At one school, the students said that whenever they got something *really* interesting to do in class it turned out that the teacher got it from a SEED seminar. So they wanted their own SEED class. They got it, and seventeen juniors enrolled in a semester-long course of SEED readings, videos, and interactivities. This was not enough for them. In their senior year, these same students presented SEED work to the rest of the senior class, who determined that their graduation gift to the school would be a SEED Day, offered to all teachers and students in grades 9 through 12. The day was led by seniors and involved SEED interactivities, readings, presentations, and videos, including *The Color of Fear* (Lee and Stir-Fry Productions, 1997). We view this as a gift to the school from students who realized their need and hunger for social, emotional, and political education that would open up the Evaded Curriculum (Bailey et al., 1992). Two features of the day were an open dialogue by seniors on Ebonics[3] and a panel of alumnae (adults) who were lesbian but had been closeted during their student years at the school.

We believe that schools' silences surrounding the emotional feelings and social relationships of people of all ages are a political phenomenon serving to keep power where it now is. Students are taught about war in history classes. This is strife as military and public, distanced from their lives and managed by powerful rulers in public life. The implication is that strife is the domain of the powers that be. Meanwhile, teasing, bullying, harassment, and other types of strife in schools themselves go unaddressed in the curriculum.

Creating communities that work is a highly charged political act. The silence surrounding social and emotional education is a politically conservative silence, saying, in effect,

> You and we cannot do anything except in our individual lives; our stories do not exist in history. Be quiet and answer the test questions on other people's thinking and actions, or on math where there are no people, or on science which is about things beyond your control. Your silence, your capacity for doing what the teacher asks, and your willingness to ignore teachers' incoherence, school-based strife, and the arbitrariness of grading and assessment practices will safeguard you. In this way, you will survive school, and that will be your reward.

Many, however, do not believe in this reward and drop out mentally, if not physically. Those who do believe in it can become passive, non-voting citizens of the United States.

Schools cannot do social and emotional education unless educators examine why we have not been doing it before. Educators John Dewey and Maria Montessori each in their own way advocated it in earlier eras; however, with the erosion and loss of progressive and practical traditions has come a loss of experiential and meaningful components in schooling. Is it possible that most adults wish schooling to fail students and students to fail school lest students call us, as adults, on our own agendas and methods of fending off their embarrassing questions about the violent and inequitable state of the world? We believe that all adults and young people can gain if students and teachers develop healthy balances of affect, political feeling, social courage, intellectual depth, and physical health. The damper on the balanced development of children comes from adult evasions that cost the whole society heavily, economically and psychologically.

We feel that schools need to exemplify, embrace, and teach what educational philosopher Jane Martin (1985) names as the "three C's" of education: care, concern, and connection. Education without these will continue to incapacitate most youth with regard to social, emotional, and political learning. Educational practice today rarely connects training of the *mind*, seen, individualistically, with the *emotions* and with the *power* relations attending both thinking and feeling. We believe that unless the political reasons for having excluded *advertent* social and emotional language are recognized, current attempts to promote Social Emotional Learning will be apolitical, ahistorical, and sentimental, despite good faith, preventing students and teachers from obtaining balanced self-knowledge, social fairness, and intellectual tenacity and depth.

Notes

1 This essay originally appeared in Cohen (1999).
2 When psychologist Jonathan Cohen invited us in 1999 to contribute a chapter to his book on social and emotional learning, we both said more or less in unison, "Social, Emotional, and POLITICAL learning!" We were frustrated by the omission of power in discussions of social and emotional learning. We use the word "political" to mean "having to do with power." To us, political awareness is to us the knowledge or awareness of how power works in the society and in individuals. In the SEED Project, we provide examples of power-reducing, power-equalizing methods of holding meetings or running a school or a class. We try for a fine balance of personal assertiveness and respect for the experience of others who have what Adrienne Rich (1984) named a different "politics of location."
3 Today, Ebonics is more formally referred to as African American Vernacular English or AAVE.

References

Bailey, S. M., Wellesley College. Center for Research on Women, & American Association of University Women Educational Foundation. (1992). *How schools shortchange girls: The AAUW report: A study of major findings on girls and education.* Washington, DC: American Association of University Women, Educational Foundation.

Cohen, J. (1999). *Educating minds and hearts: Social emotional learning and the passage into adolescence* (pp. 137–157). New York: Teachers College Press.

Kincaid, J. (1978, June 26). Girl. *The New Yorker.*

Lee, M. W. and Stir-Fry Productions (Producer, Director). (1997). *The color of fear.* [Video/DVD] Oakland, CA: Stir Fry Seminars and Consulting.

Lomas Garza, C. (1991). *A piece of my heart/pedacito de mi corazón.* New York: New Press.

Martin, J. R. (1985). *Reclaiming a conversation: The ideal of the educated woman.* New Haven: Yale University Press.

McIntosh, P. (1983). Interactive phases of curriculum and personal re-vision: A feminist perspective. *Working paper No. 124.* Wellesley, MA: Wellesley College Center for Research on Women.

McIntosh, P. (1990). Interactive phases of curriculum and personal re-vision with regard to race. *Working paper No. 219.* Wellesley, MA: Wellesley Centers for Women.

Rich, A. (1984). Notes toward a politics of location. In *Blood, bread, and poetry: Selected prose 1979–1985* (pp. 210–231). New York: W. W. Norton & Company.

Style, E. (1981). *Multicultural education & me: The philosophy and the process, putting product in its place.* Madison: University of Wisconsin Teacher Corps Associates.

Style, E. (1988). Curriculum as window and mirror. In *Listening for all voices: Gender balancing the school curriculum.* Summit, NJ: Oak Knoll School.

16

SELECTION FROM "TEACHER SELF-KNOWLEDGE: THE DEEPER LEARNING" (2015)[1] BY PEGGY MCINTOSH, HUGO MAHABIR, BOB GORDON, AND RUTH MENDOZA

I spent a good deal of time in elementary school in the 1940s staring out the high windows of Kenilworth School in Ridgewood, New Jersey, and thinking. In my time, place, race, and class, this was often called wool-gathering. That word referred to one's plucking off bits of wool that sheep had left on bushes in passing, so as to spin and weave it into usable cloth. The teachers did not fault me for woolgathering probably because I was a white child with blond hair in braids who showed up for school every day and was able to do the assigned work. But I filled every available minute in school with my own diverging thoughts.

I think I daydreamed because I was trying to get away from school, which I experienced as a wounding place, like the rest of the world. I felt scared and wounded not only by World War II but also by the wars closer to home – in family cruelty, in children's cruelty to each other on the play-ground, and in the grading and report card system that subtly set us against each other. I could do the schoolwork easily but suffered watching what happened to others who could not. I tried to daydream my way out of fear and sadness to a place of greater peace, stability, and grounding, plucking ignored bits of fleece to make my own fabric.

I see this habit now as an attempt to come to some version of alternative self-knowledge.

Having worked in schools and with educators for fifty-eight years, I've come to wish that all educators were given more time and more rewards for self-knowledge. I feel that when we as teachers have the opportunity to get to know our deep selves better, we improve our lives and the lives of those who deal with us. But daily school life, extroverted in its demands, does not give students and teachers much incentive to follow Socrates' core directive: "Know thyself."

I wish for all students and all staff in school, even if only in flickering seconds and silences during a day, stability, peace of mind, and the chance to follow their own ideas, mine their memories, and explore their feelings – and not be constantly made to divert their attention away from their own trains of thought. The act of reflecting, even in snatches, gave me to myself and allowed me to try to make sense of my life. It allowed me to find my threads of coherence in a scary and unjust world. In time, it also made me into a more engaged and effective teacher. Once I knew more about who I was, I became far more useful to others.

As a very young teacher, I had felt exhausted after class, whether in school or in college. My teaching hours felt strained and artificial, and I would end each class feeling relief that I had survived. Survived what? It was not until I got the chance to structure classes more intuitively, and without rigid lesson plans or modes of instruction, that teaching did not tire me out, but rather inspired me. I felt then that I had stopped being an instrument in the hands of other people's ways of knowing. This change felt like spiritual development to me.

Although solitary self-reflection was a priceless asset that started me on the way to a coherent life, it was too narrow to make me knowledgeable. Too few other voices reached me. Team-teaching was the first corrective. Team-teaching with a trusted, close, diverse group of colleagues at the University of Denver in the 1970s, I could help to develop inclusive pedagogy and soul-restoring courses. We did not try to "cover" subjects so much as create classes in which students could bring to school what they knew and could speak, listen, be heard, imagine, feel, and think in reflective ways. As teachers, we did the same. Developing such processes required faith in our new methods; I would sometimes feel that, by the old standards, we weren't really teaching – hardly earning our paychecks, we were having such fun – until ... Bam! We arrived back at the old task of grading, which demanded that we judge students and which reinstated the top-down relations between teacher and students as well as the competitive relations among students and a certain subservience to the named curriculum.

Despite the backpedaling that grading required, we wanted to come to class, and so did the students. Thirty years later, we were still getting love letters from graduates about what our ways of teaching gave to them. We taught that "history" is really just versions of history, and that doing research in primary sources was a route to greater political intelligence about knowledge making, but it seems they felt that, basically, we gave them back to themselves – as more fully human. We helped them heal from all the years of schooling that had ignored them as knowers and had avoided questions of power in knowledge-making.

Is it unrealistic to think that a teacher can keep growing, reflecting, and threading together the pieces of his or her vulnerable being in the midst of the demands of teaching? Can educators become italicized to themselves in a way that feels restorative? I think so. But a group setting makes all the difference in achieving this.

The SEED Project

For the past twenty-eight years, I've worked with an amazing group of educators in the National SEED Project on Inclusive Curriculum. The acronym stands for Seeking Educational Equity and Diversity. The Project prepares teachers to facilitate deeply personal group work with colleagues in their schools. We find that when teachers come to believe in mining their own memory banks and interior selves for their understanding of equity or injustice as they have experienced these in their own lives, they become more firmly grounded in school and in life – to a degree that often startles and surprises them. And when they do this in the company of other educators, the effects can be life changing.

The group work of the SEED New Leaders' Week, in particular, offers participants the experience of meeting with other educators at a place of self-reflection and self-respect, beyond competition, judgment, and the need to prove oneself. The workshop participants, immersed in print and video resources about inequity and diversity, testify to their own experiences, listen to others do the same, see patterns and systems in their stories, and keep pondering, reflecting, and connecting. Then they go home and facilitate that same process for a year of monthly meetings in their own schools.

The key questions addressed in seminars focus on how to make the curriculum, teaching methods, and school climates more multicultural, gender-fair, and inclusive of every child regardless of his or her background. The group process of personal testimony within frameworks of systemic seeing changes teachers, who in turn tend to relate to their students in newly engaging ways, respecting what they bring from their own stories. As Emily Style, SEED Co-Director for twenty-five years, came to realize in her high school classes, "Half the curriculum walks in the door when the students do."

More than half the curriculum walks in the door when teachers arrive at the SEED New Leaders' Week. In their dialogues, we ask them to draw on their experiences rather than opinions, for opinions are usually generalizations of some sort. Twenty-five years after her training, SEED leader Nancy Letts wrote,

> SEED didn't demand anything from me but to be more of what I was. It wasn't the literary criticism I expected when the books for the workshop arrived in the mail. It was my experience that counted. My gendered experience, my racial experience, my blue-collared experience. It was my life and the lives of others that counted …

SEED leader Keith Burns wrote, of learning about privilege,

Here's the magic of SEED and its ability to create vision where there was none. No one told me about my privilege. No one blatantly revealed to me that my life was something other than what I understood it to be. SEED simply welcomed me into conversations about myself and about others, about history, and about the present. And because SEED showed me *how* to take part in conversation, and because SEED showed me that conversation is as much about *listening* as it is about talking, I discovered within myself things I had not known or seen before. I discovered how much of my own experience reflected important aspects of how our human worlds of power work. And when my eyes were opened and my mind made aware, I wept at what I now saw and knew …

SEED leader Phyllis May-Machunda wrote,

When I signed up for SEED training I never anticipated how deeply this training would transform my being. SEED has rooted social justice education in my worldview, and now I am compelled to tend and share seeds of social justice throughout my life's work.

Readers may wonder whether this work can be called professional development. Years of experience make it clear that it is – though perhaps a better way to think of it is as "adult development of educators." Through the years, we've received common illustrative comments about this method of coming to self-knowledge. Teachers value the opportunity to have something for themselves and about themselves. They appreciate being part of something that touches their hearts, minds, and spirits. They say they become better at listening, empathizing, and accepting of people, become better at respecting and learning from colleagues. They appreciate the chance to unpack their personal and professional stories as a means to help shape another generation's growth through this same process. They believe that feeling validated allows them to teach their own students to feel the same way themselves. To a person, they learn to dig deeper into issues of diversity and social justice – and embrace my view that *we are all part of what we are trying to change.*

My experiences with this work, in fact, make it clear to me that focusing on self-knowledge is one of the most important elements of teacher development. How can students trust us as educators if we come to class without a sense of our intricate complex selves mediated through history and circumstances and all we have seen? Because strong self-awareness is usually neglected in teacher training programs, teachers are often thirsty for the attention to their lives that diversity work can bring, and appreciate schools that encourage and support this work.

Self-Knowledge and Intentionality

Exactly how do we introduce educators to the experiential method of testimony and listening?[2] All of us contain voices in our head from early childhood onward, telling us how to be a boy or a girl. We ask participants not to write a narrative but to transmit words that were actually said to them.

There is no abstract analysis of "gender" during the week. But the autobiographical readings always give us much to reflect upon and always reveal some repeated patterns, some female or male specific teachings, much ethnic and cultural variety, adult inconsistency, and generational differences. Mostly, they reveal culturally embedded views on class, sex, gender, race, sexual orientation, religion, and ethnicity. Each participant then becomes his or her own analyst of statements like these:

- *Wear clean underwear in case you are in an accident.*
- *Put the worm on the damn hook.*
- *Boys don't cry.*
- *Why don't you go into teaching? You can always fall back on it.*
- *Girl, get your education and never depend on a man.*
- *Why are you such a Mama's boy?*
- *Suck it up.*
- *Keep your voice down.*
- *No, your brother will wash the car.*
- *You can be anything you want in life but that dress is not appropriate.*
- *You can do anything you want but remember never beat a boy at anything.*
- *Looks don't matter; manners do.*
- *Maybe next time you could try wearing red.*
- *Don't wear red! You'll look like the whore of Babylon.*
- *She doesn't have to cut the grass because she's your sister.*
- *Wait 'til your father gets home.*

After reading our statements without interruption, which we call Serial Testimony, everyone has a large amount of primary source information to reflect on. There is no argumentation, contention, generalization, or authority to instruct anybody on what to notice and what to conclude. On principle, we do not debrief afterward, for debriefing requires generalization. But teachers recognize that they know something about all this. And if they think back on what has served them well and what has not, from their and others' early teachings on gender, there are central questions that follow: Am I doing to the next generation what was done to me? If so, what are the consequences for them? And me? And the society in the future? How do I feel about it?

Through this process, teachers raise their level of awareness of issues related to identity and society, which means they can teach from a base of greater self-knowledge and intentionality.

Emily Style writes about how the SEED process balances "the scholarship on the shelves with the scholarship in the selves" (Style, 1981). The key extroverted questions of the SEED Project are:

- What are we teaching, and why?
- Can we make the curriculum, teaching methods, and school climates more gender fair, multicultural, and engaging to all the students regardless of their backgrounds?

Key inner questions are:

- Who am I in all this?
- Where am I?
- What is my own experience?
- Can I put my life more in the service of what I say I believe?[3]

My point here is not to recruit educators into the SEED Project, but rather to underscore the reasons we dedicate ourselves to this work year after year. We know that self-exploration leads to a better understanding of who we are and how we want to teach, which in turn makes all of us better educators and more grounded human beings.

The teacher essays that accompany this article illustrate the regrounding that can occur for teachers who come to recognize the authority of their own deep experience, and bring it into their schoolwork. In a very multi-racial and multicultural group setting in the SEED New Leaders' Week, they have learned the validity of talking about and hearing about experiences that most people have been encouraged to discount or ignore in conversations about education. These neglected areas often have to do with unexamined hierarchies. They constitute what we in the SEED Project call the evaded curriculum – the curriculum usually avoided in school settings and skirted by the unreflective self. The evaded curriculum often has to do with our own experience with systemic inequity and injustice that, in both obvious and subtle ways, does its work in and around us. Exploring our own growth can create a reflective awareness about who and where we are as educators. If we do so, we have a better chance of engaging alienated students who themselves have not been encouraged by education to know in a deep, usable, and validating way who and where they are.

Making Space, Taking Time, Sharing Power

By Hugo Mahabir

One of the early readings I came across through the National SEED Project on Inclusive Curriculum is *The Alchemy of Race and Rights,* by Patricia Williams (1992), a law professor and cultural theorist who documents her thinking about race, democracy, and law in a series of autobiographical essays published in 1992. In one of her essays, Williams describes an argument she and her sister had as children on a family driving trip regarding the color of the road ahead of them. Through her story, Williams describes what it means to have two divergent points of view, and yet have them both be valid.

As Williams tells it:

> One summer when I was about six, my family drove to Maine. The highway was very straight and hot and shimmered darkly in the sun. My sister and I sat in the back seat of the Studebaker and argued about what color the road was. I said black. My sister said purple. After I had harangued her into admitting that it was indeed black, my father gently pointed out that my sister still saw it as purple.
>
> I was unimpressed with the relevance of that at the time; but with the passage of years, and much more observation, I have come to see endless highways as slightly more purple than black.
>
> My sister and I will probably argue about the hue of life's roads forever. But the lesson I learned from listening to her wild perceptions is that it really is possible to see things – even the most concrete things – simultaneously yet differently; and that seeing simultaneously yet differently is more easily done by two people than one, but that one person can get the hang of it with lots of time and effort.

The household I grew up in was a place where things were either right or wrong with very little room for ambiguity or variance, even less for multiplicity and plurality. Life was singular, facts were facts, and truth and knowledge could be ascertained with unequivocal certainty, as long as one could prove one's point or argue from evidence. The problem was that, despite this premise of objectivity, subjectivity and experience always came into it. Never was it validated for me as a child that truth is multiple – not relative, but plural – based on the experiences and standpoints of the people making the truth claims. The adults around me believed in the authority of knowledge that gave one's perceptions and assumptions about the world their validity and legitimacy. In this world, there was no room for difference. The aim was to argue your point, to the death it seemed, if necessary, in order to stake your claim to the truth. As a result, my people argued about just about everything, making it impossible to give birth to fledgling thoughts, feelings, or intuitions that didn't conform to the received opinion or fall in line with the most persuasive (read: silencing) argument.

It was in the SEED Project that I began to understand that what I had always believed and sensed as a child was true: that there is more than one answer to a question, that there are many sides to a story, and that there is always more than meets the eye. With its insistence on the basic truth of experience and the existence of multiple perspectives, many voices, and plural ways of knowing, the SEED Project leaves open the field of knowing, allowing a room of SEED participants to speak the truth of their own experience, while at the same time listening, deeply listening, to the truth of the experience of others.

Going-around-the-circle in a SEED seminar changes the balance of power within the group. In this exercise, everyone in the circle has authority and a claim to knowledge, not just those onto whom authority has been projected by the systems of an oppressive society, whether through racism, sexism, classism, or adultism. To be in a SEED circle is to be in more authentic relation to oneself and to others without the free reign of internalized authority or internalized subordination over-privileging some and under-privileging others.

In the SEED circle, everyone has time enough to speak, but not unlimited time, nor is anyone asked or expected to comment on or respond to what others testify to, nor expected to have the answers to the questions posed. Simply put, it's not about being right, but about being in right relation to others. This is an ethic and a practice that the SEED Project teaches as a fundamental part of becoming multiculturally literate and self-aware.

Changing the balance of power, or more accurately, sharing the power, is one of the most transformative processes to which a SEED seminar gives rise in the course of being in reflective dialogue with others over time. During the time spent in a SEED seminar, there is an intrinsic justice that comes to bear that we seldom experience in the world at large. Once experienced, however, it can be practiced, both in the classroom and in the workplace.

Through participation in the SEED Project over many years, my pedagogy and practice as a teacher and administrator were radically transformed, making my classroom more democratic and inclusive of all voices and ways of learning, and making my leadership dependent on "being a body in the body of the world," as Leroy Moore has put it. Through the epistemological rebalancing that the SEED seminar process cultivates, teachers can translate this ethic into classroom practice, where there is a way of being "right" about discrete areas of knowledge without being oppressive, since the aim is not to be right to the exclusion of others, but "right" for the development of all.

SEED As Change Agent – Personal, Institutional, and Community-wide

By Bob Gordon

I'm not sure what I expected when I agreed to lead a SEED Project on Inclusive Curriculum seminar. I guess I thought that it would be good and useful for my colleagues to consider such important topics as race, class, gender, and sexual identity. I know that I thought I was only signing on for one year, not a lifetime! In addition, I did not anticipate how SEED would change my school, my community, and me.

In 1992, I was not yet out as a gay man in my workplace. I decided that I didn't want to be part of any diversity program that wouldn't accept my sexual identity, so I identified as gay in my application to become a SEED leader. Through the application process, I came out to the head of the upper school, the headmaster, and several other colleagues who were personal friends. Twenty years ago, this in itself was momentous. I went to the SEED training in California as an openly gay man, bringing print materials and music related to gender and sexual identity with me. The SEED training week was overwhelming for me. In addition to all the other mind-opening experiences, it was the first time I had been openly gay in a professional setting.

Serial testimony is bedrock of the SEED process. Founder and senior associate Peggy McIntosh calls it the "autocratic administration of time in the service of democratic distribution of time." In any group, whether it is two people or twenty, each speaker is allotted a certain amount of time, two minutes for example, to share his or her thoughts and/or feelings on a given topic. Successive speakers do not respond to what others have said. Emphasis is not on judging but on listening respectfully to each person's contribution. A person may pass (continue listening). In this way, everyone has an equal opportunity to participate, and those who are the most verbally aggressive do not dominate conversation. Ever since experiencing this practice repeatedly during my own training, I have been a different person and a different teacher.

I use serial testimony regularly in my Spanish classroom. How different it is when everyone knows she or he will have a time to speak. In committees I have chaired both at work and at my church, I have instituted the same practice. It is remarkable how different these groups now feel.

My life partner (also a trained SEED leader) and I co-facilitate a "covenant circle" at our church. It is a group of about eight people who meet twice a month to consider important topics such as aging, work, friendship, or loss. We use serial testimony as part of the group's process, with excellent results.

SEED experience can be pervasive. I am disappointed when a group of friends or relatives interact in ways I took for granted before my SEED training – everyone talking at once, interrupting each other, talking over someone else by being louder, and so forth. Several times I have hurt a friend's feelings by pointing out the ways he or she is interrupting or dominating a conversation. I have to remind myself that every group is not a SEED seminar with respectful ground rules.

During the six years that I led SEED seminars at my school, change came incrementally, generally subtlely, and often in unintended and surprising ways. Some examples:

- The admissions director, with a long tenure at our institution, was in my first seminar. About halfway through the year, having considered the voices of children, of girls and women, of boys and men, and of families, he asked to speak with me. "What do you think of our admissions applications," he began. "Do you think we should change the lines for 'father' and 'mother' to something more inclusive?" That began the process of designing new admissions forms, an institutional change.

- A number of members of the English department participated in SEED in years one and two. At that point, the upper school English reading list consisted of virtually all male authors. By the third year, it had evolved to include Zora Neale Hurston, Anzia Yezierska, May Sarton, Toni Morrison, and other women writers. Although I was not privy to the discussions that preceded those changes, we had read all of those authors in our SEED seminars.

- When I began teaching at the school, there was a Fathers' Association and a Mothers' Association. The Mothers' Association meetings were during the day time, assuming, I suppose, that our students' mothers did not work outside the home, and were therefore free at that time. The topic of separate parents' associations, as well as the meeting times, came up at several SEED meetings. Various administrators and faculty members spoke with parents, and within a year there was one Parents' Association with evening meetings – not a perfect solution, but movement in the right direction.

- One spring, prom tickets went on sale as usual: $15 per person, or $25 for couples, which were understood to be a boy and a girl. Several SEED seminar participants spoke with students on the prom committee, and I talked with the faculty advisor and the dean of students. It was fairly easy to convince them that the discount for couples was not equitable, and that they should simply charge $15 per person. When a lesbian student came to me to ask if I thought she could invite her girlfriend to the prom, things got more complicated. I spoke with the dean of students, the head of upper school, and the headmaster, before finally getting the OK to tell her "yes," provided that I agreed to be one of the chaperones to "make sure everything went smoothly." This same-sex couple came to the prom surrounded and supported by their "posse" of friends. The culture of the school's prom experience had forever changed.

- The dean of students, also a participant in SEED, sponsored a weekly lunch speaker for upper school students and faculty. With my help, he invited a lesbian couple, parents of one of our students, to speak on their decision to have a child, and about the challenges involved in parenting as a same-sex couple.

- All freshmen took a required health class. The instructor, another SEED seminar member, decided that sexual identity should be included in the curriculum. With administrative approval, and again with help from me, he invited the gay male director of GLBT (gay, lesbian, bisexual, and transgender) Services at the local state university and a lesbian psychologist to speak to his students. SEED had expanded the curriculum.

Many other seemingly small but significant changes occurred that could be traced directly or indirectly to SEED. For me, the most amazing story happened on Monday of the last week of classes at the end of our first year of SEED. I came in early as usual, the first person in the building that day. On the wooden door of my classroom, in letters over a foot high, someone had scratched the word "FAG." Horrified, I quickly covered it with a poster from my room. When I heard the head of the upper school open his office door, just down the hall. I asked him to come and look at the door to my room. After seeing it, he told me to wait a minute, went to his office, and returned with a screwdriver and a hammer. He asked me to help him remove my door. I said, "But Phil, I need a door on my room." As I helped him carry the door down the hall to his office, he told me that all the doors in the building were identical. We removed his office door, installed it in my room, and put my door on his office. The ugly word now faced his desk. "But Phil," I asked, "Why would you want to see that on your door all day?" He answered, "Because it will remind me of how much work we have to do." I realized Phil was a true ally.

Phil was a member of our SEED seminar that year. He had initiated several private conversations with me during the year about how being gay affected my life, both personally and professionally. I was "the first gay person he had ever known," he told me, early on. When I looked askance at him, he self-corrected, "That I knew about, anyway." He proved to be remarkably insightful and empathetic, and was supportive of a number of changes within the school related to gender and sexual identity.

At some point, my SEED leadership moved beyond our school campus and into the community beyond. I was on radio talk shows, was the subject of newspaper articles, and participated in faculty development classes at local school districts, all related to GLBT issues. I presented workshops at my church on race and racism, privilege, and sexual and gender identity. I gave "Gay 101" presentations to students at area high schools and colleges. After my retirement from full-time teaching, I worked part-time as a consultant on gender, race, and/or sexual identity in schools, colleges, and businesses.

What began as a one-year commitment to lead a faculty seminar on equity and diversity has completely transformed the past twenty years of my life. In addition, the school where I taught has changed in many ways and is still growing as a result of SEED's ongoing presence there. Finally, the community beyond my school campus has felt the influence of SEED in ways I couldn't have imagined.

Our Stories As Windows and Mirrors

By Ruth Mendoza

Beyond their practical uses, windows and mirrors had little relevance in my daily life, or so I thought.

This was the case until the reflective nature of the SEED training, which began with filling out my application, invited me to consider the reasons behind my diversity work.

The year was 2002. The day was an ordinary morning. I was busily getting my children ready for school – making breakfast, getting them dressed, and finally brushing my youngest daughter's hair. With her braids almost done, she unexpectedly asked, "Mom, can I bring a mirror to school?"

Puzzled by her question, I paused briefly before adding the last details to her hair. The response already taking shape in my head was centered mainly on safety and the potential for the mirror to become a distraction in class. I felt justified in thinking that a kindergarten child did not need to carry such an object to school. After all, mirrors break easily and could lead to injury. I could imagine my daughter and her friends finding too-creative ways of using it in their play.

Regardless of any possible scenarios, I asked myself, why would she want to take a mirror to school? Rather than inquiring about my daughter's request, my focus became fixed on her reflection on the dresser mirror in front of us. I noticed that she too was quietly and intently looking at it. Was she not happy with how I was fixing her hair? No, of course not, I told myself, she likes her dark, long hair braided. And just like that, the answer became clear. She wants to take a mirror to school to check on her hairstyle, I decided. With only a couple of minutes to spare before leaving for school, I began to swiftly explain why bringing a mirror to school was not an option. Still looking at the mirror, my daughter broke her silence as if I were not even speaking, "Mom, every day I go to school." She pauses. "I see my friends and I see my teachers, but nobody looks like me. If I had a mirror I could look in it, and I won't forget what I look like."

My heart sank.

Her words replayed in my head incessantly at first and like a distant echo as my day progressed. My maternal instincts dictated that I should fix this problem, and fix it quickly so the burden could be lifted from my daughter, but I did not know how or whether it could be fixed. Her words taunted me. Yes, we were perhaps the only Latino family in the school and we did stand out in this predominantly white environment, but shouldn't the benefits of a great education outweigh any sacrifices made along the way? In the days and months that followed, I struggled to reconcile her heartbreaking experience with my hopes of providing my children with the opportunities that I could only dream about in my native Bolivia.

Since then I have been on a journey to find open and engaging ways in which to address issues of diversity in my school community. This journey led me to the SEED Project on Inclusive Curriculum, where I was first introduced to SEED Co-Director Emily Style's work.

While my daughter's words point to the lack of being physically reflected by those around her, Emily Style's metaphor of windows and mirrors offers a broader application (Style, 1988). It illustrates that as we undertake meaningful sharing of our experiences/stories with others, we may encounter both reflections (mirrors) of our own story, and windows into other people's experiences. The idea of finding mirrors and/or windows in each story was appealing to me as it opened a door to new possibilities, such as the possibility of breaking down stereotypes, gaining fresh perspectives, and knowing more about the particular feelings of each child.

Notes

1 This collaborative article on SEED appeared in *Independent School Magazine* as McIntosh et al. (2015). The article included a total of six teacher testimonies; three can be found here and the other three can be found on the SEED website. Additional quotes from teachers in this article were gathered for an internal, unpublished SEED document compiled by Judy Logan.
2 See Chapter 14, *Faculty-Centered Faculty Development*, and Chapter 15, *Social, Emotional, and Political Learning*, for more on the exercises used in SEED.
3 This question was inspired by "When I dare to be powerful - to put my strength in the service of my vision, then it becomes less and less important whether I am afraid" (Lorde, 1984).

References

Lorde, A. (1984). *Sister outsider: Essays and speeches*. Trumansburg, NY: Crossing Press.
McIntosh, P., Badger, Chen, J., P. Gillette, P., Gordon, B., Mahabir, H., & Mendoza, R. (2015, Summer). Teacher self-knowledge: The deeper learning. *Independent School Magazine*, 74(4).
Style, E. (1981). *Multicultural education & me: The philosophy and the process, putting product in its place*. Madison: University of Wisconsin Teacher Corps Associates.
Style, E. (1988). Curriculum as window and mirror. In *Listening for all voices: Gender balancing the school curriculum*. Summit, NJ: Oak Knoll School.
Williams, P. (1992). *The alchemy of race and rights*. Cambridge, MA: Harvard University Press.

PART V

Closing

A CLOSING LETTER

Dear Reader,

I hope that you have taken some comfort or pleasure from this collection of essays, even in these frightening and ugly times. I may have said things you have known for a long, long time, but like to see repeated – or not. You may have found that some of my language evokes your own experiences. I hope you will take up the invitation to stop apologizing. Perhaps I have reminded you of aspects of what formal education has done to you, for better or for worse. Another connection to this book may come from your deciding to face more directly matters of power that we were taught to deny or evade. My essays have been grouped here under such hopes. They come from some of the major preoccupations of my life over the last four decades.

In the four parts of this book, you will have found my commitment to these beliefs among others:

- Understanding systems of privilege and disadvantage is wise, though often upsetting. Once people have some understanding of privilege, it is up to us what we will do with unearned power, in our minds and actions. We have power we can use to make change.
- Human beings benefit when we escape from feelings of fraudulence that are imposed on us by systems of power.
- All of us would benefit from schooling and public policy that recognizes and validates the humanity of all peoples. We can contribute to such schooling and public policy.
- All teachers benefit from learning about how power works in themselves, schools, and students; without such understanding, they usually replicate existing hierarchies in their work, whether or not they mean to.

These are key commitments and beliefs running through my essays. If I spend a day neglecting them I usually feel a hollow despair about the world. Re-immersing in them, I feel I can go on and will do so.

After reading in these pages, you may have chosen to close the book and write yourself. Why not do this? You are the only world's authority on your own experience. You can make your own metaphors. I wish you well in documenting how you have survived, as the world's markets and manners attempted to weaken your connections to others and to many aspects of your plural self.

Each of the four parts of the book focused on matters I feel I would have benefited from realizing early on. What difference would it have made to me as a young person if I had learned more about power early in my life? The insights from seeing privilege systems would have affected my attitudes and behaviors for the better. Having more confidence in myself would have been useful; even though my students liked me, I often doubted myself when teaching in schools and universities. I did not yet see the fraudulence of many academic conventions that were making me feel hesitant. Beginning to see women in the curriculum would have been one step forward, and then seeing most of the world's population as valid, real, and interconnected would have been truly humanistic education. And finally, what a blessing it would have been to have teachers at every level of education who knew deeply that they were still learning.

Responses to these four preoccupations of my work have ranged from rage to placid indifference. The idea of privilege is upsetting to many but can be introduced in such a way that rage is not the result. Feeling like a fraud is common in the United States and important to analyze. Curriculum reconstruction is endlessly interesting especially to those who remember they were bored by the subject matter of most courses. Letting teachers talk this all through with themselves and preparing them to lead groups within their institutions has been the thrilling, inspiring, demanding, and rewarding work of SEED.

I am wondering when this book will come to seem obsolete, as it will, sooner or later. My guess is that the part on privilege will endure longest since it marked a turning point in the US discourses on race, helping more and more people to see racial advantage and disadvantage systemically. The specific examples I gave and my autobiographical method led to much further reaction, commentary, and research. Many teachers in schools and universities have courageously extended the understanding of privilege. This is hard work as U.S. students have been so reinforced in seeing individually, without much sense of the history that produced our current social systems.

The part on Fraudulence may evaporate in the heat of early 21st century escalations of fraudulence and fakery. The psychological points I was making may disappear in the heat of the disregard for truth-telling. It may well be that most people stop caring whether organizations and institutions are engineered to reproduce fraudulence in ranking and judging. My reason for starting this line of thought was to comfort those who feel fraudulent and to tell them I feel they are no more fraudulent than the next person. Since lying, cheating, stealing, and bragging are currently common in high places, my papers on fraud may come to seem ephemeral. I hope, however, that the final paper of the Fraudulence series will survive the shock and the cynicism. The final paper says that many different moves toward survival and growth are plurally in us; all are valid in some way. This theme is gathering momentum in cognitive science, literature, psychology, philosophy, and even theology.

Will the Phase Theory become obsolete? I think it may continue to influence education, though perhaps under different names. I hope students' low scores on standardized tests will move school systems to ask why they keep teaching to the test, when teaching to the test doesn't work. They are finding, very slowly, that students learn from personal attention, from collaborative projects, from compelling ideas, from activities, and from conversations. Students learn some subjects better when they are free of the fear of grades. I hope that Phase IV's lateral learning modes will reaffirm teachers who, as a matter of course, follow insights from John Dewey, Maria Montessori, and Paulo Freire about what works in education.

Will the SEED Project become obsolete? At this writing, the SEED Project is thriving under the leadership of Emmy Howe, Gail Cruise-Roberson, and Jondou Chase Chen, and is preparing over 150 new SEED seminar leaders each summer. The problem of teacher time may continue to squeeze what was our three-hour seminar expectation during the first three decades of the project. I think there will be many experiments with seminar length and timing, and a further expansion of SEED in non-school sites. I think that the use of Serial Testimony will continue to distinguish SEED from many other adult development projects. SEED continues to be one of the few national K–12 projects for teacher development that has a central focus on social justice. I think that more parents and in some cases students will want SEED seminars of their own. The combination of plenary sessions and small groups will probably continue to be a potent mix for serious discussions inside and outside of school. Teachers who feel isolated, and crave non-competitive opportunities to talk with one another about their teaching and about their lives, will continue to want SEED seminars. I feel much gratitude to all SEED leaders and participants who have taken the SEED journey of inner and outer exploration. They have survived disconcerting realizations about how habits from our white-and-male dominated institutions were lodged in us from our earliest years. They have also had the redeeming experience of learning more about their own and others' lives, hearts, minds, and souls. I feel this increase in knowledge empowers us in a humane way, and is good for us, for our communities, and for our world.

So now dear Reader, I wish you well in your own reflections and actions.

I thank you for your company on the journey.

Arms 'round,

Peggy

FURTHER READING

Adichie, C. N. (2013). *Americanah*. New York: Anchor Books.

Alexander, M. (2012). *The new Jim Crow: Mass incarceration in the age of colorblindness*. New York: The New Press.

Allen, P. G. (1986). *The sacred hoop: Recovering the feminine in American Indian tradition*. Boston: Beacon Press.

Anderson, M. (1983). *Thinking about women: Sociological and feminist perspectives*. New York: Macmillan.

Anzaldua, G. (Ed.) (1990). *Making faces, making soul / hacienda caras: Creative and critical perspectives by women of color*. San Francisco: Aunt Lute.

Asian Women United of California (Eds.) (1998). *Making waves: An anthology of writings by and about Asian American women*. Boston: Beacon Press.

Baldwin, J. (1963). *The fire next time*. New York: The Dial Press.

Baldwin, J. (1985). *The price of the ticket: Collected non-fiction, 1948–1985*. New York: St. Martins/Marek.

Banks, J. A., & Banks, C. A. (2004). *Handbook of research on multicultural education*. San Francisco, CA: Jossey-Bass.

Bateson, M. C. (1989). *Composing a life*. New York: Grove Press.

Bauer, M. (Ed.) (1994). *Am I blue?: Coming out from the silence*. New York: Harper Collins.

Beck, E. T. (1982). *Nice Jewish girls: A lesbian anthology*. Trumansburg: The Crossing Press.

Bell, D. (2018). *Faces at the bottom of the well: The permanence of racism*. New York: Basic Books.

Bigelow, B. E. (Ed.) (2004). *Rethinking our classrooms: Teaching for equity and justice*. Volume 2. Revised Edition. Milwaukee, WI: Rethinking Schools Ltd.

Billings, D. (2016). *Deep denial: The persistence of white supremacy in United States history and life*. Roselle, NJ: Crandall, Dostie, & Douglass Books, Inc.

Blau, J. R. (2004). *Race in the schools: Perpetuating white dominance?*Boulder, CO: Lynne Rienner.

Bonilla-Silva, E. (2010). *Racism without racists: Color-blind racism and the persistence of racial inequality in the United States*. Lanham, MD: Rowman & Littlefield.

Brant, B. (1984). *A gathering of spirit writing and art by North American Indian women.* Rockland, ME: Sinister Wisdom Books.

Brod, H. (1988). *A mensch among men: Explorations in Jewish masculinity.* Freedom, CA: Crossing Press.

Brodkin, K. (2010). *How Jews became white folks: And what that says about race in America.* New Brunswick, NJ: Rutgers University Press.

Bulkin, E., Pratt, M. B., & Smith, B. (1988). *Yours in struggle: Three feminist perspectives of anti-semitism and racism.* Ithaca, NY: Firebrand Book.

Calderón, JL. (2012). *Occupying privilege: Conversations on love, race & liberation.* Ridgewood, NY: Love-N-Liberation Press.

Case, K. (Ed.) (2013). *Deconstructing privilege: Teaching and learning as allies in the classroom.* New York: Routledge.

Chou, R. S., & Feagin, J. R. (2008). *The myth of the model minority: Asian Americans facing racism.* Boulder: Paradigm.

Coates, T. (2015). *Between the world and me.* New York: Spiegel & Grau.

Collins, C., & Yeskel, F. (2000). *Economic apartheid in America: A primer on economic inequality & insecurity.* New York: New Press.

Collins, P. H. (1990). *Black feminist thought knowledge, consciousness, and the politics of empowerment.* New York: Routledge.

Crass, C. (2015). *Towards the "other America": Anti-racist resources for White people taking action for Black Lives Matter.* St. Louis, MO: Chalice Press.

Crenshaw, K. (1996). *Critical race theory: The key writings that formed the movement.* New York: The New Press.

Dace, K. (Ed.) (2012). *Unlikely allies in the academy: Women of color and white women in conversation.* New York: Routledge.

Davis, A. Y. (2015). *Freedom is a constant struggle: Ferguson, Palestine, and the foundations of a movement.* Chicago: Haymarket Books.

DeGruy Leary, J. (2009). *Post traumatic slave syndrome: Americas legacy of enduring injury and healing: The study guide.* Portland, OR: Joy DeGruy Publications

Delpit, L. (2006). *Other people's children: Cultural conflict in the classroom.* New York: New Press.

Derman-Sparks, L., & Phillips, C. B. (1997). *Teaching/learning anti-racism: A developmental approach.* New York: Teachers College Press.

DiAngelo, R. J. (2018). *White fragility: Why it's so hard for white people to talk about racism.* Boston: Beacon Press.

Du Bois, W. E. B. (1986). *W. E. B. Du Bois: Writings.* New York: Penguin.

Dyson, M. E. (2017). *Tears we cannot stop: A sermon to white America.* New York: St. Martin's Press.

Dyson, M. E. (2018). *What truth sounds like: RFK, James Baldwin, & our unfinished conversation about race in America.* New York: St. Martin's Press.

Ehrenreich, B. (1990). *Fear of falling: The inner life of the middle class.* New York: Harper Perennial.

Feagin, J. R., & Vera, H. (1995). *White racism: The basics.* New York: Routledge.

Fine, M. (1997). *Off white readings on race, power, and society.* New York, NY: Routledge.

Frankenberg, R. (1993). *White women, race matters: The social construction of whiteness.* London: Routledge.

Freire, P. (1970). *Pedagogy of the oppressed.* New York: Continuum.

Frye, M. (1983). *The politics of reality: Essays in feminist theory.* Trumansburg, NY: Crossing Press.

Gates, H. L. (1986). *"Race", writing, and difference.* Chicago: University of Chicago Press.

Gatto, J. T. (1992). *Dumbing us down: The hidden curriculum of compulsory schooling.* British Columbia, Canada: New Society.

Gibbs, J. T. (1988). *Young, black, and male in America.* Dover, MA: Auburn House.

Giddings, P. (1985). *When and where I enter: The impact of Black women on race and sex in America.* Toronto: Bantam Books.

Gilligan, C. (1982). *In a different voice: Psychological theory and women's development.* Cambridge, MA: Harvard University Press.

Giovanni, N. (1994). *Racism 101.* New York, NY: Morrow.

Gordon, L. (1989). *Heroes of their own lives: The politics and history of family violence: Boston 1880–1960.* New York: Penguin Books.

Gould, S. J. (1996). *The mismeasure of man.* New York: W.W. Norton & Company.

Gwaltney, J. L. (1993). *Drylongso: A self-portrait of Black America.* New York: New Press.

Hacker, A. (1995). *Two nations: Black and white, separate, hostile, unequal.* New York: Ballantine Books.

Harding, V. (1981). *There is a river: The Black struggle for freedom in America.* New York: Harcourt Brace Jovanovich.

hooks, b. (1984). *Feminist theory: From margin to center.* Cambridge: South End Press.

hooks, b. (1989). *Talking back: Thinking feminist, thinking black.* Boston, MA: South End Press.

Howard, G. R. (1999). *We can't teach what we don't know: White teachers, multiracial schools.* (Multicultural Education Series). New York: Teachers College Press.

Irving, D. (2014). *Waking up white, and finding myself in the story of race.* Cambridge, MA: Elephant Room Press.

Iyer, D. (2015). *We too sing America: South Asian, Arab, Muslim, and Sikh immigrants shape our multiracial future.* New York: The New Press.

Jobin-Leeds, G. (2016). *When we fight, we win twenty-first-century social movements and the activists that are transforming our world.* New York: The New Press.

Jordan, W. D. (1968). *White over black American attitudes toward the Negro, 1550–1812.* Chapel Hill: University of North Carolina Press.

Katz, J. H. (1978). *White awareness handbook for anti-racism training.* Norman, OK: University of Oklahoma Press.

Kendall, F. E. (2013). *Understanding white privilege: Creating pathways to authentic relationships across race.* New York: Routledge.

Kimmel, M., & Ferber, A. (Eds.) (2016). *Privilege: A reader.* Boulder, CO: Westview.

Kivel, P. (2017). *Uprooting racism: How white people can work for racial justice.* Gabriola Island, British Columbia: New Society.

Klein, S. S., Ricahrdson, B., Grayson, D. A., Fox, L. H., Kramarae, C., Pollard, S., & Dwyer, C. A. (2007). *Handbook for achieving gender equity through education.* Mahwah, NJ: Lawrence Erlbaum Associates, Inc.

Kohn, A. (2017). *No contest: The case against competition.* Boston, MA: Houghton Mifflin.

Kozol, J. (1991). *Savage inequalities: Children in America's schools.* New York, NY: HarperCollins.

Lauter, P. (1990). *Selections from Walt Whitman and Emily Dickinson: A supplement to the Heath anthology of American literature, Vol 2.* Lexington, MA: DC Heath and Company.

Lee, E., Menkart, D., & Okazawa-Rey, M. (2008). *Beyond heroes and holidays: A practical guide to K-12 anti-racist, multicultural education and staff development.* Washington, DC: Teaching for Change.

Lewontin, R. C., Rose, S. P., & Lamin, L. J. (1984). *Not in our genes: Biology, ideology and human nature.* New York: Pantheon Books.

Lindbergh, A. M. (1972). *Bring me a unicorn: Diaries and letters of Anne Morrow Lindbergh*. New York: Signet Books.

Lipsitz, G. (1998). *The possessive investment in whiteness: How white people profit from identity politics*. Philadelphia: Temple University Press.

Loeb, P. R. (1999). *Soul of a citizen: Living with conviction in a cynical time*. New York: St. Martin's Press.

Logan, J. (1997). *Teaching stories*. New York: Kodansha International.

Lorde, A. (1984). *Sister outsider: Essays and speeches*. Berkeley, CA: Crossing Press.

Lowe, M., & Hubbard, R. (1990). *Woman's nature: Rationalizations of inequality*. New York: Pergamon Press.

McIntosh, P. (1982). Warning: The new scholarship on women may be hazardous to your ego. *Women's Studies Quarterly*, 10(1), 29–31.

McIntosh, P. (1986). Women's studies international at Nairobi. *National Women's Studies Association Perspectives*, 4, 12–13.

McIntosh, P. (1988). Curricular re-vision: The new knowledge for a new age. In C. S. Pearson, D. L. Shavlick, & J. G. Touchton (Eds.), *Educating the majority: Women challenge tradition in higher education*. New York: American Council on Education/ Macmillan.

McIntosh, P. (1993). Foreword. In J. Logan, *Teaching stories* (1st ed.) (pp. xiii–xvi). New York: Kodansha International.

McIntosh, P. (1996). Miss Muffet asks a systemic question and frightens herself away: Questions like "Why did the serfs stand for it" stand at the threshold of systemic thinking. *Holistic Education Review*, 9(4), 15–20.

McIntosh, P. (2004). Afterword: The growing influence of right-wing thought. In A. L. Ferber, *Home-grown hate: Gender and organized racism* (pp. 227–234) [Afterword]. New York: Routledge.

McIntosh, P. (2005). Gender perspectives on educating for global citizenship. In N. Noddings (Ed.), *Educating citizens for global awareness* (pp. 22–39). New York: Teachers College Press.

McIntosh, P. (2007). Crashing into more of white privilege. In M. J. Benitez, & F. Gustin, *Crash course: Reflections on the film Crash for critical dialogues about race, power, and privilege*. Emeryville, CA: Institute for Democratic Education and Culture – Speak Out.

McIntosh, P. (2009). Foreword. In K. Weekes (Ed.). *Privilege and prejudice: Twenty years with the invisible knapsack* (pp. ix–xiv). UK: Cambridge Scholars Publishing.

McIntosh, P. (2012). Reflections and future directions for privilege studies. *Journal of Social Issues*, 68(1), 194–206.

McIntosh, P. (2012). Too much history between us. In K. Dace (Ed.), *Unlikely allies in the academy: Women of color and white women in conversation* (pp. 91–100). New York: Routledge.

McIntosh, P. (2013). Teaching about privilege: Transforming learned ignorance into usable knowledge. In K. Case (Ed.), *Deconstructing privilege: Teaching and learning as allies in the classroom* (pp. xi–xvi) [Foreword]. New York: Routledge.

McIntosh, P. (2015). Deprivileging philosophy. In B. Bergo & T. Nicholls (Eds.), *I don't see color personal and critical perspectives on white privilege* (pp. 13–24). University Park, PA: Pennsylvania State University.

McIntosh, P. (2015). Real-izing personal and systemic privilege: Reflection becoming action. In E. Moore Jr., M. W. Penick-Parks, & A. Michael (Eds.), *Everyday white people confront racial and social injustice: 15 stories* (pp. 13–24). Sterling, VA: Stylus Publishing.

McIntosh, P., & Minnich, E. (1984) Varieties of women's studies. *Women's Studies International Forum*, 7(3), 177–184.

McIntosh, P., Christiansen, D., & Lewis, V. (2008). Volume III. *Lessons from The Color of Fear*. Emeryville, CA: Institute for Democratic Education and Culture – Speak Out.

Millett, K. (1977). *Sita*. New York: Ballantine Books.

Moore, E.Jr., Penick-Parks, M. W., & Michael, A. (Eds.) (2015). *Everyday white people confront racial and social injustice: 15 stories*. Sterling, VA: Stylus Publishing.

Moraga, C., & Anzaldúa, G. (1983). *This bridge called my back: Writings by radical women of color*. New York: Kitchen Table, Women of Color Press.

Morrison, T. (1992). *Playing in the dark: Whiteness and the literary imagination*. Cambridge, MA: Harvard University Press.

Mura, D. (1995). *When the body meets memory: An odyssey of race, sexuality, and identity*. New York: Anchor Books.

Nelson, C. & Wilson, K. (Eds.) (1998). *Seeding the process of multicultural education: An anthology*. Plymouth, MN: Minnesota Inclusiveness Program.

Nieto, S. (2013). *Finding joy in teaching students of diverse backgrounds: Culturally responsive and socially just practices in U.S. classrooms*. Portsmouth, NH: Heinemann.

Noddings, N. (Ed.) (2005). *Educating citizens for global awareness*. New York: Teachers College Press.

Olsen, T. (1978). *Silences*. New York: Delacorte Press.

Perry, T. (1994). *Freedom's plow: Teaching in the multicultural classroom*. New York: Routledge.

Pharr, S. (1996). *In the time of the right: Reflections on liberation*. Berkeley, CA: Chardon Press.

Pipher, M. (1994). *Reviving Ophelia: Saving the selves of adolescent girls*. New York: G. P. Putnam's Sons.

Pollock, M. (2008). *Everyday antiracism: Getting real about race in school*. New York: New Press.

Rich, A. (1978). *The dream of a common language: Poems 1974–1977*. New York: W.W. Norton & Company.

Rich, A. (1979). *On lies, secrets, and silence: Selected prose, 1966–1978*. New York: W.W. Norton & Company.

Rich, A. (1986). *Blood, bread, and poetry: Selected prose 1979–1985*. New York: W.W. Norton & Company.

Rich, A. (2018). *Essential essays: Culture, politics, and the art of poetry*. New York: W.W. Norton & Company.

Roberts, T. (2015). *Joan Chittister: Her journey from certainty to faith*. Maryknoll, NY: Orbis Books.

Roediger, D. R. (1992). *The wages of whiteness: Race and the making of the American working class*. London: Verso.

Roediger, D. R. (1994). *Towards the abolition of whiteness*. New York: Verso.

Rosenwasser, P. (2013). *Hope Into Practice, Jewish Women Choosing Justice Despite Our Fears*. Penny Rosenwasser.

Rothenberg, P. S. (1988). *Racism and sexism: An integrated study*. New York: St. Martin's Press.

Rothenberg, P. S. (1998). *Race, class, and gender in the United States: An integrated study*, 4th ed. New York: St. Martin's Press.

Rothenberg, P. S. (2002). *White privilege: Essential readings on the other side of racism*. New York: Worth.

Rothman, J. (2014, May). The origins of "privilege." *The New Yorker*. Retrieved from https://www.newyorker.com/books/page-turner/the-origins-of-privilege

Ruddick, S. (1995). *Maternal thinking: Toward a politics of peace*. Boston: Beacon Press.

Ruether, R. R. (1974). *Faith and fratricide: The theological roots of anti-Semitism*. New York: Seabury Press.

Schniedewind, N., & Davidson, E. (1983). *Open minds to equality: A sourcebook of learning activities to promote race, sex, class, and age equity*. Englewood Cliffs, NJ: Prentice-Hall.

Schuster, M., & Van Dyne, S. (1985). *Women's place in the academy: Transforming the liberal arts curriculum*. Totawa, NJ: Rowman & Allenheld.

Segrest, M. (1993). *Memoirs of a race traitor*. Boston, MA: South End Press.

Shaheen, J. G. (2009). *Reel bad Arabs: How Hollywood vilifies a people*. Northampton, MA: Olive Branch Press.

Sleeter, C. E. (1996). *Multicultural education as social activism*. Albany, NY: State University of New York Press.

Smith, B. (1983). *Home girls: A Black feminist anthology*. New York: Kitchen Table: Women of Color Press.

Smith, L. (1961). *Killers of the dream*. New York: Doubleday.

Spelman, E. V. (1988). *Inessential woman: Problems of exclusion in feminist thought*. Boston, MA: Beacon Press.

Starhawk. (1987). *Truth or dare: Encounters with power, authority and mystery*. New York: Harper & Row.

Steele, C. (2011). *Whistling Vivaldi: And other clues to how stereotypes affect us*. New York: W.W. Norton & Company.

Steinem, G. (1983). *Outrageous acts and everyday rebellions*. New York: Holt, Rinehart, & Winston.

Stevenson, B. (2014). *Just mercy: A story of justice and redemption*. New York: Spiegel & Grau.

Steyn, M. E.(2001). *Whiteness just isn't what is used to be: White identity in a changing South Africa*. Albany:State University of New York Press.

Stout, L. (1996). *Bridging the class divide and other lessons for grassroots organizing*. Boston, MA: Beacon Press.

Style, E. (1981). *Multicultural education & me: The philosophy and the process, putting product in its place*. Madison: University of Wisconsin Teacher Corps Associates.

Style, E. (1988). Curriculum as window and mirror. In *Listening for all voices: Gender balancing the school curriculum*. Summit, NJ: Oak Knoll School.

Sue, D. W. (2010). *Microaggressions in everyday life: Race, gender, and sexual orientation*. Hoboken, NJ: Wiley.

Sullivan, S. (2006). *Revealing whiteness: The unconscious habits of racial privilege*. Bloomington, IN: Indiana University Press.

Sullivan, S. (2014). *Good white people: the problem with middle-class white anti-racism*. Albany, NY: State University of New York Press.

Takaki, R. (1989). *Strangers from a different shore: A history of Asian Americans*. Toronto: Penguin Books.

Takaki, R. (1993). *A different mirror: A history of multicultural America*. Boston, MA: Little, Brown and Company.

Tatum, B. D. (1997). *"Why are all the black kids sitting together in the cafeteria?" and other conversations about race*. New York: Basic Books.

Terkel, S. (1992). *Race: How blacks and whites think and feel about the American obsession*. New York: New Press.

Thandeka. (1999). *Learning to be white: Money, race, and God in America*. London: Continuum.

Thompson, B. W. (2001). *A promise and a way of life: White antiracist activism*. Minneapolis: University of Minnesota Press.

Tochluk, S. (2016). *Living in the tension: The quest for a spiritualized racial justice*. Roselle, NJ: Crandall, Dostie & Douglass Books.

van der Valk, A. (2014). Peggy McIntosh: Beyond the knapsack: Learn how serial testimony places the emphasis on student experience. *Teaching Tolerance* (46). Retrieved from https://www.tolerance.org/magazine/spring-2014/peggy-mcintosh-beyond-the-knapsack

Villanueva, E. (2018). *Decolonizing wealth: Indigenous wisdom to heal divides and restore balance*. Oakland, CA: Berrett-Koehler Publishers.

Ward, J. (2000). *The skin we're in: Teaching our teens to be emotionally strong, socially smart, and spiritually connected*. New York: Simon & Schuster.

Weis, L., & Fine, M. (1993). *Beyond silenced voices: Class, race, and gender in United States schools*. Albany, NY: State University of New York Press.

Wellman, D. (1977). *Portraits of white racism*. Cambridge: Cambridge University Press.

Whaley, L., & Dodge, L. (1999). *Weaving in the women: Transforming the high school English curriculum*. Portsmouth, NH: Boynton/Cook.

Wilkerson, I. (2010) *The warmth of other suns: The epic story of America's Great Migration*. New York: Random House.

Williams, P. J. (1993). *The alchemy of race and rights*. London: Virago.

Wise, T. J. (2007). *White like me: Reflections on race from a privileged son*. Berkeley, CA: Soft Skull Press.

X, M., & Haley, A. (1964). *The autobiography of Malcolm X*. New York: Ballantine Books.

Yancy, G. (2008). *Black bodies, white gazes: The continuing significance of race in America*. Lanham, MD: Rowman & Littlefield.

Yezierska, A. (1925). *Bread givers*. New York: Doubleday & Co, Inc.

INDEX

Note: 'n' indicates chapter notes.